Pelican Books

The Radical Therapist

The Radical Therapist

edited by the Radical Therapist/
Rough Times Collective

Penguin Books

Penguin Books Ltd, Harmondsworth,
Middlesex, England
Penguin Books Australia Ltd, Ringwood,
Victoria, Australia

This selection first published by Penguin Books 1974
Copyright © The Radical Therapist Inc., 1974

Made and printed in Great Britain by
Hazell Watson & Viney Ltd
Aylesbury, Bucks
Set in Linotype Plantin

Contents

III. Women, Men and Children

IV. Self Help and Communities

Introduction

The *Radical Therapist* began as an idea in a cold North Dakota winter. Therapy, like other professional fields, had spawned several radical groups and caucuses in previous years, but no journal had emerged as a rallying ground for all the people involved. That's why we began the *Radical Therapist* in early 1970. If we hadn't started it, others would have. It was in the air.

Wherever you look, therapy has failed. The only persons consistently helped are the therapists, whose lives are comfortable. State hospitals are collecting bins and processing plants; psychoanalysis serves a fancy élite group, and it's debatable if it helps even them. Other forms of therapy are hit-and-miss – the field is swollen with people selling their wares, but the wares are often shoddy and the marketplace is corrupt. Most therapists are men; most patients, women. Therapy thus reinforces and exemplifies the sexist practices of this society, making it hard for a woman to get real help. Most therapists are white and middle-class, thus making it hard for lower-class, black, brown, and red people to get counselling in a non-oppressive way. Family or group therapy may deal well with interpersonal dynamics, but it grapples less fully with the real social conditions under which people live. New touchy-feely encounter therapy helps people become freer in themselves, but ignores social or political change. And all this in a society that, as R. D. Laing points out, systematically drives people out of their minds from childhood on, a society that regards as 'normal' a meshwork of dehumanized, mechanical, and rigid patterns of destructive behaviour.

The therapist touts himself as a magician. But he doesn't follow through. Instead of allying himself to the tradition of healing (witch, witch doctor, GP, priest), he allies himself to the *status quo* – and bolsters it. He sells his skill like a vendor of fried chicken. He uses his prestige to discredit and slur social protest, youth, women's liberation, homosexuality and any other different kind of behaviour. Therapists' rewards come from helping the system creak on.

Claiming to be 'detached and clinical', therapists never are. They can't be. Their words and acts demonstrate their bias. Current therapy's emphasis on the individual cools people out and/or puts them down. It cools them out by turning their focus from society that fucks them over to their own 'hang-ups'. It puts them down by making them 'sick' people who need 'treatment' rather than oppressed people who must be liberated. *Therapy is change not adjustment.*

In 1971 we put out our first US anthology of the *Radical Therapist* – a collection of articles from the first year of the newspaper. Although the book was well received, we were ourselves critical of it, and of all our past issues, because of the change in direction that had taken place in our ideas. We have always had different positions on the *RT*'s role in making a revolutionary, but there was originally a *de facto* agreement to aim our work at professionals, students, and intellectuals, in the belief that they held the key to radical work in mental health. We have found, however, that while some of these people are open to change most of them are too comfortable in their professionally detached attitudes, pseudo-hip life-styles and removed position from world revolution.

At the same time we have come to realize more and more that psychology and psychiatry are simply another expression of an oppressive society, we have to see our work not so much as reform within a profession but as one part of a whole socialist movement. We see mental hospitalization as coming from the same established power that drops bombs over Hanoi. We see the culture of imperialism in therapy as well as in Saigon's brothels. We see more and more people who are misfits in society – outraged women and gays, 'psychotics', high-school dropouts, Vietnam veterans – all people whose lives are in contradiction to the system. Psychology is more than a professional field – it is an ideology, a belief in 'appropriate', 'normal' behaviour with coercion to back up that belief. From thorazine and electroshock in the hospitals to adjustment by therapists, proposed lobotomies for rebellious prisoners and racist IQ theories, psychology as a whole is corrupt and oppressive, responsive only to the needs of the ruling class.

What does it mean to build a revolutionary new world? This is a complex question, involving ongoing struggle and constant change. In its broadest outline, this new world would be one in which no one makes profit from another, where men do not dominate women, whites non-whites, parents children, and authority is not parcelled out in hierarchies. To build such a world we need a mass movement, one which is composed of more than just intellectuals. A total revolution to end such a system comprises many types of organizing: in factories, communities, schools, prisons, and hospitals; third-world, female and gay organizing; the setting up of counter institutions; and many others.

We have gone through many changes in ourselves and our editorial policy for the most part quite gradually – academic theoretical articles have given way to news and analysis of actual projects; the name of the newspaper has been changed from the *Radical Therapist* to *Rough Times* – 'Radical' is a term used by too many people who don't want to rock the boat, our concerns are larger than just therapy and 'therapy' is a concept implying the possibility of personal change without political change. Reactions to our changes have been as predicted – some professionals were upset, and felt left out; many patients, expatients, prisoners, and organizers saw *RT* moving ahead in a better direction. We know that more changes will come, that changes always come. It may be hard to be continually sure of our direction, but we have a better sense of it now.

This collection of articles, which we are very glad to make available to an English public, is taken from the first two years of our publication and combines the best from our two US books, the *Radical Therapist* and *Rough Times*. While some of the articles are North American in content, we feel that their lessons are universal – psychology and psychiatry have developed along similar lines in both countries and differences are those of detail rather than basic premises. If you want to keep up with RT, we publish eight times a year – overseas subscriptions are $10 a year; some London bookshops carry us too. We welcome contributions of material from readers. When writing to us, please enclose return postage by Universal Postal Union Coupon. Our address is PO Box 89p, Somerville, Massachusetts 02144, USA.

ROUGH TIMES Collective:
Phil Brown
Michael Galan
Nancy Henley

Acknowledgements

'Detherapizing Society', copyright © Richard Kunnes M.D.; 'Lobotomies and Prison Revolts', first printed in *Liberation News Service*, 3/8/72; 'Therapist Turned Woman', first printed in *Off Our Backs*, December 1971; 'The Myth of the Vaginal Orgasm', copyright © Anne Koedt, 1970; 'Gay Liberation Manifesto', first printed in *Chicago Seed*, by Carl Wittman with some help from Miller Francis; 'Madness and Morals', by Morton Schatzman, first printed in *Counter Culture*, ed. Joseph Berke (Peter Owen, 1970).

I. Towards a Theory of Radical Therapy

1. Radical Psychiatry: Principles

Claude Steiner

Psychiatry is the art of soul healing. Anyone who practises the art is a psychiatrist. The practice of psychiatry, usurped by the medical profession, is in a sad state of disarray. Medicine has done nothing to improve it; as practised today, medical psychiatry is a step sideways, into pseudoscientism, from the state of the art in the Middle Ages when it was the province of elders and priests as well as physicians.

Psychiatry as it is predominantly practised today needs to be changed radically, that is 'at the root'.

Psychiatry is a political activity. Persons who avail themselves of psychiatric aid are invariably in the midst of power-structured relationships with one or more other human beings. The psychiatrist has an influence in the power arrangements of these relationships. Psychiatrists pride themselves on being 'neutral' in their professional dealings. However, when one person dominates or oppresses another, a neutral participant, especially when he is seen as an authority, becomes an enforcer of the domination and his lack of activity becomes essentially political and oppressive.

The classic and prime example of this fact is found in psychiatry's usual role in relation to women where, at worst, psychiatrists promote oppressive sex roles and at best remain neutral, therefore supportive of them. The same is true of psychiatry's traditional role in relation to the young, black, and poor; in every case psychiatry's 'neutrality' represents tacit support of the oppressive *status quo*.

There are four types of psychiatrists. Alpha psychiatrists are conservative or liberal in their political consciousness and in their practice and methods of psychiatry; the largest majority of medical psychiatrists fall into this category. Beta psychiatrists are conservative or liberal in their politics and radical in their methods. Examples of this type are men like Fritz Perls and Eric Berne and the human potentialities psychiatrists, usually not physicians, who expand the boundaries of psychiatric practice, but tend to be unaware of the manner in which oppression is a factor in psychic suffering and ignore the political nature of their work. Gamma psychiatrists are radical in their politics but conservative in their practice. Examples of this are Laing and others (as a special case, Szasz, whose awareness of the politics of psychiatry is quite heightened) who practise old, outmoded methods of therapy based on Freudian or neo-Freudian theory with emphasis on individual psychotherapy, 'depth', and 'insight'. The fourth kind of psychiatrist is the radical psychiatrist, who is radical both politically and in his psychiatric methods.

The first principle of radical psychiatry is that in the absence of oppression, human beings will, due to their basic nature or soul, which is preservative of themselves and their species, live in harmony with nature and each other. Oppression is the coercion of human beings by force or threats of force, and is the source of all human alienation.

The condition of the human soul which makes soul healing necessary is alienation. Alienation is a feeling within a person that he is not part of the human species, that she is dead or that everyone is dead, that he does not deserve to live, or that someone wishes her to die. It may be helpful, in this connection, to remember that psychiatrists were originally known as alienists, a fact that seems to validate the notion that our forefathers knew more about psychiatry than we. *Alienation is the essence of all psychiatric conditions. This is the second principle of radical psychiatry.* Everything diagnosed psychiatrically, unless *clearly* organic in origin, is a form of alienation.

The third principle of radical psychiatry is that all alienation is the result of oppression about which the oppressed has been mystified or deceived.

By deception is meant the mystification of the oppressed into believing that she is not oppressed or that there are good reasons for her oppression. The result is that the person instead of sensing his oppression and being angered by it decides that his ill feelings are his own fault and his own responsibility. The result of the acceptance of deception is that the person will feel alienated. A good example of this is the depressed youth who does not wish to participate in a war, but is forced to do so and told that he's doing it for the benefit of his country, the benefit of his brothers and sisters, or even for his own benefit. If he neglects to see that he is oppressed in this situation and comes to believe the mystifications about it, he will then turn from someone who is angry at his oppression to someone who is alienated and believes that he is a coward. Another example is the woman who, angered by her husband's domination, ceases to enjoy sex with him. Again, if she fails to recognize her oppression she will conclude that she is at fault; that she is 'frigid', while if she becomes aware of the source of her anger she will recognize that her loving nature is intact.

Thus, the difference between alienation and anger about one's oppression is unawareness of deception. Psychiatry has a great deal to do with the deception of human beings about their oppression.

$$OPPRESSION + DECEPTION = ALIENATION$$
$$OPPRESSION + AWARENESS = ANGER$$

What, then, are the methods of radical psychiatry? *The radical psychiatrist sees anyone who presents himself with a psychiatric problem as being alienated, that is being oppressed and deceived about his oppression, for otherwise he would not seek psychiatric succour.* All other theoretical considerations are secondary to this one.

The basic formula of radical psychiatry is :

$$LIBERATION = AWARENESS + CONTACT$$

The formula implies that for liberation two factors are necessary. On the one hand, awareness. That is, awareness of oppression and the sources of it. This type of awareness is amply illustrated by the writings of Laing and the writings by radical feminists and blacks, and so on. However, this formula also implies that pure awareness of oppression does not lead to liberation. Awareness of oppression leads to anger and a wish to do something about one's oppression so that a person who becomes so aware changes from one who is alienated to one who is angry in the manner in which some black people and women have become angry. Anger, therefore, is a healthy first step in the process of liberation rather than an 'irrational', 'neurotic', or otherwise undesirable reaction. But liberation requires contact as well as awareness. That is to say, contact with other human beings who, united, will move against the oppression. This is why it is not possible to practise radical psychiatry in an individual psychotherapy context. An individual cannot move against his oppression as an individual; he can only do so with the support of a group of other human beings.

Thus it appears *radical psychiatry is best practised in groups* because contact is necessary. Because people seeking psychiatric help are alienated and therefore in need of awareness *a radical psychiatry group seems to require a leader or leaders* who will undertake to guide the liberation process. To avoid the leader's oppression of group members *each individual member should propose a contract with the group* that indicates his wish to work on a specific problem. Liberation from the leader's guidance is the ultimate goal of radical psychiatry and is indicated by the person's exit from the group.

Contact occurs between people in a number of different forms. Basically contact is human touch, or strokes, as defined by Berne. But contact includes also when people become aware of their oppression, permission, and protection. Permission is just what the word implies, a safe-conduct for a person to move against his oppressor and to 'take care of business'. This permission needs to come from a person or persons who at the moment feel stronger than the one who is oppressed, usually the leader. Along with the permission, the person who is to move against the oppression needs to know that he will be protected against the likely retaliation of the oppressor.

This, then, is the vital combination of elements in radical psychiatry: awareness to act against deception and contact to act against alienation. It should be re-emphasized that *neither awareness by itself nor contact by itself will produce liberation*. As an example, it is very clear that contact without awareness is

the essence of the therapeutic encounters of the 'human potentialities' movement. The potency of human contact and its
immediate production of well-being, as found at Esalen and the
present R A P Centre, is rightfully eyed with suspicion by therapists in the Movement because without awareness human contact has a capacity to pacify and reinforce the mystification of the
oppressed. It is equally clear that pure awareness, whether it be
psychoanalytic or political, does not aid the individual in overcoming oppression since the overcoming of oppression requires
the banding together of the oppressed.

2. Detherapizing Society

Rick Kunnes

The title of this article is uncoincidentally similar to Ivan Illich's *Deschooling Society*. In fact it's a paraphrase of many of Illich's key points. 'Learning' and 'feeling good' have become institutionalized and repressive. School and Therapy claim to help, to enhance, to care for and educate their clients. Both institutions do very little of these things, and in fact more likely miseducate and maltherapize.

While therapy is not the pervasive and all-encompassing institution that school is, at least number-wise, their analogous functions and parallel ideologies are nevertheless numerous.

A person completing two to three years of one-to-one therapy, at the rate of twice a week, will have had a therapy costing an amount ten times the median annual income of half of humanity. Therefore, to be therapized, is indeed to be in a privileged class. Unfortunately, even at these prices, individual well-being and social equality cannot be enhanced by the ritual of the conventional, or indeed any therapy system.

I wish to be clear that I am talking about literally any form of therapy, not only therapy as a private, fee-for-service business, and therapy as a community mental health programme, but also any radical therapy which dichotomizes people into therapists and therapized roles.

Therapy has the effect of imposing consumer standards. The consumer-patient aspires to the emotional life and social style of the therapist. It is difficult to go beyond the therapeutic-consumer society unless we understand that therapy inevitably reproduces such a society, regardless of the nature of the therapy.

Once a person has accepted the need for therapy, she or he is easy prey for other institutions. Once people have allowed their imaginations to be formed by the therapeutic setting and the therapist, the person-client-patient is conditioned to institutional planning of every sort. Therapy smothers the horizons of their imaginations.

The existence of therapists and therapy, in part, produces the demand for it. Once we have learned to need therapy, all our activities tend to take the shape of client relationships to other specialized institutions.

Therapy training centres teach by implication that the value of therapy increases with the amount of time spent in therapy ... for both the therapist and patient. The person addicted to therapy seeks security in compulsive therapizing, pushing, or consuming therapy. The person who experiences well-being as the result of a therapeutic process wants to reproduce it in others.

People who submit to the standard of others (in this case, therapists) for the measure of their own personal growth, soon apply the same ruler to themselves and other potential consumers. They no longer have to be put in their place, but put themselves into assigned slots, squeeze themselves into the niche into which they have been therapized to seek, and in the very process put their fellows into similar places.

In the 'therapeutic' world the road to happiness is paved with a therapeutic-consumer index. Therapists and therapeutic institutions sell therapy – a bundle of goods made according to the same process as merchandise and having the same structure. The production of new therapies begins with allegedly scientific *research*, on whose basis therapeutic *engineers* predict future demand and tools (e.g., drugs and community mental health centres) for the assembly line, within limits set by budgets and taboos. The *distributor*-therapist delivers the finished product to the *consumer*-patient, whose reactions are carefully studied and charted to provide research data for the preparation for the next model, which may be 'client-centred', 'short-term', 'conjoint', 'pharmacologic', 'leaderless group', and even 'radical'.

The result of this production process looks like any other modern staple. It is a bundle of planned meetings, a package of values, a commodity whose 'balanced appeal' makes it marketable to a sufficiently large number to justify the cost of production.

Consumer-patients are taught-urged to make their desires conform to marketed values. Thus, they are made to feel guilty if they do not behave according to the predictions of consumer-client-patient research, by 'getting well', not 'acting out', 'performing better' at school or work or sex, 'feeling better', 'seeking employment', 'getting/staying married', *et al.*

Even when accompanied by declining returns in comfort and well-being, Therapeutic Systems, Inc. pushes the person-client-customer to greater levels of consumption and expenditure. If nothing else, the therapeutic milieu teaches the value of escalation – the value of the American way of doing things. As Illich says:

> The Viet Nam war fits the logic of the moment. Its success has been measured by the number of persons effectively treated by cheap bullets delivered at immense cost, and this brutal calculus is unashamedly called 'body count'. Just as business is business, the never ending accumulation of money, so war is killing, the never ending accumulation of dead bodies.

In like manner, therapy is therapizing, and this open-ended process is counted in therapy-hours, or therapy-years, or days hospitalized. The various processes mentioned above are self-justifying. By economic standards, the country gets richer and richer. By death-accounting standards, the nation goes on winning its wars forever. And by therapeutic standards, the population becomes 'healthier' or 'better' or 'improved'.

The therapeutic setting pushes the person-patient-consumer to hunger for a steady absorption of therapy. However, the therapy consumed never yields the joy of having or feeling something to one's complete satisfaction. Each therapeutic issue or subject matter is raised and 'dealt with', with the instruction to go on consuming one more issue or subject. And last year's issue or subject, along with last year's manner and mode of dealing with it, are always obsolete for this year's consumer. The therapeutic racket builds on this demand. Therapeutic reformers promise each new generation of patient-consumers the latest and the best. For example, in recent years radicals have become intrigued with the democratizing potentials of videotape. When reformist psychiatrists and other élitist and nondemocratic therapists began turning increasingly to half-inch videotape, it did indeed begin to look like the 'greening' of therapy. Unfortunately, when one examines the therapeutic settings of such renowned therapy video-freaks as Milton Berger, M.D., one can't help but become rapidly disillusioned about Berger's and others' therapeutic efficacy and radical politics.

Videotape is considered to have a radical potential because it can be used and viewed by anyone. The artificial dichotomy between taper and viewer is removed and with it the mysticism of mass media. Videotape can turn the passive viewer into an active articulator of her/his surroundings, increase real communication, enhance community, and decrease alienation – all of which is therapeutic, and none of which has anything to do with the way therapists have used video.

Obviously, therapy which simply follows fads cannot be meaningful. On the other hand, therapy which simply 'evolves through time' is not, in and of itself, an improvement, particularly when that evolvement is along lines of advancing capitalism. The overarching trends in therapy systems have, in general, pretty much paralleled the trends in the economic and industrial system, namely a trend towards 'technologization' and glamorous mechanization. In psychiatry the setting of therapy is going from couches to cameras (albeit, video cameras). Therapy, Inc. has joined the electronics industry to become part of a therapeutic industrial complex. Though there has been an evolution in the technology of therapy, the politics of therapy remains the same. The artificial dichotomy between 'patient' and professional remains. The camera in the hands of the therapy professional is a one-way tube, controlled authoritarianly by the professional, mystifying and pacifying the 'patient'. Treatment and therapy remain under élitist control and are not a subject for collective decision making. The therapeutic setting is manipulated by the professional and the 'patient' objectified. Berger, *et al.*, don't seriously use feedback mechanisms, but rather the old broadcast model of a leader or master of ceremonies with a passive audience or 'patients'.

Professionals like Berger are earning over $100,000.00 per year by charging their 'patients' exploitative fees, fees so high that only the relatively well-off can afford to be treated. In such circumstances it's difficult to speak of videotape as 'serving the people' or of bringing 'power to the patients'. The money Berger, et al., take doesn't go to support the Black Panthers or other oppressed peoples, but for the maintenance of a fancy office and fancier equipment.

The techniques of videotape remain potentially radical, and as such we applaud their use as an adjunct, not to therapy, but to building communities. We continue to oppose the political context of contemporary therapy and the politics of its therapists. A pig therapist dispenses pig therapy, whether the 'patient' is on the couch or in front of the camera. In the hands of a Berger, videotape has become not the 'new morning' of a democratic milieu, but the latest form of technological rip-off.

In a capitalistic-expansionistic-consumptionistic society, both the therapeutic dropout, who is forever reminded what she or he missed, and the therapeutic graduate, who is made to feel inferior to the new breed of patient-consumers, sense where they stand in this ritual of rising deceptions, but nevertheless, usually continue to support a society which euphemistically calls the widening frustration gap a 'revolution of rising expectations'. But growth conceived of as open-ended consumption and eternal progress can never lead to maturity. Commitment to an unlimited quantitative increase vitiates the possibility of real psychological development.

Arnold Toynbee has pointed out that the decadence of a great culture is usually accompanied by the rise of a new Church which extends hope to the proletariat, while servicing only the needs of the ruling class. Psychotherapy seems suited to be that new Church of our decaying culture. No institution could better veil from its participants the deep discrepancy between social principles and political reality in today's world. Secular and scientific, it is of a piece with the modern mood. Its classical, critical veneer makes it appear pluralistic, if not anti-religious. Its subjects and subject-matter are defined by so-called scientific research. No one completes therapy – yet. Therapy never closes its doors on anyone (assuming the consumer's money is available) without first offering her or him one more chance at remedial, adult, continuing and ongoing therapy.

Therapy combines the expectations of the consumer, expressed in its claims, with the beliefs of the therapist-producer, expressed in its ritual. Therapy, as practised, fuses the growth in humiliating dependence on a master with the growth in the futile sense of omnipotence that is often typical of the patient-becoming-therapist, who wants to go out and therapize people to save themselves.

The Therapeutic Way of Life is not only a new Church. It is also one of the fastest-growing labour markets. The engineering of consumers has become one of the economy's principal growth factors. For example, 50 per cent of all hospital beds in the US are for 'mental illness'. Thirty to fifty per cent of many states' annual budgets is for 'mental health'.* The major drug companies which specialize in tranquillizers are the highest profit-making US corporations on a percentage basis. Community mental programmes have defined the whole world as their community of consumers.

As production costs decrease in rich nations, there is an increasing concentration of both capital and labour in the enterprise of equipping communities for disciplined consumption. During the past decade, capital investments directly related to therapy systems greatly rose. Therapy programmes give unlimited opportunity for legitimated waste – so long as its destructiveness goes unrecognized and the cost of palliatives goes up.

If we determine the number of people involved in 'therapeutic' settings, either on the consuming or pushing end, we realize that this arena has become a major employer of people's time and effort.

Alienation, in the traditional scheme, was a direct consequence of work becoming wage-labour, which deprived people of the

---

* Bertram Brown, M.D., Director of the National Institute of Mental Health, has said :

'Mental Health is big business ... It is usually the biggest public employer in the states ... Many states' mental health expenditures exceed 30 per cent of the state governments' annual fiscal budget.'

opportunity to create and be recreated. People are now pre- and post-alienated by therapy systems that isolate them from the world of work and pleasure. Therapy makes alienation preparatory to life, thus depriving therapy of reality and work of creativity. Therapy prepares one for the alienating institutionalization of life by pushing the need for one to be therapized. Once this lesson is learned, i.e., the need to be therapized, people lose their incentive to grow in independence and close themselves off to the surprises which life offers when it is not pre-determined by institutional definition.

Of course, therapy is not the only modern institution which has as its primary purpose the shaping of people's vision of reality. Advertising, mass media, schools and universities, and the design components of engineered products play their part in the ruling class's manipulation of people's demands. Therapy oppresses by making learning about oneself, about others, and about nature, depend on a pre-packaged process. Therapy can touch us so intimately that virtually none of us (i.e., therapists and therapized,) usually expect to be liberated from it by something else. We can only imagine other therapies, radical or otherwise.

The discovery that the development of a truly therapeutic milieu in our communities requires no therapy or therapists can be neither manipulated, nor imposed. Each of us, pushing or consuming therapy, is responsible for her or his own detherapizing. Collectively, we have the power to do it. People could not free themselves from the Crown until at least some of them had freed themselves from the Church – in our circumstances, Therapy.

Therapy systems are a good example of a new kind of enterprise, succeeding the guild, the factory and the corporation. The multinational corporations which have dominated the economy are now being complemented, and may one day be replaced, by supernationally planned service agencies, such as the multinational community mental health-social services centres. These enterprises present their services in such a way that people feel obliged to consume them. The services are internationally standardized, redefining the value of their services periodically. The apparatus of 'mental health care' defines a peculiar kind of health, whether the service is paid for by the state or by the individual. As Marcuse says, 'Health is a state defined by an élite.' Graded states of improved mental health fit the patient-consumer on the same international, endlessly escalating pyramid of quantification, no matter who directs the therapy. However, a liberation movement, which starts in the therapy setting and is nevertheless grounded in the awareness of therapist and patient as simultaneously exploiters and exploited, would parallel and augment other revolutionary movements.

Therapy has become a social problem. Now it is being attacked from many quarters. Scientists and governments, universities and agencies sponsor unconventional, if not mindless and exploitative, experiments all over the world in order to validate and evaluate, support and rationalize, therapy systems. They resort to unusual statistical devices in order to keep the faith and save face.

Our options are clear enough. Either we continue to believe that therapy is a product which justifies unlimited investments of time and money or we tear down the barriers that now impede opportunities for the development of a truly therapeutic community. The barriers are the political and economic institutions of Amerika. Those barriers can be torn only by political activity and revolutionary violence.

If instead we opt for more and better therapy, society will be increasingly dominated by totalitarian therapists (cf. Dr Kenneth Clark's APA speech on pills for peaceful presidents). Therapists will increasingly play overtly repressive roles. Pedagogical therapists will drug their pupils more in order to teach them better the lessons a repressive society wants them to learn, and the students, as patients or not, will drug themselves to gain relief from the pressures of therapist-teachers.

In summary, rituals, such as therapy, can hide from their participants discrepancies and conflicts between social principle and political reality. As long as we are not explicitly conscious of and actively fighting against the therapeutic process, we will remain politically unconscious.

3. On Training Therapists

Michael Glenn

The psychiatrist in training is embedded in a medically orientated matrix with a closed-guild tradition, whose model is master and apprentice. He is assumed to be inexperienced and naïve, a stumbling creature whose every step must be watched and checked. The model of supervision approximates that of therapist/patient, and the supervision constantly resorts to unbeatable ploys, like commenting on the trainee's psychological hang-ups. Mathematicians, businessmen, artists, actors, teachers, historians: all are acknowledged to have some sense of the world and of their place in it by the time they are thirty: yet the therapist in training is encouraged to see himself as grossly inadequate, ill-informed, and bumbling.

The professionalism of the medical model, with its aura and mystique, permeates psychiatric training. One is constantly mystified and perplexed. The completion of training allows the now-professional psychiatrist to begin mystifying others, even though he usually has no idea how he does it. He seems to become mature, capable, and a member of the guild in good standing the moment the diploma enters his hand.

Its model makes psychiatry invincible. Attempts to change are readily discredited as psychopathology, delayed adolescence, and acting out. The trainer rarely encounters the trainee as another person, a brother or sister. Training is marked by psychological put-down, intimidation, and guilt-invoking techniques. Its graduates then repeat their experience with their clients. Such a dehumanizing, destructive system must be changed.

Szasz, Laing, and others have shown how psychotherapy dehumanizes both patient and therapist. Goffman has shown this in asylums. The same is true for therapist training, which effects the professional annihilation of trainees by incorporating them into a corrupting structure, which they must accept to succeed.

They must play the game correctly. But learning to play the game correctly often ties them to its rules for life. It is a Medean shirt which cannot easily be removed once it is put on.

There are several features to this.

Professional mystification and the psychiatrist's role

Psychiatrists, being physicians, have endured years of psychological brainwashing called education. They have learned that, to be able to make an exorbitant income, they must assume a social mask of Responsibility and Omniscient Doctor. They are our society's shamans, though lacking in the latter's sense of true drama.

Medical training has certain values: (1) It lets the young psychiatrist see the system as it really is; (2) It helps him learn to act decisively in emergencies; (3) It gives him experience with ultimate, profound situations; (4) It provides him with a range of human experience – albeit as observer – usually forbidden others not in the guild; (5) It gives him status in the system.

In return, however, medical training tyrannizes the young psychiatrist in several ways: (1) It foists an image of the physician on him; (2) It keeps him an observer, not a participant; (3) It makes him seem/feel infallible; (4) It inculcates in him values of sacrifice and responsibility, while at the same time insisting he owes himself all the luxury he can later obtain, thus encouraging him to accept materialistic values as the true measure of his worth; (5) It estranges him from others.

Medical training supports the conventional values in this society: the *status quo*, traditional sex roles, the search for profit. The physician becomes a petit entrepreneur. He has to behave the correct way. He becomes a defender of the church, the family, the community, the nation. His role today is a far cry from what it was in the nineteenth century, when physicians were often, as sceptics and scientists, in the vanguard of social change. Now, comfortable and fat, they challenge little and accept much. They hang on to what they've got.

In addition, medicine is mystifying. Doctors have kept their numbers down. They conceal facts from patients. They hide behind the garb of their professionalism, as if they possess arcane secrets. The public goes along with them and attributes all kinds of knowledge and power to them which they do not possess. Use of drugs, treatment of illness, prognosis of common maladies: all these are kept as secrets for the medical profession only. Mystification augments their status. But, based on a lie – that only they are capable of holding the secrets – it makes the 'profession' ever paranoid, ever watchful, ever more secretive. Of course physicians resent pressure 'from below' to demystify.

The doctor's morality is conventional: thus oppressive. Physicians act to heal and patch up: not to challenge the fabric of the system which sustains them. Psychiatrists, at the top of the 'mental health' heap, may indulge in liberal causes without fear, especially in a liberal university or town setting; but they run into trouble if they become politically concerned beyond that. (I can cite five known instances of therapists being dismissed after becoming involved in community politics.)

The psychiatrist in training learns to treasure his élite identity, to pull rank on 'ancillary' and 'para-professional' personnel. His lengthy training lets him charge higher fees in private practice. He is a ubiquitous authority, assured prestige if he only behaves right.

The same is true of other therapist professionals. Each pecks on those beneath him; and all peck on the clients. Mystification of their skill maintains their invincibility.

Who needs medical training?

What is the rationale for psychiatrists – or any therapists – being physicians? How relevant is medical training?

Four years of medical school followed by an internship give the young psychiatrist the following: months of anatomy and biochemistry, histology, pathology, urology, surgery, cardiology. But he receives *no* sociology, psychology, anthropology, politics, or notions of human interaction. To be a physician, he endures all kinds of special training, which he only forgets later. Indeed, he has to *unlearn* his taught bias later on.

If the medical model is really important, all therapists could receive training in it. Certainly notions of public health, emergency care, and common maladies are useful to everyone who works with people. But the bulk of medical school's professionalism, formality, and specialization is irrelevant to the therapist's work.

The usual arguments for psychiatrists having to be physicians – thus distinguishing them from psychologists, nurses, social workers, etc. – are rationalizations for historical accident and caste privilege. Emotional difficulty was defined by physicians as a *medical* illness: thus it had to be treated by a physician specialist in emotional illness. The medical model makes psychiatry oppressive: people are defined as 'patients', they are told they have 'diseases', they are locked up, shocked, socially denigrated, and ostracized because they are 'sick'. The psychiatrist becomes society's cop.

Do people with problems in living really have an 'illness'?

The medical model makes psychiatrists a healthy élite. It makes the patients an oppressed class. Other therapies too, insofar as they participate in the one-up, one-down relationship, join psychiatry as oppressive.

The issue of prescribing drugs is a red herring. Because only physicians can prescribe the drugs needed to treat emotional 'illness', they maintain a monopoly on their role. This issue is so contaminated with drug-company commercialism, 'diagnostic', and mystifying guild élitism that any sensible discussion of it is impossible. The simple fact is, if drug use is important, most people can learn about it in a rather brief time.

Others argue that psychiatrists need medical training to 'catch' brain tumours and other 'organic' diseases which might masquerade as depression, conversion reactions, etc. The argument is weak. If such training is important for a therapist to have, it can be taught most therapists in a rather brief time. It doesn't take five years of medical training to recognize organic disease.

Medical school is about 80 per cent a waste of time for the young psychiatrist. It should be scrapped.

Repression of trainees

In most psychiatric training centres, the residents, young adults, are powerless. Their curriculum is not theirs to make; their routine is set up for them to follow. 'Others, wiser than they' determine what they shall and shall not do. Resident advisory councils are false fronts.

The ideal therapist in training is intelligent and afraid: indecisive and obsessional, he can be made to feel inadequate and guilty with ease. Over and over again, in my own training, administrators and supervisors would push residents down, dismissing their grievances as adolescent psychopathology, criticizing their efforts at assuming responsibility for their own education. The amazing thing is how readily the residents accepted this image of themselves. They got themselves into therapy. They forswore social activism to uncover the 'causes' of their rebelliousness within themselves. A more thorough job of mystification and brainwashing was never achieved!

Here, at random, are some incidents from my own experience:

1. An activist resident who organized the community against the university's 'mental health centre' – an imperialistic fraud – was fired for 'clinical incompetence'. The other residents refused to create a stir to defend him.

2. The director of the emergency room service decided that third-year residents would have to see every patient the first-year resident saw. This rule had not been observed for years. Rather than discuss the situation, the director insisted his will would be followed. Residents' arguments could not move him. Yet the residents would not consider a strike or collective action to dramatize their opposition. Their attitude was: Why make waves; we'll soon be out.

3. A resident rotating through a state hospital criticized its programme to its director. The latter complained to a supervisor, and the resident was severely upbraided for 'unprofessional behaviour'.

4. A paper written about the state hospital system was bottled up by the administration and refused imprimatur.

5. An anonymous letter circulated among the supervisory staff which demanded higher salaries for residents and threatened to call the press unless its demand was met was angrily denounced by several of the staff at a residents' meeting. The unknown author – it was unclear to the residents if any of their number had ever written it – was called 'seriously disturbed' and told to get himself into therapy. The issue of salaries was not discussed, except when the director advised any resident who wanted more money that he could go elsewhere. The anger and fear of the staff was incredible.

6. The grapevine in the programme proclaimed that, so long as a resident didn't rock the boat, he could leave the programme and make $40,000 a year. Most of the residents swallowed the bait. What earthly incentive could they then have for challenging the system!

Our programme emphasized one-to-one treatment, psychoanalytic insight, and hospital care. Family and group work was almost nonexistent; and the 'community programme' existed in a vacuum, whose instructors never discussed what was going on in the actual community outside but instead prepared the residents for administrative posts.

It was frightening how few residents saw any value in opposing a system which they all agreed was oppressing them. Their attitude was to wait until they were out and on top themselves. Their salvation, in other words, lay in their future capacity to bilk, brainwash, co-opt and alienate others. They preserved the illusion that, so long as they disagreed inwardly, they could go along with the outward demand and still preserve their integrity.

Unless training programmes are changed, therapists will continue to serve their own interest, not that of the people. They will be men of good will in an oppressive structure.

Therapy and politics

Therapists are politically naïve. They come through a professional education which gives them little understanding of social and political issues. Psychiatrists probably suffer the most through their long isolation in medical school, where they remove themselves from their society and give themselves the illusion they are gods. They are ignorant of their place in society; they are ignorant of what is going on in the real world; they are victims of a narrow horizon.

Many therapists go into debt to complete training. Making money to them is important. Staying within the system they can rise out of debt and become affluent in a matter of years. It is no wonder they guard their possessions jealously and are angry at those who 'impatiently' press for change.

The life-style of the therapist – certainly the psychiatrist – proclaims his place in the *status quo*. He lives comfortably. off in the suburbs, or in a town house. His children are in private school. He has a maid to free his wife. He owns colour TV sets, cars, boats, land in the country, stereos, tailor-made clothes, season opera tickets, a fine portfolio of stocks; and takes vacations around the world. *How can he ever be an instrument of change, then?* He owes allegiance to the system in which he prospers.

Thus it is that he becomes an oppressor, an enemy of the people. While he eats high off the hog, others starve. Even when he is 'liberal' he rarely risks his security for his ideas. Within the present system, it seems, he has no choice. That is why the system must change.

Therapy is not a branch of medicine, nor is it a social science

Therapy is a discipline in its own right, dealing with human feelings and human relationships in a human society. It was a historical accident that therapy became incorporated under its various disciplines.

If we accept this, it then becomes clear how unfortunate and divisive are the distinctions between the various therapy fields. For some therapists to have medical training and others social work training and others experimental psychology training, etc., means that the field of therapy is being partitioned like Poland in the eighteenth century. Therapy demands its own institutions, its own training programmes, its own practice. The therapy fields belong together, brothers and sisters under one roof.

Current training programmes prepare young therapists for roles which already exist in the system: institutional roles, private practice roles, research and teaching roles. But they don't prepare them for re-examining and challenging the system itself.

The young therapist may see this, but he isn't sure how to deal with it. Staying clean has its advantages. Going outside the system is a hardship. Only a few will take the risk, and they can be easily isolated.

New training programmes are needed if any change is to occur.

Alternative training programmes

Alternative institutions have risen dramatically in recent years. Spurred on by Goodman and others, free universities, free clinics, and new life-styles have emerged. Roszak documents the movement's strength. Berke presents its rationale. Domhoff underscores its political importance.

Rather than confront the present system head on and be massacred by its flunkies, many today are working 'to let grass push through cracks in the concrete': putting energies into new forms and new ways and letting the system collapse of its own dead weight. Some attempts have already been begun. Others will soon arise and solidify. The following is a sketch of what they will involve:

1. Training will not divide people into categories such as 'psychiatrist' and 'social worker'. All people in the programme will be therapists. They will be trained as such. Further skills can be obtained elsewhere.

2. Training will be open to all people, not made a class privilege. Those from poorer communities and minority groups will have ready access to the training their communities need. There will be an end to honky experts who come as colonialists to tell people how to live.

3. Training will be funded by local communities.

4. Training will be demystified and deprofessionalized. What is necessary to know will be taught, straight out. What is unnecessary will be trashed. Therapists will be workers in their communities, like any other worker. Their skills are needed for the common good. But their skills will not make them a 'professional' élite.

5. Training programmes will be interdisciplinary, dealing with psychology and politics, sociology and art, the mass media, the analysis of power, theories of interaction, and contemporary history.

6. The model of training will change from hierarchical, obsessional, master/pupil interaction to a more open, popular, democratic form. All whose ideas and insights are valid will be heard. Age itself will carry no guarantee of wisdom.

7. New techniques will be evaluated openly, without fear of change. Therapy training centres will be like free universities, not trade schools. Free inquiry and dissent will be encouraged, not put down as 'pathology'. Therapists will become politically involved in the overall struggle against oppression.

8. The number of therapists trained will increase, thus benefiting the people by more available, more adequate, more relevant care.

9. Incomes for practising therapists will be appropriate to their work. No one will grow wealthy from the people's suffering.

10. Modes of collective practice and communal living will be tried, in the belief that the therapist's life-style strongly affects his work. Therapists will not live aloof from their clients, distanced by class and interest, élite oppressors helping only from 'above'. They will be part of their community.

11. Therapy will be available to all, not sold to those who can afford it like fried chicken or any other commodity. It will be geared to the needs of communities, not the needs of professionals.

Let us push ahead, towards a radical therapy.

4. Radical Psychiatry and Movement Groups

Claude Steiner

Radical psychiatry's main goal is to help human beings overcome alienation. Because overcoming alienation requires contact with other human beings in groups it is important that radical psychiatry provide guidelines for the healthy functioning and survival of groups. When people who are interested in radical changes organize groups they quite naturally wish to organize them along lines which differ from the authoritarian and alienating basis on which oppressive, establishment groups are usually organized. As a consequence the structure of such groups is usually uncertain and indeterminate, and the cohesiveness of such groups against external attack is weak. There are two types of attacks upon movement groups which have become classic examples: one of them is the levelling of hierarchies; the other is the game 'Lefter Than Thou'.

Lefter Than Thou

It is a phenomenon completely familiar to everyone who has worked in a radical organization that in the course of events it happens that one or more people will attack the leadership by professing to be more revolutionary or more radical than the leadership. Since it is always possible that this is the actual state of affairs, namely that the leadership of the group has become counter-revolutionary, many an organization has been totally torn apart by this kind of argument; in many cases organizations that were doing true and valuable revolutionary work.

How is one to distinguish a situation in which a splinter group is for one reason or another simply attacking the leadership illegitimately, or whether such a group is in fact justified in its attacks?

I would like to cast the illegitimate attack of the leadership of a group by a splinter group in the mould of a Bernean game. The game is called 'Lefter Than Thou'. The thesis of the game is that a group of people doing revolutionary work which has a certain amount of momentum always includes a sub-group of people with revolutionary aspirations but who are incapable of mustering either the energy or the courage to actually engage in such activities.

'Lefter Than Thou' players are persons who are dominated by an extremely intolerant and demanding conscience (or Parent) on the one hand and are not able to mobilize their sacred Child to do any work on the other. Criticism of the activities of the group and the decisions of the leaders becomes a substitute for revolutionary work. This criticism occurs, usually, at meetings where work would ordinarily be discussed, and it always replaces effective action. 'Lefter Than Thou' players are either effective in dismembering the organization and wind up without a context in which to work, or they are expelled from the organization by the effective leadership of it and find themselves again in a situation in which no work can be done. In both cases they have a clear-cut justification for their lack of activity, and this is the pay-off of the game.

It is a hallmark of 'Lefter Than Thou' players that they are angry, often 'Angrier Than Thou'; it is quite possible, however, to distinguish the anger of a 'Lefter Than Thou' player from the anger of a person who is effectively reacting to his oppression.

'Lefter Than Thou' players are most always children of the middle class. On this basis it is easy to see why a group of black militants can hardly be accused of playing 'Lefter Than Thou' while a group of white college students who accuse these black militants of not being radical enough is suspect.

Whether a person plays 'Lefter Than Thou' or not can be determined by making a simple assessment of how much revolutionary action he takes other than at meetings over, say, a period of a week. It will be seen that if observed closely, the activity of a 'Lefter Than Thou' player occurs mostly in the form of an intellectual 'head trip' at meetings and hardly ever in the real world. 'Lefter Than Thou' players will excel in destructive arguments or sporadic destructive action when sparked or impelled by others. But it will be seen that they lack the capacity to gather momentum in creative or building work and that they lack the capacity to work alone due to the extreme intransigence of the Pig Parent in their head which will defeat, before it is born, every positive, life-giving effort.

It appears, therefore, as if that extraordinarily divisive game 'Lefter Than Thou' is played by persons whose oppression has been largely oppression of the mind. This form of intellectual oppression, a Calvinist 'morality of the intellect', is usually accomplished in a liberal context in the absence of societal or familial application of force, a context in which action or force is actually disavowed so that the chains that bind the person are strictly psychological or within the head, yet most paralysing indeed. When anger is felt it is not expressed physically but in the form of destructive talk.

Movement groups are especially vulnerable to destructive talk as their leaders are often in awe of and mystified by intellectual accomplishment. It must be remembered that a game has to be played by the Victim as well as the Persecutor. The Victim in this case being the leaders of the group under attack who, ordinarily, are more than willing to submit to the persecution of the 'Lefter Than Thou' player. This willingness to respond to 'head trips' and intellectual arguments is a characteristic of certain cultural subgroups, so that while a 'Lefter Than Thou' player would be scoffed at and ignored in a very clearly action-oriented movement group, 'Lefter Than Thou' players have a capacity to affect the decisiveness of the guilt-ridden intelligentsia.

This game is a liberal, intellectualized form of the aggressiveness that has been observed among the oppressed poor and the black. It is a well-documented fact that crimes against persons occur mostly between members of oppressed subcultures. Fanon in *The Wretched of the Earth* illustrates how the savage, homicidal and capricious criminality that has been observed among

Algerians dissolved when the war of liberation became established. The supposed fact that Algerians are born criminals, taught even to Algerians by the faculty of Algiers, was not only not a fact but a mystification of their oppression. The actual fact of the matter is that the oppressed, when they have no access to their oppressors, either because their oppression is mystified or because their oppressors are not within reach, are likely to wind up at each other's throats. 'Lefter Than Thou' is a case of the frustrated and mystified oppressed seizing the throats of their brothers and sisters because of an incapacity to engage in positive, creative revolutionary action.

The measure of a revolutionary's worth is the work that she or he does. When a person questions the effectiveness of the leadership of a group or the work of a group, the first question to that person should be, 'What work are you doing?' It will be found that in most cases the critic is a person who is doing very little or no work. If that person is, in fact, contributing a great deal of work outside of the discussions at meetings, then the challenge of the validity of the leadership's goals and methods is again open to question. Thus, the demystification of a critic's actual work output is a very important tool in the maintenance of a cohesive movement group.

Another usual attack upon movement groups which is also quite effective is 'levelling'.

Levelling, hierarchies, and leadership

The greatest single evil in mankind is the oppression of human being by human being. Oppression ordinarily expresses itself in the form of hierarchical situations in which one person makes decisions for others. It has been the wish of many to eradicate this greatest of all evils from their lives. In order to do so some people have completely levelled hierarchical situations and have attempted to function socially in the total absence of leadership, in the hope of building a society without hierarchies in which the greatest evil – oppression – cannot find a breeding ground.

With the spectre of the worst pig, authorization hierarchy

haunting them, people have attempted to work in organizations which have been levelled of all hierarchies. In my opinion such organizations, when they involve more than about eight persons, have an extremely low chance of survival. When 'levellers' enter an organization and impose willy-nilly a no-hierarchies principle they usually bring about the ultimate destruction of the group.

I will attempt to demonstrate the fallacy of levelling of hierarchies, and will attempt to present an alternative to levelling which I believe is capable of making rational use of the valuable qualities of leadership in people while preventing that extension of leadership into oppression which is such a scourge upon humankind.

First let me define some terms:

I will call oppression the domination by force or threats of force of one person by another.

I will call levelling a situation in which, at least publicly, no leader is recognized and no hierarchy is allowed in a group, even though leadership and hierarchy may in fact exist.

I will call a hierarchy a situation in which one human being makes decisions for other human beings.

I will call a leader a person in a group who is seen as possessing a skill or quality which causes others to wish to learn or profit from that quality.

Hierarchies come in a great variety of forms, from the murderous hierarchies in a capricious war to the mother-child hierarchy, including the hierarchies between teacher and student, man and woman, black and white, master and slave, factory owner and exploited worker, foreman and journeyman, craftsman and apprentice. Some of these hierarchies are alienating and dehumanizing. Others are not. To relate to all hierarchies as if they were all dehumanizing and evil is a great error, bordering on mindlessness. Hierarchies should be analysed in terms of whether they affect human beings well or badly.

There are at least three human hierarchies which are of obvious value to humankind and which clearly would not profit from being levelled.

The first and most basic hierarchy is the hierarchy between mother and child. Here one person makes decisions for another person and it is difficult to see how levelling this hierarchy would be of any advantage to humankind. When this mother-child or parent-child hierarchy is extended beyond its fruitful and natural reach, namely when it is imposed by force or threats of force and beyond the period in which the child needs parental protection and when it is extended to large aggregations of people, then this parent-child hierarchy becomes the model for the military, the great corporations and so on.

Another such is the hierarchy between a human being who is in great physical pain or need (the sick, the hungry, the wounded, the deranged) and another human being who has the means to fulfil that need. When a person is in dire physical need he may wish that another human being will make decisions for him. Again, this natural hierarchy which is conducive to well-being can be extended into one that is damaging as has been the case with the hierarchy that has been created by the medical profession and the attending psychiatric and other mental health professions. Again, the continuation of the need beyond necessity, the continuation of ministration beyond necessity, the encouragement of the preservation of the hierarchy even in the absence of physical need, have resulted in a hierarchical medical establishment which at this point may be doing more against human health than for it. This may sound startling but if one separates medical knowledge which is vast and potentially helpful from medical activity which is self-serving and oppressive one can see that the medical establishment is not only not fully serving humanity but holding back potential help from it.

A third hierarchy is based on differences of skill between human beings in which one person who can be considered a craftsman is sought out by another person who wishes to learn her craft. This hierarchy in which one person places himself below the other in knowledge is desirable to both. The apprentice, by recognizing his need to learn and by riveting his attention to his master, is likely to acquire a skill more quickly and more thoroughly than a student who questions the master's knowledge. On the other hand a teacher who is given the attention and recognition of an apprentice finds his teachings the greatest rewards for his life effort. Both the craftsman and the apprentice profit from this process, and it is hard to see how either of them, especially the student, is damaged by it. Again, this natural hierarchical situation can be extended beyond its necessity so that certain persons are forever kept in an inferior position to others with respect to their skills. This, of course, is the basis for most universities and professional schools and is again an example of where a natural hierarchy can be extended into an oppressive and evil one.

It is characteristic of humanizing hierarchies that they are first, voluntary; second, bent upon their own destruction or self-dissolving.

All three of the above mentioned beneficial hierarchies can be extended into oppressive ones. The tendency toward dehumanizing hierarchies that may exist in human beings can be overcome by human beings who decide that they wish to do so. That very same tendency can be empowered by the human intelligence, and has been, to the point of building monstrous hierarchies which may now consume us. As human beings we have the choice between mindlessly extending natural hierarchies to the point where they will devour us, or equally as mindlessly levelling and abolishing them, or using our intelligence, wherever it suits us, to create groups with humanizing, beneficial hierarchies when needed.

I wish to postulate an intelligent principle of authority which discriminates between hierarchy and oppression and which I hope will be useful to people working in movement organizations.

The first principle of human hierarchies is that they be voluntary and that they be self-dissolving, that is that the eventual historical outcome of the group's work be to make the hierarchy unnecessary.

The second principle of human hierarchies is that leaders shall be responsive and responsible.

In order for a hierarchy to be voluntary it cannot involve oppression or coercion by force or threats of force. As a consequence, no one shall use force or threats of force in any situation relating to human beings within a movement or an organization of which he's a member. Intimidation of group members by psychological means (pigging) must be avoided by developing an atmosphere of mutual protection between group members.

Responsive leaders are leaders that are available for criticism by group members. Thus leadership can be extended only as far as it remains possible for all group members to make extended face-to-face contact with the leaders.

Finally, a responsible leader is one who feels the impact of his or her actions and takes responsibility for them. This is a human quality which can only be assessed by observation. Responsibility is judged from the leader's previous actions and can only be ascertained over a period of time during which his or her work is open to scrutiny and during which the important quality of responsibility is observed.

The same kind of guilt that operates in the leadership when faced with 'Lefter Than Thou' players comes into effect when confronted with a leveller.

The self-doubt of a leader is the greatest aid to the leveller. Oppressors don't respond to such attacks at all, but good leaders are prone, because of their basic wish to be responsive and responsible, to allow the attacks of a few to vitiate their useful work for the many. Thus when faced with such attacks leaders should responsibly investigate their work and responsively obtain feedback from all the group's members before abdicating their leadership. Only if this analysis reinforces the levellers' argument should a leader allow that most precarious process, levelling, to occur in the group.

5. Civilization and its Dispossessed: Wilhelm Reich's correlation of sexual and political repression

Phil Brown

Currently the work of Wilhelm Reich is becoming very popular: especially *The Mass Psychology of Fascism,* of which three editions have been printed in the last year and a half. The questions which Reich deals with for the most part are sexuality in 'human nature', the possibilities of freedom in the context of human civilization, and authoritarianism (especially fascism) in light of sexual repression. Fascism is seen very much as the result of authoritarian patterns, primarily sexual, in society. The problem stems from Freud's work and Reich is not the only one to answer it – Fromm and Marcuse have dealt with the matter extensively.

What is Freud's original theory which gives rise to these inquiries and critiques? After Freud had laid down a complete system of psychopathology he turned to socio-historical theorizing. Following up on *Totem and Taboo* with its primal horde, murder of the primal father, and the resultant repressive mores of civilization, Freud wrote *Civilization and Its Discontents*, a very bad translation of *Das Unbehagen in der Kultur* (discomfort or *malaise* in society). This was his definitive work on the nature of civilization and its requisite social control. For Freud, the pleasure principle, as enticing and pleasurable to the individual, is to be controlled by the reality principle which dictates correct social conformity so that society may 'advance'. This is a psychologization of the earlier *The Ego and the Id*: the ego mediating the 'bad' id instincts with the aid of the moralistic superego. Freud asserts that civilization cannot progress if the instincts are not sublimated, channelled to another pathway. This means primarily the sublimation of Eros, sexuality. Civilization, for Freud, is nothing more than an institution 'to protect men against nature and to adjust their mutual relations', a tool with which humanity can aspire to 'higher psychical activities – scientific, artistic, or ideological'.

Freud sees humanity as basically evil – he replaces original sin with instincts – and repression (especially sexual) is the way to control people. He invents Thanatos, the destructive, aggressive death instinct – as if Eros were not enough. Now, Freud sees the need to control this mystical aggressiveness as well as a 'normal', 'healthy' libido; control 'like a garrison in a conquered city'. (Is this a revolutionary anti-Victorian or a Junker militarist?)

Sexuality was a great threat to Freud, and he psychologized to such an extent that he demanded authoritarian social control to guarantee the success of familial sexual repression on a widespread societal scale. In 1933 his wish came true, but the Nazis were ungrateful and Freud was disappointed.*

Marcuse, in *Eros and Civilization,* wrote a 'philosophical inquiry' supporting most of the beliefs of *Civilization and Its Discontents.* Nearly the only difference was the hope for a 'non-repressive reality principle', but no idea is given of how that will be brought about. Although Marcuse well understands 'repressive desublimation' (the fetishist sexualization of non-sexual objects, as in advertising), he doesn't give any indication of how to fight against it. Marcuse is basically pessimistic about people's ability to live lives which they themselves control. He tries to get us to believe that Freud's view contains within it the possibilities of liberation, that it contains hope for a non-repressive culture, but this is not the case for either Freud or Marcuse – the latter picks out of context to prove Freud's 'humanism', and his choice of pickings is not too attractive: mainly a collection of Freud's parenthetical *mea culpas.*

Even Marcuse's fantasy of a non-repressive reality principle is distasteful and as mechanistic as Freud ever was: 'The body in its entirety would become an object of cathexis. . .' What does this

---

* 'Freud was able to justify the renunciation of happiness on the part of humanity as splendidly as he defended the fact of infantile sexuality. A few years later, a pathological genius – making the best of human ignorance and fear of happiness – brought Europe to the verge of destruction with the slogan of "heroic renunciation".' (*The Function of the Orgasm.*)

mean? Do we hear even one word about the quality of people's lives, save that quality is important? No – Marcuse's system is in the realm of pure ideas: free, but useless.

Fromm switches back and forth from this pessimism to a half-hearted optimism, but he at least challenges Freud's mysticism concerning instincts. *Escape From Freedom* views humanity as afraid and somewhat unable to live in free relationships, but *The Sane Society* reverses that into some hope for social change, since Fromm sees society as the most important variable in determining the conditions of the psyche. Although he, along with Horney and Sullivan, led a direction within psychoanalytical circles which demanded a certain materialist basis, none of them offered a real radical outlook. Nevertheless, they were important, and Marcuse's attack on them as 'neo-Freudian revisionists' is the worst kind of 'lefter-than-thou' game, since Marcuse himself retreats into orthodox, conservative Freudianism.

The one person whom Marcuse did not have the courage, or capacity, to answer in such a manner was Wilhelm Reich, who had gone far beyond the neo-Freudians in search of an answer to the question of society and sexuality. Reich had begun a favourable association with Freud and the 'inner circle' of psy-choanalysis, but there was no way for it to last, especially upon Reich's publishing of *The Mass Psychology of Fascism*. This book followed his disagreement with Freud over *Civilization and Its Discontents*, and reasserted in more radical form the correl-lation of sexual and political repression discussed in *The Sexual Revolution*. He pressed the point that sexual repression is not instinctually based, but rather a result of socio-economic conditions.

Reich spends a good deal of time in *The Function of the Orgasm* refuting *Civilization and Its Discontents*. Concerning the reality principle, Reich states: 'Freud neither questioned the irrational in this "reality", nor did he ask which kind of pleasure is compatible with sociality and which kind is not.' The sexual sublimation required by civilization 'dams up' sexual life-energy and causes psychic disturbances on both the individual and mass levels. Reich was very upset at the psychoanalytic position that all instincts must be sublimated or rejected, a position 'based on a fundamental misconception of sexuality'. Psychoanalysis was at a dead-end: its 'psychologizing of sociology as well as of biology took away every prospect for a practical solution to these enormous problems'. Reich saw Freud as never changing his views on the immutability of human structure and existence, and proposed to do Freud's unfinished work in a biological/sociological investigation.

Reich prefaces *Mass Psychology* by showing how the surface of society is a mask of perverse distortions of all 'genuine expressions of life'. But he not only opposes this function of society; he sees it as changeable:

> We, however, decline to accept the error of idealist philosophy, namely that this human structure is immutable to all eternity. After social conditions and changes have transmuted man's original biological demands and made them a part of his character structure, the latter reproduces the social structure of society in the form of ideology.

This mass sublimation, and idealist approaches to it, have been partly responsible for the development of fascism, the highest form of authoritarian social structure – 'the organized political expression of the structure of the average man's character ... the basic emotional attitude of the suppressed man of our machine civilization and its mechanistic-mystical conception of life'.

This is, of course, the exact opposite of Freud's views: civilization and its requisite sublimation are an evil rather than a benefit in Reich's eyes. Where Freud blames the individual for not resisting socio-sexual sublimation, Reich holds the person responsible for *not* resisting it.

What method will Reich use to investigate the mass psychology of fascism? Not psychoanalysis, for his disagreement with it was too fundamental, although he maintained certain Freudian elements for many years thereafter. Marxism too he rejected – not because of a failure in Marx's thought, but because of the failure of the so-called Marxist parties to comprehend fascism on account of their vulgar orthodoxy and refusal to deal with repressed sexuality*. Also important is Reich's moving to a purist

* For an understanding of the failure of the Communist Party in Germany to grasp the importance of sexuality in the political struggle, see Reich's *What is Class Consciousness?* (Socialist Reproductions, London).

position in which class structure does not count: 'There are no class distinctions when it comes to character.' Marxism is, in fact, rejected more strongly than psychoanalytic theory.

Reich turns to his own method of character-analytic vegeto-therapy with a comprehension of the individual in a social environment, involving a loosening of the 'armour' of the musculature and the genitals in order to liberate bound-up sexual energy.

Strongly fighting against economic determination, Reich formulates the theory of ideology becoming a material force. This occurs as a continuation of actual social conditions which engendered certain human behaviour, but this behaviour is no longer practicable for new social conditions: 'The psychic structures lag behind the rapid changes of the social conditions from which they derive, and later come into conflict with new forms of life.'

Reich follows, generally, Marx's ideas of consciousness, but adds the Gramscian theory of cultural hegemony – the psychological oppression in advanced capitalist society in which ruling class ideology becomes the dominant ideology through the transmission of it by social institutions.

For Reich the most dangerous and omnipresent sublimation is that of sexuality, conducted mainly through the family. Sexual repression of the basic life/sexual energy in children leads to the masses of people accepting this nuclear kernel of authoritarian society, and makes them ripe for fascism.

Why is the family the conductor of this authoritarianism, and why is the family the nucleus of society? Using Engels' interpretation (*The Origins of the Family, Private Property and the State*) of the social anthropology of Morgan and Bachhofen, Reich traces patriarchy from its birth as guardian of surplus value and division of labour to the present when it functions to control the economic unity of the family in the path of the *status quo*. Sexuality, as the basic life energy, is repressed, this repression being the most effective means of control by the authoritarian patriarchy:

The interlacing of the socio-economic structure with the sexual structure of society and the structural reproduction of society takes place in the first four or five years and in the authoritarian family. The church only continues this function later. Thus, the state gains an enormous interest in the authoritarian family: it becomes the factory in which the state's structure and ideology are moulded.

Continuous sexual repression makes children fearful, shy, respectful of authority out of coercion and fear, docile, malleable, afraid of their own sexuality. Built up from the nuclear family, mass sexual repression lends itself to authoritarian statism. Reich sees militaristic personality coming out of dammed-up libido, coupled with fear of officers and other hierarchical persons as authoritarian father-figures.

Thus, ideology, once a response to material force, becomes a material force itself. Reich did not clearly see how this could fit into a Marxist framework, which is why I stated earlier that Reich did not utilize a *conscious* Marxist methodology; nevertheless, it fits to a certain extent, particularly when viewed in terms of Luxemburgian spontaneity (*Mass Strike*) and Gramscian cultural hegemony (*The Modern Prince and Other Writings*).

It may seem that Reich has replaced economic determinism with sexual determinism. But that is mainly relevant to his later years when he worked on orgone theory, after having ceased work on socio-political matters. What is important is that a thorough understanding of the role of the family in society, coupled with seeing sexual repression as the most intense form of family authoritarianism, leads to grasping the crucial role of sexuality in society.

Children for the most part are brought up in sterile atmospheres where anything sexual in nature is stifled, displaced, or perverted by the parents. Childhood masturbation is punished, and the child receives threats of the most dire consequences for giving him- or herself pleasure. 'Polymorphous perversity' (including masturbation as mentioned above, but more as well: mutual sexuality, anal eroticism, etc.) is treated likewise. Parents' sexuality is mystified and hidden, often made to seem dirty to the children. From Freud comes the primacy of the 'Oedipal' situation, reflecting society's fear of the liberating possibilities of childhood sexuality. The 'Oedipal' myth is a psychologization of the concrete reality of the father-dominated, sexually repressive family in which the child rebels against abstract authority. The wide acceptance of this myth is a functional proof of the seriousness of the situation which engenders it.

Such a full-blown mystery cult is of great use to the fascists, especially since they realize that it is a part of the fascist background and mentality. The Nazis utilized pent-up sexual frustration and fears; they mystified the family even more than it was before. Sexual purity was raised to a pinnacle – only procreation was desired or tolerated. Religious mysticism was employed, with the nation replacing the church and the leader replacing God. In their invention of the Hellenistic origins of the 'Aryan' race, the Nazis embraced ascetic gods, shunning Dionysus who represented unbridled sexuality. Classism and sexism came together: fascism crushed the workers' movement and then equated the suppressed class with 'alien races', with whom the fear of interbreeding is based on fear of the mythic sexuality of the masses. This is not uncommon in authoritarian systems – Cleaver's brilliant observations in *Soul on Ice* show how the oppressed blacks have been mystified by white sexuality anxiety inventing legends of black sexuality, a situation still very widespread in the US. The French held the same attitudes towards the Algerians – as Fanon points out (*The Wretched of the Earth* and *A Dying Colonialism*), the psychological make-up of the oppressor will be reflected in that of the oppressed by identification and by social conditioning. The sexual reality of societal oppression is a thousand times mirrored in the sexual reality being distorted under the authoritarian rule.

Reich sees the 'emotional plague' of sexual repression in the masses as ready to embrace the *Führer* as representative of the authoritarian sexual suppression of society. But it need not be a Hitler – the plagued people will also be similarly enslaved in a society with a fine liberal veneer. Under that veneer is the irrationality of authoritarianism, this irrationality being inevitable since 'sexual inhibition prevents the average adolescent from thinking and feeling in a rational way'. Irrationality becomes a key concept in the Reichian critique: it plays the role of blocking out logical thought processes with which people could see beyond the given belief system.

Unfortunately Reich didn't seek to fight this irrationality with mass political actions. He wanted mass practice of 'sex-politics', widespread application of 'sex-economy' (natural regulation of biological sexuality) through free mental hygiene clinics.

Another sexist illness shows up in authoritarian systems to a greater extent than in liberal ones: fear, prohibition, and punishment of homosexuality. This can be seen as resulting from a fear of pleasurable, non-procreative sexuality and the danger that such sexuality presents to the nuclear family. It also involves people's fear of the abolition of sexual roles into which they have been conditioned.

Male supremacy, as a major repressive factor in civilization to date, is based on the sexual enslavement (as the superstructure of an economic base) of the female sex. It is a basic feature of the nuclear family, and must be used to maintain that institution: 'Sexually awakened women, affirmed as such, would mean the complete collapse of the authoritarian ideology.' Women's use as 'child-bearers' is pressed by the fascists in 'battles for births' to propagate the 'pure race', and in liberal nations it is always the most reactionary elements who oppose birth control and abortion. The oppression of women, economically and sexually based, involves seeing them as sex-objects to be used by men, thought incapable of pleasure, certainly not considered as equal sexual partners. The woman must concede to a sexuality which is penis-oriented, and of no relation to her own needs. Reich did not see through the myth of vaginal orgasm, but such insight is not impossible in a more revolutionary restatement of the Reichian model.

To protect the authoritarian family and society, homosexuality becomes a major political question: the night of the long knives progresses into the seemingly placid days of the bourgeois state, and gays bear the hardest brunt of the state's anti-sexuality. Reich, for all his brilliant insight into certain sexual matters, failed to understand the oppression of gays. He had a fanatic anti-gay attitude, never questioning this or seeing it as part of the emotional plague which he was always ascribing to others.

Pluralistic sociology and psychology attempt to separate sexual repression from the 'outer' society, fearing the realization of a totalistic conception of society. Psychoanalytic theory is a party to this, substituting reductionist psychopathology for social criticism.

Reich fought such approaches, but unfortunately wound up placing most blame on the individual, having given up on the possibility of a mass movement. Had Reich continued to write about sexual politics, he might have ended up in the same camp as Marcuse and Fromm, seeing the individual as incapable of attaining freedom, either alone or in a mass movement. Thus, it is probably better that Reich stopped where he did, although it is unfortunate that such a brilliant person could not go further.

There are other faults with Reich. Of great importance is his reliance on the medical model, by which he sees the necessity of 'curing' the masses. This is the typical élitist contradiction that we find in so many people who have good analysis, but are still bound by professionalism and distrust of the masses.

Beyond Reich's failures, he has left us some brilliant thought which can be of great use to our Movement. The present development of revolutionary politics in this country has been greatly influenced and advanced by the realization of sexual politics as a motive force. The message which Reich wished to bring to the German workers – a message of sexual awakening and anti-fascism – must come out in our approach to the masses here.

II. Mental Illness as Oppression

6. On Professionalism

Michael Glenn

Since its beginnings, the *Radical Therapist* has been in a paradox. People have identified themselves as radicals and as therapists. As radicals, they participate in a worldwide movement for social change. As therapists, they learn and practise useful skills, but also gain professional status from their special position in an oppressive society; they join the élite.

When the *Radical Therapist* began, each group of professionals in the country was being challenged by an inner 'radical' caucus, exposing and attacking the groups' own racism, sexism, élitism, and cooperation with Amerikan imperialist interests. We joined in attacking the mystique of The Profession. We appealed to others within the professions to work for social change.

It's time to re-examine this goal. By and large, therapy still continues to serve the *status quo*. A few modest changes have not altered the overall picture. Some therapists have utilized their professional identity to legitimize their views on public issues – the war, racism, unfair abortion laws, etc. They denounce professional privilege, but use it themselves. Their function has been to be a counterbalance to reactionary professionals who serve the Establishment by justifying racist, anti-youth, anti-radical, and sexist practices. This work is important, but it has not attacked professionalism itself.

Some therapists we know have moved away from therapy, have even stopped 'doing' it for a living, and have become involved in more overtly political and community work. This is a serious challenge to us all. We have thought about it, and have come to understand that these people are doing important work, but that other important work remains to be done in institutions, in straight jobs, and in providing therapy care. We do not urge everyone to drop out, even though some of us will choose this route.

We feel that people in straight jobs and people in alternate jobs and people in community organizing can all do revolutionary work. We feel it's crucial, though, to examine the notions of being a therapist when we evaluate their work.

Professionalism has been denounced by people arguing that all people should be equal, thus possess equal skills, and no one is more equal than anyone else. This argument is naïve. We do believe that therapy skills exist, and that they can be learned and taught. Further, they can be useful to people involved in revolutionary work. These skills need to be shared. Knowledge needs to be opened up. The mysteries can be dissolved.

The matter of *skill* vs *role* is important. Therapists may learn valuable skills in their training; others, without that training, may also learn these skills in understanding how people feel, how people interact, how to listen without laying a trip on someone, how to intuit people's conflicts, how to deal with those in extreme emotional turmoil, etc. It is important to maintain the skills which are useful and to bring them to others who can use them.

Social role is concerned with people's titles, their salaries, their fronts: and thus with the formal, rigid aspects of therapy which oppress people. Role makes therapists jailers of the people, drug-pushers, committers, brainwashers, mythmakers, and so on. Role keeps therapists alienated from others not of their sex or class or race. Role is tied up with the therapists' power and prestige: and is thus fantastically threatened by any talk of social change. About the only revolutionary use of role we can see, is where therapists use their role and power to challenge the *status quo*: to raise awareness, to educate, to gain access, to challenge myth.

It is important today for people to survive. Thus many therapists will have to make a living 'doing' therapy. We don't go along with trashing people for having straight jobs: therapists are workers, too. What seems crucial for us is the kind of work therapists do, and the kind of lives they lead, and the way they treat one another and others. Having a job isn't 'revolutionary' in itself; it's survival. It's what we do that counts.

Here, we are thinking of several specific ways 'radical therapists' can do meaningful work. Other ways can be thought of,
too, depending on the actual situation people are in:

1. Being available to sisters and brothers in emotional distress,
from political collectives, the 'movement', communes, and
people's liberation groups.

2. Working in institutions, straight and otherwise, and speaking up about oppression wherever we see it.

3. Spreading information about 'radical therapy' to others and
gathering in discussion and task-oriented support groups.

4. Challenging commitment procedures, working for patients'
rights, attacking the hierarchical structure of mental hospitals
and training programmes.

5. Working with community groups under their control, using
our skills as the people direct, and sharing our skills with them.

6. Attacking racism and sexism in groups and families and in
individual clients we may see.

7. Trying to understand where other people besides our radi-
cal/intellectual selves are, and meeting them there.

8. Working for alternatives.

9. Using professional credentials to protect people where
necessary.

10. Sharing skills and knowledge with others, thus demystify-
ing and deprofessionalizing ourselves.

11. Trying to live our own lives according to our principles, as
best as we can.

12. Teaching courses to nonprofessionals, talking to colleagues,
working with the communities we live in.

13. Attacking therapy bullshit whenever we encounter it.

We will listen to people who have actually done something,
not to those who just talk.

We would like to see therapy skills shared. The *Radical Therapist* should be relevant to more than professionals and profes-
sionals-in-training. It should relate to the movement against
oppression, the liberation movements, and to the needs of
people in our communities. In this sense, the *Radical Therapist*
articles should be clearly written without academic bullshit, and
we should be printing articles on issues of popular concern –

drug use, movement psychology, families and communes, sexuality, the process of freaking-out, oppression. The answer to the problem of professionalism is sharing what we know with non-professionals and working to abolish the distinctions of social role which dehumanize us all.

7. The Myth of Skill and the Class Nature of Professionalism

Nancy Henley and Phil Brown

We should not accept as a given that therapists have 'useful skills', or at least socially useful ones (though they have some reprehensible ones). We're all aware that some therapists are quite simply pigs, living off the damaged psyches and dollars of the people. Others are at best no help to those who seek their help. Some 'good' therapists do help people, putting them in touch with themselves and their political reality, but of course so do other 'good' people, untrained as therapists. Thus there is no 'good' skill that being a therapist confers; and where 'good' skill exists, nothing that makes it the exclusive property of therapists. Even to label an ability to deal with human problems as a skill, removing it from the realm of ordinary human accomplishments, is adding to the mystification. It is one of the maddening facts of our time that people believe themselves incapable of dealing with the most ordinary human conflicts without the aid of a 'specialist'.

The pernicious suggestion that 'therapy skills', even 'radical' ones, may be learned and taught pushes the mystification process ever forward, with only slightly different phases. A new breed of superheroes will arise, the movement therapists, a specialization within a specialization – *still* a group with privileged access to information, for they have been 'taught'. True demystification means that we must cut through the 'special knowledge' bullshit, and begin not learning from each other (as therapists) so much as from the people whose lives we affect so deeply and so unilaterally.

The skills model is a liberal cover-up for power, in therapy as in other professions. What therapists have is a monopoly not of knowledge, but of power. Even those therapists who feel themselves most powerless in their workplaces must admit the contrast of their power with that of those whom they are to 'help'. And very often the power that mental health professionals wield is only that given them as servants of the more powerful, for preservation of the class structure is a very important use of the mental health establishment today.

The class nature of the mental health system is evident from many viewpoints. In an institution, the internal hierarchy not only mimics that of the outside society, but shows a high correlation with the class backgrounds of its occupants. Ward attendants are chosen from the oppressed classes to administer state control, just as are prison guards, policemen, etc. (This does not excuse their behaviour – the point is made simply to show how the ruling class utilizes a small part of the working class to fight the majority.) The class basis is most evident in state hospitals, where patients are the most restricted and oppressed, and where there is the highest percentage of patients from working-class backgrounds.

Given the understanding that a model based on the passing on of skills among the initiated cannot break through a system designed to perpetuate class structures, what can mental health professionals, in their roles as establishment intellectuals, do? Maoist thought offers a good outlook for the role of intellectuals. While many intellectuals from the old régime worked for the Revolution, they were not too anxious to change afterwards and give up their previous privileges. A dialectic process must occur, then. New intellectuals will arise from the peasantry and proletariat, old intellectuals will be re-educated, and the two groups will interact with each other. We can see this process at work in Joshua Horn's *Away With All Pests*, where prerevolutionary doctors worked together with new doctors, para-medical workers, and 'untrained' people. Medical problems were approached not as simply scientific matters, but as political concerns also. Interaction between all groups involved insured a transmission of knowledge in all directions, along with socialist methods of criticism/self-criticism.

Earlier, Gramsci, the great Italian Communist, expounded on the problem in a broader sense. In 'The Formation of Intellectuals' and 'The Study of Philosophy' he speaks of every class bringing its own groups of intellectuals with it in its ascendance. Additionally, the ruling class recruits intellectuals from the masses. Thus, because of the bourgeois culture, in which the dominant thought in all fields is coloured by the necessities of the bourgeois state, even the oppressed become brain-workers for their oppressors. This is not to say that the ruling class connives to directly create mass culture. Rather, the institutions of the bourgeois state perpetuate beliefs, attitudes, and 'preferences' which are consistent with the requisites of bourgeois culture, which in turn props up the bourgeois state.

As Gramsci saw it, intellectuals could be 'organically' created by the working class; or 'traditional' intellectuals (those who feel more of an historical continuity than a class relation) can be won over to the revolutionary forces. This winning over, of course, is a difficult task. But whatever background the intellectual comes from, she/he must 'never forget to remain in contact with the "simple people" and moreover, *find in this contact the source of ... problems to be studied and solved*' [our emphasis].

The task of the intellectual today is no easier than when Mao and Gramsci faced the problem in different revolutionary situations. Much of the impetus for certain intellectuals to honestly serve the people will not come from a moralistic, reasoned-out basis – it will come from their seeing that their interests are tied in with those of the masses of people. In a sense that is more direct today, since the incredibly large number of intellectuals in this country are less privileged than used to be the case. Unemployed teachers, psychologists, engineers, etc. can hardly cling to a false notion of superiority for too long before unemployed workers understand the game.

Some of us have been lucky enough to have helped, and been helped by, those we love and who love us. But as yet, most people do not have the political consciousness that allows for this, and thus depend on traditional forms. They have had to go to strangers and make a purchase of friendship for this help.

In day-to-day living we are faced with the appeals of those who have been scarred by life in Amerika and the social relationships demanded by a capitalist society. Obviously we cannot send them away with the admonition that therapy is bullshit. Rather, we must respond to the need they feel for a 'specialist', without being clouded with notions of our proficiency ourselves, so they are able to perceive their own ability to understand and deal with their problems. To do this we must have increased understanding of the political basis of mental health problems today, *especially* those now considered apolitical, personal, internal ones. *If we understand people's fears, and see a commonality in our respective struggles, they will cease to see us as 'specialists' and we will cease to see them as 'patients'.*

More and more professionals today are creating collective situations where their 'services' are available free or for donations by those who can afford it – but the donation goes to the support of the collective, not in payment for service rendered. Unfortunately this is not occurring in therapy, being restricted mainly to lawyers and medical professionals. *We must collectivize emotional support and help, and end the mercenary nature of professionalism.*

Intellectuals must give up professional/class bias and privilege – not as a realization that the masses of people in a revolutionary situation will not tolerate it. Therapists have begun to feel that already – many women are leaving male shrinks once they realize what the game is all about; gays leave straight shrinks; third-world people leave white shrinks.

But we should not see these people, and others, only in the context of going to private shrinks and community clinics. Many are shoved into the wards of state hospitals where they have less access to 'liberation'. It is more important – in terms of the power nexus and class relation – to organize in these wards than to try to talk young shrinks into being 'groovy'. *The slogan 'Free All Political Prisoners!' must be applied to mental patients.*

'Radical therapists' should raise high the motto: 'We want to put ourselves out of business!'

8. Professionalism:
A Reply to Henley and Brown

Ken Cousens

The article on 'The Myth of Skill and the Class Nature of Professionalism' by Nancy Henley and Phil Brown, although it made some good radical intellectual points about the class nature of professionalism, potentially creates a dangerous myth that skills are a myth. They are intellectuals creating theory from their own heads rather than from practice. Neither of them has gone through the experience of being trained as therapists. That theory should come from practice is a Marxist approach and is and was a distinguishing point between Marxism and bourgeois utopian thinkers who dreamt up theories. My criticism of them comes out of a part of my own political practice.

Their article used loaded New Left patriotic words like 'mystification', 'power', and 'professionalism', and somehow linked them with the word skill. There is no question that skills can be and are manipulated and used by the ruling class to maintain power positions and class oppression to further fascist designs. When the ruling class doesn't succeed with these subtle things they turn to fascist violence with guns and bombs. We clearly label the use of guns in fascist hands as tools of oppression just as we label guns well used in the hands of revolutionaries as tools of liberation. By the same reasoning, how can we not label skills in the hands of revolutionaries as tools of liberation? But by Phil and Nancy's argument of guilt by association, skills are only tools of oppression, that is if skills exist at all for them.

Skills do exist in my frame of reference. Because of some medical skills I have, movement people used to come to me as a 'good untrained person' for psychiatric reasons, and I was able to help some. Since I have been involved in learning and applying psychiatric skills although I may still feel inadequate, I find myself being considerably more useful to people either directly or at least helping them decide whether it is something they can work out themselves or need some help with. I can only say from my own experience of depending on natural ability and now trained ability, that there really is a significant difference in my level of usefulness.

Nancy and Phil say that to 'label an ability to deal with human problems as a skill, removing it from the realm of ordinary human accomplishments, is adding to the mystification'. We all have abilities; the question is the degree and in what area. A form of mystification occurs when there is an arbitrariness of how those people with certain abilities are chosen to develop them into skills. Can you imagine the NLF selecting sharpshooters randomly because shooting is a human skill and we all should be able to be sharpshooters? We can bet that they select them from those with the best raw abilities and develop their skills. In China, doctors are selected from their communes by voting on who is likely to be the best doctor for the commune. They are then sent to medical school for training to develop their natural abilities into medical *and psychiatric* skills. It is beyond my reasoning to understand why this shouldn't apply to the developing of psychiatric skills here. (It is a given that the present selection method has a tremendous class, race, and sex bias.) This doesn't mean that those who want to develop their skills to a higher level through the process of practice and training create mystification.

Their statement that 'the pernicious suggestion that therapy skills, even radical ones, may be learned and taught pushes the mystification process ever forward', really mystifies me. It not only contradicts the training programmes in China, but also my political practice of the last three years of working in collectives which taught a variety of skills to movement people. The only way I can understand Nancy and Phil's position is to say that psychiatric skills are somehow different from other skills we are able to develop like karate, first aid, how to make a leaflet, or organize a demonstration, auto mechanics, etc. To take this position, however, would be really to mystify psychiatric skills. Again, from my own practice I do not find the general process of developing psychiatric skills from raw abilities any different from the process of learning these other skills. Contrary to Nancy and

Phil's position, I have found that the teaching and learning of those skills like psychiatric skills will usually de-mystify them.

Their point about the danger of a new breed of 'superheroes will arise, movement therapists, a specialization within a specialization . . .' is quite relevant. Partly because of the ego-tripping of the *Radical Therapist* there has developed a mystique of 'the radical therapist'. Another part of this is that this literary mystique plays into the needs of movement people who want to see themselves as special, different from the rest of the population. The more I use my psychiatric skills to serve the people, the more I have come to see movement people are really human beings with human problems like everyone else. There are some differences because one has to understand how human problems interact with the political framework we in the movement are working in. This may seem like an obvious statement, but when you have heard statements of specialness from people that 'they (other therapists) can't treat me because I am a 'radical' more than just a few times you get scared. It is true that bourgeois, fascist mental health workers often do not understand a Left political life-style, but beyond that, there are liberal therapists, or new technique therapists (who often call themselves radical for their technique and not their politics) who are quite capable of incorporating a Left political frame of reference into the therapy process. If movement people will only allow a politically radical therapist to work with them, they will severely constrict their resources. An example of this is a collective in Detroit which was desperately looking for help from people with psychiatric skills but had discounted all nearby potentially useful people by rejecting liberal therapists with 'you can't help us because we are radicals and you don't understand our problems'. After much struggle with a member around the myth of their specialness he was able to agree that there might be several liberal therapists who could relate to their human problems in a non-fascist way and who had the potential, with the help of the collective, to understand the political components of their problem.

The reason that I feel so strongly that it is a dangerous myth that skills are a myth not only comes out of my personal practice but also the experiences of other movement people. Huey P.

Newton said: 'The spirit of the people is greater than the man's technology.' This is a right-on statement, but in practice it has sometimes been turned around to mean that because we are revolutionaries our spirit will overcome the man's technology. This not only leads us into the delusion that if we can wish or demonstrate hard enough, the man will hand over his power, hand over his guns, skills, bombs; and also means that we do not need to develop skills to fight our struggle. Anyone who has been in the movement a short time is aware of the shortage of skills, including personal survival or support skills. Hence, Nancy and Phil's myth serves to cover up our vulnerabilities rather than allowing us to identify and work on them. Skills develop out of practice and not wishful thinking.

Perhaps the most tragic illustration of this is the early, unfortunate deaths of two Weather people in the New York town house explosion. (From the movement news accounts I am making some assumptions about what happened.) Partly because they were in the early phases of developing their technology, but also because of a righteous revolutionary zeal of their spirit being greater than the technology, safety, and fatigue, they had a tragic accident.

Another example of the danger of the myth of the 'no skills myth' is the binds it puts on individuals and collectives who feel the collective should be able to solve their or the collective's problems. I have had several real unhappy individuals sneak out of their collective setting to talk with me. They felt even worse because their collective couldn't really help them . . . and it was supposed to (the *Radical Therapist* said so). It was unfortunate that their pain and difficulty had to get really bad before they could overcome their guilt and let practice overrule theory and seek solutions outside of their collective. Not only do these people suffer, but their collective has to suffer unnecessary failure feelings because they are ruled by their moral 'shoulds' rather than their practice. These collectives also tended to develop covert activity around these issues rather than open struggle because of the guilt around the 'shoulds'. This doesn't negate Nancy and Phil's right-on statement that 'one of the maddening facts of our time is that people believe themselves incapable of dealing with the most ordinary human conflicts without the aid of a specialist'. It is very important that collectives and individuals become self-reliant, as the North Koreans say . . . develop *Juche*. The way to do it, however, is not to ignore the reality of skills, but to develop those skills to avoid the dependency that comes from lack of knowledge and skills. In particular, if we assume that movement people, like other people, sometimes have more than 'ordinary human conflicts', it becomes critical that we develop at least the skills to make a distinction between the ordinary and that which may require more than just what the collective can give them alone. The point is that untrained people are quite capable of handling ordinary human problems, but contrary to the implied thinking of Nancy and Phil that – because we are human we do not need skills to handle, or even distinguish more than ordinary human or collective problems – there are certain problems or resources that need more than a collective can reasonably offer and we do need additional skills to distinguish and treat these. Like in any other area – first aid, karate, auto-mechanics, house building, etc. – where we are forced to go beyond our daily experience, we need to learn, grow, and develop skills or be forever at the mercy of the oppressors.

It is rather a long response to an article, but I find it harder and harder to suffer the unnecessary failures of people – myself amongst them – who sincerely allowed their lives to be ruled by the theory and god of *should* of radical intellectuals, rather than the political realities of their own practice. The dialectical process of growth becomes stunted if we allow our practice of *is* to be overwhelmed by our theories of *should*.

9. In Defence of Individual Therapy

Tim De Chenne

In the radical movement today individual therapy is acquiring the status of a new taboo. Although many still see a place for the therapeutic dyad in a radical approach, suspicion of the individual context is widespread and growing. For example, in the 'Radical Psychiatry Manifesto' Steiner offers an eloquent and compelling indictment of individual therapy:

Extended individual psychotherapy is an élitist, outmoded, as well as nonproductive form of psychiatric help. It concentrates the talents of a few on a few. It silently colludes with the notion that people's difficulties have their source within them while implying that everything is well with the world. It promotes oppression by shrouding its consequences with shame and secrecy. It further mystifies by attempting to pass as an ideal human relationship when it is, in fact, artificial in the extreme.

While admitting that the dyadic structure is 'of great value in crises', Steiner maintains that it 'should become the exception rather than the rule'.

In 'Radical Psychiatry: Principles' Steiner points out that liberation requires not only awareness of oppression but 'contact':

... that is to say, contact with other human beings who, united, will move against oppression. That is why it is not possible to practise radical psychiatry in an individual therapy context. An individual cannot move against his oppressors as an individual; he can only do so with the support of a group of other human beings. (See above, p. 18.)

An honest appraisal of individual therapy must begin by admitting that, in many respects, Steiner is on firm ground. First, one-to-one therapy has been, and still is, a primarily élitist affair.

Therapists reside in the higher socio-economic strata of society. The preference of therapists for white, better-educated, higher-incomed clients is well-documented (Meltzoff and Kornreich, 1970). There is little doubt that many therapists are interested only in clients who can pay, who come from a familiar sub-culture, and who are not so disturbed as to present real problems.

Second, it is also clear that even by its own standards individual therapy has been somewhat less than a raging success. The situation is not so dismal as Eysenck would have us believe – taken as a whole 'therapy' does seem to promote traditionally desired outcomes more than no therapy at all (Meltzoff and Kornreich, 1970). However, the margin of success is so slim as to be no source of pride, and there is always a question over the adequacy of the improvement criteria employed. It must also be recognized that the extension of therapy over a period of years serves mainly the finances of the therapist and that the point of diminishing returns in a dyadic process occurs much more rapidly than our orthodox colleagues would like to admit.

Finally, it is amply evident that the actual conduct of individual therapy aims primarily at adjusting the deviant, and mostly ignores the paramount social issues which are the major factors in a nonorganic 'pathology'. Although every *theory* of personality considers the social matrix of humankind, the actual practice of therapy usually ends in the silent collusion to which Steiner refers. This collusion takes different forms. In psychoanalysis, for example, it hinges on dealing mostly with the past and on interpreting such legitimate complaints about the environment as 'externalization', 'rationalization', or 'projection'. Too many individual therapists operate as if they accept the immutable facticity of social arrangements, and are unwilling to join with their clients in a concrete struggle against an intolerable life space.

Turning to the other side of Steiner's argument, it can hardly be denied that the group context offers advantages for a radical approach; the superior power of concertive action is inarguable. Members in a radical group, with the help of leaders and other members, can come to an awareness of the social pathology which lies at the heart of their problems in living. They can be supported in their concrete actions against or away from such pathology. The encounterlike aspects of a radical group can help to fashion, in the group itself, alternative modes of being with others: avoiding one-upmanship, stressing honest self-disclosure and interpersonal sensitivity.

But it is also true that a therapy group, radical or otherwise, can offer disadvantages to its members. A group often develops a scapegoat from among its membership. A group always develops norms which – if for no other reason than their normativeness – can lead to a sense of artificiality 'in the extreme'. Further, it is sometimes difficult for a group member to truly obtain enough *space* to work slowly through his problems in living.

It seems to me that the group approach will continue to absorb much of our energy, and rightfully so. But I believe it will become evident that individual therapy is an indispensable part of our efforts, and that we can make it work for us. Instead of saying that 'radical psychiatry is best practised in groups', we can then say that most aspects of a radical approach are best suited to groups, but that other aspects are best handled in a one-to-one structure. Instead of saying that individual therapy should be the 'exception to the rule', we can then say that it is part of the rule. A radical individual therapy can take its place *within* the radical group or therapy collective as a valuable and necessary structure. It will continue to provide a kind of 'curative intimacy' not available in the group setting, no matter how open or sensitive the structure.

Implicit in these arguments is my contention that it is possible to be a radical therapist in the dyadic context, that there is nothing inherently 'counter-revolutionary' in the one-to-one structure. Suspicion of the individual context has begun to leave the radical line and circle back into the reactionary. Viewing the individual therapist as nothing but hopelessly co-optive is a way of saying that things must be as they always have been. We need never pretend that one-to-one therapy is an 'ideal' human relationship, any more than is group therapy. But we can make the individual context less artificial, more responsive to the needs of humankind.

About a year ago a therapy collective was formed in the community surrounding the University of Chicago. We call ourselves

'Changes'. There are about fifty of us, a good portion of this number being graduate students in the social sciences. A description of our efforts/problems/goals would require an article in itself. But it seems to me that one of the lessons we have learned is that there is still a place for individual therapy in a radical approach; that what I have labelled the 'curative intimacy' of the one-to-one encounter is still a potent and valuable force in the radical movement.

We must begin by centring the individual therapist *within* the therapy collective or radical community. People coming to the group then have available to them both the collective and individual structures. Hopefully the new people partake of both – but involvement with only one of the two should at least be an available alternative.

Within the group individual therapists can distribute their energies differently. First, they can pass along basic therapeutic skills to others in a convenient and informal setting. Second, the financial and other resources of the collective can help them abandon the traditional 'economism'. Therapists must put an end to the professional whoring which accepts enormously overpriced payments for a service sold in fifty-minute units. They must stop being 'friends for hire'. Therapists (particularly psychoanalysts) frequently assert that payment by the 'patient' is important, that it gives her heightened respect for the situation, or stronger motivation, etc. But as of yet we are still awaiting empirical verification of this assertion. It strikes me as rationalization *par excellence*.

Abandoning economism also means abandoning the therapist's store – namely, the office setting. We must be willing to walk out from behind the counter and into those times and places more supportive of our efforts. The goal is to meet with people in an individual context when they need it, for as long as they need it, and in places where true meetings are possible.

These considerations were addressed to the external structure of dyadic encounters. It is also evident that the internal structure of individual therapy must undergo change. It is only of late that we have become fully sensitized to the political arrangements implicit in many therapy techniques. For instance, in his little masterpiece 'The Art of Psychoanalysis' Haley has given us a humorously accurate portrait of therapeutic power games. But the kind of one-up-manship pervading traditional therapies need not persist in other arrangements. We need not accept the supposedly enlightened despotism of psychoanalysis or the alienating technocracy of behaviour modification. Political structures are changeable.

To me a 'politicized' therapy is one which reflects or rather actualizes on a small scale the political philosophy of the therapist. In a recent article (Noel and De Chenne, 1971) we have tried to outline a 'multicentred' system of therapy operating more on the basis of a participatory democracy. Space does not permit a complete detailing of the approach, but the elements of the system which are important for a radical outlook are easily statable. For us a democratic framework means a system which is explicit, teachable, mutual, and negotiable. By *explicit* we mean exactly that – the therapist's attempt to clarify where he or she is coming from. It means laying out in clear language what the therapist hopes will go on in the sessions, and why this kind of activity is considered important. By *teachable* we mean that the therapist does not give merely a cursory theoretical introduction, but that the system be presented and carried out in such a way that the client may learn to do what the therapist is doing. The goal here is not only that the client will change but will himself become an effective agent of change. Of course, all of this requires a more 'symmetric' relationship than is typically offered by a therapist; hence our *emphasis* on mutuality. By this we mean simply that the therapist allows herself to be explored – that a large part of her role involves self-disclosing and helping the client relate to those disclosures. This kind of mutual relationship obviously takes us away from the old model of the isolated therapist, a model which so often leaves the client feeling condescended to and manipulated. Finally, a democratic framework is always *negotiable* and so we advise therapy participants to make a point of frequently examining their interaction, talking about what is right and wrong with them, and groping toward possible solutions.

These ground rules can form the foundation upon which more

specific therapeutic techniques may lie. Our own approach, for example, utilizes to a large degree the client-centred or 'experiential' response, since we consider this an extremely helpful way of being with another person. But other techniques can obviously fit within a democratic framework. I suppose that even the unconscious/interpretive orientation of the analyst *could* find a place here; but I dare say that no analyst alive *would* ever opt for a truly explicit, teachable, mutual, and negotiable system.

It seems to me, then, that the individual therapist need never 'silently collude'. The meeting of a therapist with one other person need not imply that the person was the source of his own difficulties and must adjust to the blissful normality of his environment. All it need imply is that two people wish to be together for their mutual growth. We may begin towards this goal by joining with our clients in their concrete life struggles – and by inviting them to join in our larger struggle. We may go further by leaving the storefront and economism behind, and allying ourselves with the efforts of a therapy collective or radical community. We may go still further and attempt to actualize within the structure of our therapy the participatory democracy we strive for on a larger level.

Bibliography

HALEY, JAY, *The Power Tactics of Jesus Christ*. New York: Avon Books, 1969.

MELTZOFF, JULIAN and KORNREICH, MELVIN, *Research in Psychotherapy*. New York: Atherton Press, Inc., 1970.

NOEL, JOSEPH R. and DE CHENNE, TIMOTHY K, 'I-we-thou: Multicentred Counselling and Psychotherapy' in *Psychotherapy: Theory, Research, and Practice*. In press.

STEINER, CLAUDE, 'Radical Psychiatry Manifesto' (*Radical Therapist*, June–July 1970, vol. 1 no. 2, p. 12.)

STEINER, CLAUDE, 'Radical Psychiatry: Principles' (see above pp. 15–19.)

10. Letter

'C.B.'

[*C. B. spent several years in mental hospitals and is now out.*]

Dear —,

Today I am feeling broken as a human being and your letter which we received today made me think twice about the reason for this. Is it my illness creeping back again, as it often does, or is it a result of the system which purports to 'help' those who are ill? I feel less able to cope with the world than ever before.

To be snatched from a world in which you feel you have a place (no matter how small) and purpose (no matter how insignificant) to a hospital is a most jarring experience. People need to feel they are contributing to the environment in which they live. You are in the hospital to 'get better' and that's the only purpose. It would be sufficient if the patients were given some responsibility to this end. In the hospital you must 1) get up in the morning (in some places even this is not required); 2) eat, if you want to, at specified times, the food that is planned and prepared by others; 3) take your medicine which is handed out at specified times by a uniformed nurse; 4) attend activities, if indeed there are any, that have no purpose other than to keep you 'occupied'; 5) go to bed.

It's a pretty dull existence in which everything you need is handed out in neat little packages – even the therapy – not when you may need it most, but again at specified times. I guess any institution needs to keep a schedule, but, God, it's deadly for the patient. Pretty soon the patient begins to look around for some way of changing the careful orderliness of the routine and soon finds out that if you cause enough ruckus you can get 1) a needle; 2) in some places a straitjacket; 3) an isolation room; or 4) if the place is well staffed, someone to stay not less than three feet from you; or 5) sodium amytal which sort of puts you out of it in a high which makes the place more bearable. Not all outcries are made out of boredom and this wish to break the terrible efficient orderliness of the place, but I think a good deal of them are. What patients want is some recognition of themselves as individuals – even the routine of making a ruckus doesn't satisfy the need for being recognized and appreciated as an individual who may have something positive to contribute. Instead they are reduced to making a fuss to change the routine. And even this is unsatisfying after a while. . .

Some people think that the means of dealing with upset patients is cruel. Really, it isn't so – they are to the upset patient a means of getting a response that means his problem (even if not the real one) is recognized and dealt with. To the sick patient it is a form of love – the only kind he can extract from his environment.

In the hospital you learn that there are a very minimum number of things you must do to exist. This is the terrible message of the hospital. You don't even need to wash or brush your teeth to get along. All motivation is drained, for your very minimum needs will be taken care of for you. This attitude is carried with you when you leave. It doesn't really matter what you do or don't do.

On leaving the hospital there is the added problem of feeling guilty for not doing more than the minimum, but it is already engrained in you that nothing is really essential. I guess what I am talking about is the fostering of dependencies of already dependent people – the taking away of all motivation to do for yourself. Even taking medicine (although I admit it's sometimes necessary) means to the patient that he is sick and can't control his own behaviour. In the hospital the rewards for being 'sick' are so much greater than the ones for being 'healthy'.

G—: The first hospital I entered. Essentially it was a drying-out place for alcoholics and a waiting station for those going on to other hospitals. I suppose its function was diagnostic. Therapy – if any – was provided by the patient's own doctor. Most of my time there was spent pacing the floors. Most of the anxiety there was not knowing what to do to help myself get better. I was still under the illusion, which Dr B— had led me to believe, that I would only be in the hospital a few weeks. I was anxious to get help so that I could return to the outside as soon as possible. There was no help. Only endless conferences about where I would next be sent. The weeks dragged into a whole month – a long time for someone to just wait to get help.

P—: I would characterize this place as the one, which in my experience, gave the greatest rewards for being sick – especially for acting out. I entered on a fairly 'well' ward. For some reason I still don't know, I was sent up to the —th floor, which had patients who were more obviously sick. There was more staff, more medicine, more things you couldn't take with you on the ward. Oh yes, every time you changed wards your belongings were gone through with a fine-tooth comb to see if you had any forbidden items. And you yourself were looked over. It seemed almost a challenge to smuggle in certain items. There was the feeling that you were a dangerous person, not to be trusted in the least bit. This certainly makes you want to give them what they expect – a wild unmanageable patient. And there were other rewards for being cuckoo too. You got much more attention in all sorts of ways. There was the pulse chart – you had your pulse taken twenty million times a day and the yes, no chart for your BMs. Every detail of your life was down on paper and what's more you couldn't see what was written about you, nor could you know your 'diagnosis'. I have said that these things are rewards, but in the end they are really not helpful in getting you better and out of the hospital. These things cater to the already sick person and his feelings about himself. For instance, the person who feels impulses to harm himself will feel more inclined to carry out these ideas if he feels that other people are afraid that he will not be capable of stopping himself. He will carry out the expectations of others. There were other floors, too, each with different rules, and so I spent two years shuttling between the unrestricted and restricted floors. P— is a private hospital and I gather runs on private funds from the families of the patients there. It is exorbitantly expensive. My uncle stopped paying them because he no longer wanted me to stay there. It took them six months to get me into a state hospital and during that time my bills mushroomed. The final bill was $40,000 which my uncle refused to pay. They later tried to sue my mother but settled it out of court. I don't know what the final settlement was. My feeling is that no hospital, no matter how wealthy the patients, should charge such exorbitant prices. My illness was only fostered: why should I pay high prices for that? It was physically comfortable with private rooms, and the food was edible (and fattening). That was all.

M— State Hospital: I first entered on the admissions ward. It was a huge place, less physically comfortable than the two previous ones, but in some ways better. At first I had to wear a state gown. I had not one thing of my own. Everything that was personally mine was taken away. I had a bed in the infirmary of the admissions ward – one of those high hospital beds with the rails on it. I felt it was the end of the line. I felt so hopeless that I lay in bed for months getting up only to smoke four cigarettes a day and to have shock treatments three times a week. I didn't even have enough will to live to feed myself. So I was fed by someone on the staff. Not even one thing was expected of me – not even to feed myself. There wasn't enough staff and what there was I wouldn't speak to, so they didn't bother to talk to me, though that might have helped eventually. After all I was still alive and could hear most of the time. They didn't even respect my feelings enough to tell me that I was to start ECT. The morning after I arrived they herded me off with all the other patients to another building. I didn't even know where I was going. We waited (about fifteen or twenty of us) while we went in one by one. As you entered the room the ones who had already had their treatments were out on the beds. It was only then that I knew I was to have ECT. Quite a shock – literally and otherwise. This went on, I later figured out, for ten weeks or more. Even after the shock treatments (it felt like the punishment I deserved) there was more lying around in bed with no one to speak to. Finally I came to one day and decided that – felt that – I wanted to fight all this. The only fight I knew was against myself and, there being a limited number of night staff, I was put into a straitjacket more politely called a camisole. That was after the usual needle of thorazine – three of them in one night – which further fulfilled my wish for self-punishment.

The next morning I was carted off to the chronic ward. So far I had received no therapy other than the ECT. I really did feel that this was what I deserved. It's a punishment in that it dehumanizes you, but also a reward in that at least you are getting some sort of reaction out of the people around you. Again my things were combed over. I was stripped naked, notes were taken on scars and other identifying features, and I was again placed in a state gown. The ugliest things – worse than potato sacks. Finally I got my clothes back and a therapist. He was a resident – so that didn't last long. Things hadn't been going well. It was at that point I think that they gave up on me, for after the resident left I was not assigned another therapist. I had given up too! I was shuffled from one meaningless activity to the next. One of the activities I remember as a child – a rhythm band. We pounded on sticks or clappers for an hour each week. For most of us it was a most degrading experience – to have someone stand up in front of you and tell you to beat the sticks in time to some horrible march music or other.

Without further treatment, someone decided that I needed to be rehabilitated so I was sent to the bag factory. For someone with a college background to be sent to fold bags (we got paid for it) was degrading enough. Everyone around you hallucinating . . . but for all this we were paid (if you worked hard enough) $5 a month. I felt after a month or so working there that if that was all I was good for the rest of my life I'd rather not live, so for the second time in that hospital I rebelled in the only way I knew how – against myself – and ended up in the infirmary on ECT again. I don't know how long I was on them that time. I expect not as long as before. The one good thing about M— is that if you were well enough you could at least wander around the grounds with another person. This brought me into contact with the thousands of the world's forgotten people at M—. Most of them were obviously out of their minds and had spent years at the place and were fully institutionalized. I identified with them and at times felt that theirs was my fate also. Everything was provided them by the state. All their social activities were planned out and everywhere we went we were herded like cattle except in our 'free' time on the grounds.

I was lucky I was still wearing the clothes that had been mine before I went into the hospital. They were old and out of date, but at least they were mine. I was also lucky in that I had an allowance. There was a store on the grounds where we could get snacks and even meals. Our only pleasure then became the very primitive one of eating.

About the staff – I was lucky in that the staff on my ward was pretty good. My group leader was a very decent and humane sort of person as was the head nurse. The rest were mostly condescending but at least they weren't physically abusive as they were on some wards. As I got better I was given the privilege of sometimes having coffee with the staff and I used to listen to their problems, which was a switch from anywhere else I had been. It had the effect of making me feel worthwhile in some sort of way. It bridged the gap between patient and staff and we became friends, sort of on an equal footing. The two of them were decent, though simple people, with real human concern. Mrs S— I remember did administer those thirty or so needles I got one week. Boy was I sore. I had done some acting out and the doctor who didn't know me very well thought that maybe I should have more shock treatments, go to the violent ward, or have the four shots a day. He decided on the latter. That was real punishment! But being sick I thought it was what I deserved again.

I was beyond pain. It seemed I could endure any kind of physical pain without even wincing or saying ouch! I even had some stitches put in without a local anaesthetic, and it didn't seem to hurt. I guess I had cut the nerves.

Being in a state hospital where the length of your stay is limited only by your lifespan is a very depressing feeling, but even more depressing than that is getting so acclimatized to being dependent and taken care of that you begin to look forward to the few activities that are available to you without a thought to the outside. Indeed it's rather frightening after being dependent for so long to think of making it on your own in the outside world. M— is particularly removed. It's a community unto itself – even has its own electric power plant, laundry, etc., etc. The atmosphere is depressing – nobody leaves unless they run away. This is almost always true once you get beyond the admissions ward. I only know of one or two persons who have left my ward and only one other besides myself has stayed out. People have left, but only to return in a week or month in worse condition than when they left. Something must be wrong with the system somewhere.

Eventually I felt I was well enough to look for a job in town. Like most hospital towns, the townspeople are very much afraid of the hospital and of the patients it houses. This is another aspect of mental health in which work needs to be done – public education. Needless to say no one would give me a job in M— and I spent long hours answering every ad and going to places where there is a frequent turnover. It was disheartening to finally make the decision to return to the world only to be turned away.

I finally entered a sculpture course at the community college. One of the aides used to pick me up – she was a student there – and the teacher found out somehow that I was a patient at the hospital. She made things difficult for me after that in subtle ways, criticizing my work, etc. One day the local newspaper came to get a story about the class and the photographer wanted to take a picture of me and my sculpture. She kept saying, 'No, not that one. This one is really a better one,' etc. The photographer ignored her and took my picture anyway – and ran the picture of me and the story in the newspaper. That was a good one on her! But it just goes to show the prejudice that does exist. . .

B—: The most frightening thing I found about B— was that there was no one to introduce you to the routines of the ward. It took me three days of questioning to find out where and when to wash out my underwear! The aides had no patience with explaining things to you. You are plopped on the ward and that's it. If you don't do things that you should you are in for verbal and physical abuse by the aides. Needless to say, the place is a real snakepit – with mice and no doubt rats (though I never saw any rats). My glasses and all personal belongings were confiscated. You have to protect yourself against the other patients. I was attacked twice – I think because I looked so scared. Stealing was rampant. You had to carry all your things with you including toothpaste, comb, cigarettes, etc., and sleep with them under your bed at night!

The admission procedure was horrifying. Some aide, who should have been on the ward herself, stripped me of all my clothes but my pants – with men walking around – it was most humiliating. She kept yelling at me to hurry and when I wasn't fast enough to suit her she started pushing me around. I had my temp. taken – 101. It was noted in the chart but nothing was done about it.

We had to sleep in the hall. The only way I got a bed the first night was having another patient fix one up for me – again I didn't know the procedure. She was the only kind person there. She sort of had a deal with the staff for doing those extra things, I guess, in return for some kind of special treatment.

B— was the most dehumanizing place of all. Apparently I was on the worst ward there. I have heard since that all the wards are not as bad as that one – the patients not so wild, the staff not so abusive – but it's still B— and I think the place lives up to its reputation. I went to B— in a paddy wagon with the little men in white coats (I never really thought they existed) and a police escort. It really made me mad because as upset as I was I think I could have gone with a friend and admitted myself instead of being committed. That really is a rotten feeling to feel that you have been put in an institution against your will without being able to get out. I was fortunate in being there only three days. Even those three days have left their imprint on me.

The K— Day Care Centre: This place is going in the right direction it seems to me. The programme is run by the democratic process... It's very frustrating having to make decisions all the time and even harder to stick by them...

The staff is there to point out ways of looking at problems through questions. The emphasis is always on feelings. It gets to be a little wearing after a while... Gradually though things do happen. At first it was a shock to know my own diagnosis, but after all it's just a label for what I have been going through for years. We make our own decisions, we are responsible for being there, we take our own medicine, we make our own lunches, plan them, clean up after ourselves. In other words we are given more responsibility for our own lives. We are not treated as dangerous or helpless individuals. . .

Therapy is change not adjustment. This I think is the basic idea of the clinic. The idea is not to quickly patch up an individual so that he may return to a job or whatever, but to make an individual content with himself and free to express himself creatively. . .

P.S. The night I wrote this H— and I stayed up all night – I had no emotion while writing this until the next morning when H— had left for class. Then I became upset and was urged to go to the clinic. I showed them there what I had written. My doctor believed that it was good and that copies should be made to give to the administrators of the clinic. Dr R—, one of the administrators, read it the next day. His reaction was completely different. He was defensive and thought that the feelings I expressed were just written by a sick individual. He kept asking, in a very 'professional' noninvolved tone, what I had done to make myself more independent. It was a real put-down. I felt very angry and depressed until I started to realize that it was his problem not mine. . . Dr R—'s reaction to me is just what I have been talking about – the condescending attitude of professional workers.

I'd be interested to have your reaction.

11. Ordeal in a Mental Hospital

Anon.

At the age of seventeen and a half I considered myself as having some problems that were somewhat different from the problems of others: I felt inferior but could still function. I did well in high school and graduated. I had been taking dancing lessons for about ten years and always thought that when I graduated high school and started working I would see a psychiatrist. Things in my household were really bad. There was always someone screaming and fighting. My family consisted of myself, my younger brother, my mother and father.

Finally our whole family started seeing a psychiatric social worker. I liked him and told him I just could not tolerate living at home: my mother was constantly telling me that I was crazy and a myriad other such demeaning things. The social worker agreed with me that I should not live at home and placed me in a residence for emotionally disturbed girls (which is a whole other story!). It took an entire year before I could move in. One of the reasons I agreed to go there was that I could smell the sickness, and felt I belonged with messed up people.

One thing I learned very quickly, since I didn't really have a self identity, was that sickness is very catching. One girl who was my friend at the residence, when talking about myself said to me, 'You're sick.' I replied, 'What do you mean, I'm sick? I just have some emotional problems.' She said, 'Can't you accept the fact that you're sick?' And that's one of the catching attitudes I am talking about, among many, many others.

I have wanted for a long time to share some of the things I am about to write with other people.

I experienced great despair and utter hell by being in a mental hospital for eleven months, by being treated as an object of that bureaucracy.

I will go into some detail about my hospitalization, about how it hindered rather than helped me.

After four years at the residence I was really feeling helpless. The girls there were very hostile to me because I was so shy and afraid. At the point before hospitalization I was in many emotional states of disturbance such as depression and anxiety and had in general very low self-esteem. I had gone from job to job. The therapist I was seeing and had been seeing for two years discussed the idea of going to a hospital. I myself had brought the idea up, since the majority of the girls at the residence were coming from or going to hospitals. I could not seek any comfort from my therapist. I thought it was because she was a woman.

This leads me to my story about the hospital.

O.K. Now this was supposed to be an open hospital ('supposed to' meaning that I'm not sure). Passes were given and there was no solitary confinement. I suppose that is what was meant.

I had heard good reports about this hospital. One of my friends from the residence was there and I asked her to write me about everything that went on there. Her answers were quite reassuring and made me feel hopeful.

I had to wait about a month before I was accepted. From the minute I was there even entering admissions I began to notice things. My mother was there with me and there was a pot of coffee presumably for the staff. My mother asked if she could have some coffee. The desk receptionist okayed that, but when I went to take a cup the receptionist told me I couldn't have any.

This enraged my mother – she could see instantaneously the manner in which I was going to be treated. At this time I expected people to be turned off by me and wasn't enraged at all. Now I am! After eleven months there and four years later...

My father was also there during admissions. He was asked to sign some papers which entitled the hospital to have complete control over me. He just did not want to. The social worker insisted, but he didn't, thank goodness! I wanted him to because I just wanted to get in there already, and this was just delaying it. If only I knew then that signing those papers meant giving my mind and body to them for their purposes, including shock treatment, etc., as will be seen, I would have felt differently.

A nurse's aide took my luggage and I said good-bye to my parents. I don't recall how I felt about that departure, since I hadn't lived with them for five years.

My friend had told me some of the rooms were in cottages and some in 'Long Hallways'. She said that the better off you were the more chance they would put you in a cottage. I immediately asked the aide if I were going to a cottage or a Hallway, and she said a Hallway. I became frightened and questioned it. The aide said that it used to represent differences but at the present time there weren't any.

The first thing I remember happening after that was a few patients around me asking me if I were nervous. I said, 'Yes! Definitely!' One particular girl said, 'Well, at least you're honest.'

The aide showed me to my room but first checked my luggage – every last bit of it – and took out my scissors.

I had been prepared through my friend for the fact that during the first two weeks there they don't give you any medication. (I had been taking tranquillizers for a few years.) I immediately bought two cartons of cigarettes. Before I went into the hospital a pack would last me a week. I now smoke about three packs a day.

After I unpacked, the psychiatrist I was to have gave me a physical examination. He had an accent and at first I couldn't understand him, and was resentful of a Doctor of the Mind examining me. Yes, I know a shrink is also a medical man, but it just felt strange.

One of the few things I was told was that I was assigned to a special group, meaning which 'status' I had. The different groups had different numbers, according to the amount of freedom one had. At first an aide is assigned to be with you every place you go, even to the toilet.

I felt fairly friendly toward a few people and I saw my doctor for about one hour every day for two weeks – but! Every June your doctor is changed, since they are residents and must gather up new knowledge from different people. As I spent more and more time with this doctor I began to really respect him and felt a lot of confidence in his ability to help me.

Those two weeks I felt as if the hospital was like a womb. I loved all the people and the spacious green lawns and even the building – loved it all! The doctor even took me off the Group after a week and I had freedom.

Then there was a doctor change. I felt the next one would be equally adequate and I looked forward to meeting him. But then Holocaust! Downhill after that. At this point was the beginning of a hell I never experienced before and never have after.

Sure if you have a half-way decent memory and are motivated you will want to do something beneficial to you to earn a good living. In fact about two years before when I was in college I had an acquaintance in my English class who told me that he was going to be a psychiatrist. I asked him why. He replied, 'You make a lot of money that way.'

Yes, there are many reasons why psychiatrists go into practice – some for very sick power games. A lot of reasons.

People seek help in many ways. It is only recently that people have more of a choice of the kind of therapist they want to presumably grow from.

This next doctor as far as I am concerned was quite neurotic, besides not having an ounce of concern for human feelings. He couldn't even look at me directly – eye to eye. I felt he was afraid of me. When he first approached me he stumbled on some chairs and didn't know which chair to sit on. It seemed to take him a few minutes to decide.

He asked me how I was feeling. I told him I was depressed and he said, 'Oh! You mean you're feeling *blue* today!' He made me very uncomfortable. I didn't even realize then that I was angry at his euphemism. But I thought I would get over it. The point is – would he get over *his* neurosis?

He looked kind of strange and I became frightened. I told him something was holding me back from talking to him, and he said nothing.

Every session the same thing would happen. I felt choked. I wanted and needed help, but just could not trust him. In the meantime – since you only saw your doctor once a week or sometimes twice – numerous other things were happening.

One was assigned to a day's activities. They had a tremendous

Occupational Therapy building. You were forced to go to activities no matter how you felt. There were activities from 9.15 till about five at night. Then supper from 6.00 to 7.30, then some free time. Every evening you had to go to an activity which brought the other units together, sometimes the whole hospital.

Before I went to the hospital I felt afraid of people. . . As soon as I started with my new doctor, who I will call Dr A., I was in a total state of terror and became completely withdrawn. One guy did pursue me and he was the only person for five months that I talked to.

It got to a point where I would hide in my closet during activities and just not go to any of them. Also in these five months I couldn't sit down : I just stood in my room with every part of my body stiff with tension; I also do not remember any of my dreams, which is rare for me. I couldn't stand to look at my body. When I changed into pyjamas I would do it very quickly, and not dare look down. I also could not cry – it's obvious to me now that I was holding back a tremendous amount of rage and everything I was doing was to control this rage, because acting out in the hospital is forbidden – you get punished in some way for any deviant thing.

At one session with Dr A. I said something suggesting that I did not like him. He said, 'That's not a very nice thing to say to me.'

Aside from walking the hallways for five months, I was constantly writing letters. First I wrote to the staff head, and after a few letters he set up an appointment for me to have a consultation with Dr A. and him.

At that conference, it was the first time in months that I could talk to someone, I mean really talk and feel heard; in fact he made me laugh, which was something I had almost forgotten existed. It was exhilaratingly good. He asked me about my past and we talked for a while. At the end he said, 'There is no reason why you can't work with Dr A.' I protested and he just asked me to leave his office.

After I was back on my unit I cried and screamed for about an hour. The other patients were at activities so only one nurse heard me. I cannot begin to express the relief and at the same time the bitter disappointment I felt, but it was the first time in five months that I cried. It wasn't even a good cry, because I was crying to no one and no one was going to help me.

Other bizarre things happened to me which I still can't explain. One of which was that I was afraid to walk; I had to hold the wall or I thought I would fall or faint. At one point I could only see black, and other times everything seemed bleak and grey.

We had large patient-staff meetings which I was terrified of and for eleven months did not say a word in.

At my next session with Dr A., he said, rather smugly, 'Well now, you're stuck with me, and you had better accept that I am your doctor.' I couldn't.

Time passed and I got worse and saw no way out. At one point I tried a small-scale suicide stunt just to make someone realize what was happening. You see, I knew it was my reaction to Dr A. that was causing most of this; because every weekend when I was sure he wasn't at the hospital, *all* of these symptoms went away.

I couldn't go on like this. I took some sleeping pills, no prescription kind. I took ten of them, and was on my way out to town to buy more and kill myself. About three quarters of the way out I changed my mind, and just knew I didn't want to die. I ran back to a nurse and told her I had taken the pills. She immediately ran to staff and the next thing I knew I was about to have my stomach pumped. As I waited there I began to feel dizzy from the effect of the pills. When I entered the room and saw the apparatus I was horrified. 'Dear,' Dr A. said, 'you think *I* like this?'

So I had my stomach pumped. Well, what was left?!!

Soon after Dr A. approached me as I was outside the canteen on the lawn. He said they might have to send me to a state hospital.

BOOM!!!
DOOM!!!

Immediately I called a psychologist (one I had seen for a summer a few years earlier). I told him my situation. He called the hospital and got some information and assured me they wouldn't do this. But nothing was happening. I was in checkmate. No one would help me and I knew I just couldn't continue.

So I started a new project. I started writing letters to the Head of the whole hospital. I must have written about ten letters. I told him, which I believed then and believe now, that the hospital had some possibilities for help, but I was getting nowhere and was just suffering, and told him about my 'relationship' with Dr A.

The Head of the hospital finally wrote me a letter and set up an appointment, with just him and me. I had to practise what I would say and a friend of mine came to visit and we discussed it. She said, 'Whatever you say don't mention to him that you want your first doctor back' (the one I liked so much), because for five months every time I went to staff, they would say to me, 'The reason why you can't get along with Dr A. is because you have a crush on your first doctor.' At the conference I told the Head the whole story. I mentioned that I got along with my first doctor but did not put any emphasis on it. He said it would be the first time in the history of the hospital that something like this would be done. But he would do it.

Well, what was in store for me now? !

O.K. Next. At that point I didn't trust anyone, especially doctors. When I entered the room I immediately said to him, 'I don't know if I am able to talk to you.' He seemed angry and said, 'You had better talk to me Miss X because they're not going to change your doctor again.' He said that therapy is for you to talk ... period ... and final. So I thought this was the only thing to do with him – talk, talk, talk – and get no response. In the six months that I saw him, he couldn't have said more than five sentences. He was like an iceberg. Every time I saw him I got depressed and had to lie down for about five hours. My insides felt cold. If there were only some warmth from him. None.

Once I said to him, 'I feel like I'm your slave.' And he said very seriously, 'Yes, you are. I am your master and you are my slave.' I said, 'Are you for real?' He said, 'Yes, I am.' B O O M ! ! ! D O O M ! ! ! I always had a great fear of being controlled, and had felt it at various times in my life, especially from my mother.

Another crucial factor about the whole type of treatment (which also was very bad for me) is that you are told not to discuss any problems you have with another patient. They thought it would interfere with your doctor-patient relationship and of course there the doctor was GOD. He ruled everything you did.

The whole treatment was supposedly to keep occupied and forget your problems. Well I pulled another stunt. I decided I would jump off the Empire State Building. So one day I just left and went to the top, and saw how ridiculous and impossible it was anyway. I went downstairs and called my doctor. He merely said something like come back to the hospital immediately. We have plans for you.

In the meantime no physical contact was allowed. They termed it no P.C. The guy who I mentioned before tried to kiss me once, and since I was so terrified of the Whole System, I just cut off my sexual feelings. Because if they did find two people kissing they would 'restrict' them from each other. Meaning those two persons couldn't be alone together any place without the eye of a nurse or an aide watching.

I remember once at a patient-staff meeting I felt like I was choking from all the constriction in my throat. I left the meeting and ran down the hall crying. A nurse came after me, one that I liked, and put her arm around me and assured me that I would not choke. My God, it was the first time in eleven months that someone touched me like that. It felt so beautiful; it was as though someone were drowning and was saved and got air into their lungs.

I would say this is the majority of what I went through. But I was able to talk to more people after I stopped seeing Dr A. and saw what the hell was really going on around me.

A new patient had come in. She was so depressed that she couldn't eat, move, or speak. She had to carry a small but cumbersome oxygen tank around. They forced her to go to the evening's activities, a dance on the night she came in. There she sat with an attendant at her side. I thought it was ridiculous for her to have to be there and it probably made her feel terrible.

This girl seemed much improved after a few days. The oxygen was off, smiles gleamed from her face that now having come back to life was quite pretty. The last I saw of her was when she was playing ball on the unit.

The next day she was gone. Where to? 'Shipped' as the term was known. Sent to a State Hospital. Why? Well, in the 'professional' opinion of the staff she wasn't making enough progress to stay in an 'open hospital'.

Then there was a young girl who used to go into catatonic states. She was in the midst of doing something and would be stuck in that position. The patients passed her by (did they feel uncertain of what to do?). Someone tried to talk to her, to touch her, but she wouldn't move. Her doctor refused to see her more than every other week; plus she couldn't stand him. She just didn't receive any help.

I soon learned that others too shared my fear of being shipped to a state hospital. The way they used the term 'shipped' like you were luggage or baggage.

Another threat always there was shock treatment. That was pretty gory. There was a man who had a fear of losing his breath and of suffocating. I didn't know him too well but he was quite outgoing and witty and seemed like a nice and honest person. The 'Staff' advised shock treatment. In the early part of the treatment something is given to collapse the chest so you won't break bones. This man was terrified. One night with his pyjamas on he hid out in the grassy fields. He stayed there all night. The next morning he was literally dragged back to take his treatment.

The doctors all wore dark suits and the whole team of them dragged him down the hall. For a while afterwards men in dark suits frightened me.

Another woman who took shock treatments found great comfort in talking with her favourite nurse before the treatment. On this particular occasion the nurse couldn't be found and the treatment was scheduled. With her screaming protests to talk to the nurse they dragged her off down the long corridor.

There was a new man there who as soon as he entered the hospital begged and pleaded for someone to hold his hand. He was panicky. A few patients did; I did too. But this went on for a while and the patients became less and less willing to help him. I became friendly with him. I used to go into his room and we would talk about our maladies. He was in perpetual panic, and dreaded that it would never end. He had a wife whom he really seemed to love. It appeared that they had a very beautiful and affectionate relationship. After visiting hours, when she had left, he would tell me how worried he was about his family (he also had two children) and if he ever got better how he would support them. If only I knew more, and could have helped him in some way.

At the patient-staff meetings he was so witty and brilliant. It seemed that he didn't even know just how funny he was. I told him I thought he was and he seemed to simply dismiss it. He used to write television scripts.

His roommate was a young boy who I really liked; he used to really console me after my sessions with my doctor.

H. (I think I will call the new patient that) and his young roommate did not get along. The young boy couldn't take H.'s situation. H. had a woman doctor who I really don't know much about, except that she seemed very stern with him. There were times when H. would literally run after her and she would just reply coldly, 'We'll talk about it in the next session.' One day H. told me that the doctor told him that it would take a very long time for him to get better – if ever. This got me furious. There was something in the way H. told me this that smelled of disaster.

About a day or two later people were beginning to realize that H. wasn't around, and they were worried. My Great Master [sic] The Doctor (Dr B.) who was administrative Head told the nurses and some patients that we had to have a special meeting. We all gathered around fearfully. And Dr B. seriously stated that H. had taken his life. That was all he said. I started to cry in disbelief. I moaned and shook my head back and forth saying, 'No! No! Please no!'

I was heartbroken – I just can't express the feeling I had about H.'s doctor. The hate. Which is an understatement.

H.'s roommate was very affected by it and we 'eloped' as they call it when one left the hospital without a pass. We went to town and bought liquor. We sat in a field where we wouldn't be seen and just drank to get over our mutual misery.

There was so much other shit happening: like someone was taken to a State Hospital by the police for smoking marijuana given to him by an aide who was then fired. And another boy who I really liked who also smoked. No one knew about it though. But he felt he should be honest so he admitted to smoking also. His punishment was immediate dismissal from the Hospital, where he seemed to be getting help. We kept in touch for a while and the letters he wrote me were real heartbreakers; he was suffering.

Probably if I thought more I could think of more horrors. But I guess this is enough to make me know that people will read this and try to rectify these things. People acted out all they could for help; I also did but did not get any. If it wasn't for my ability to express myself on paper I don't know where I'd be today.

It's surprising to me, but I haven't given up on psychiatry; but there are very few good therapists around.

It's four years later, and so far I have gotten into one kind of sado-masochistic relationship with men after another. Does one wonder why? Obviously I had fears of men before, but, well you could take it from there...

I have a strong will now to live and to help other people. I have had some college before and I plan to go back. I've joined Women's Liberation. It has made me feel that there are a lot of other women around who feel they are oppressed and dissatisfied about the System. We are working for improvement in many ways, such as in local community action. I was alone in my struggle in the hospital; I am not alone now.

I am still into therapy and am understanding more about myself and other oppressed people. If more people were in touch with their own feelings there would be more love instead of all this destruction. Also I've noticed that the government seems as afraid of radicals as the hospital seemed afraid of patients.

I have no real answers – but at last I'm growing, and have still a lot to learn.

Also: shortly after I left the hospital I gradually began to lose my voice.

At first it started to quiver and shake. Gradually it got so I couldn't talk at all. I went into speech therapy and that didn't help. I went to a voice doctor and he said that if I continued to try to speak in the choked-up way that I was, I would lose my voice for ever.

I started seeing a bioenergetics therapist and have been seeing him for the last year and a half. I scream and beat beds and cry there – all the emotions that I felt so strongly in the hospital and would not be able to express – *would not be allowed to*. I am expressing them now.

So far as hospitals go – they are places that make you feel sick. Sicker than you ever were before in your life.

12. Lobotomies and Prison Revolts

Letter Reprinted in Liberation News Service *18/3/72*

State of California – Human Relations Agency
Department of Corrections
Sacramento, California
8 September 1971

Mr Robert L. Lawson
Executive Officer, California
  Council on Criminal Justice
1108 – 14th Street, Room 500
Sacramento, CA 95814

Subject: Letter of Intent – Proposal for the Neurosurgical Treatment
of Violent Inmates.

Dear Mr Lawson:

The problem of treating the aggressive, destructive inmate has long
been a problem in all correctional systems. During recent years this
problem has become particularly acute in the California Department
of Corrections institutions. To date, no satisfactory method of treatment of these individuals has been developed. This letter of intent is to
alert you to the development of a proposal to seek funding for a programme involving a complex neurosurgical evaluation and treatment
programme for the violent inmate. The programme would involve the
neurosurgery staff of the University of California at San Francisco
Medical Center. Initially, following screening at the California
Medical Facility at Vacaville, a period of acute hospitalization would
be involved at the UCSF Hospital for a period of five to seven days.
After this, during a period of two or three weeks, the patient would
undergo diagnostic studies, probably on an outpatient basis, being
transported as necessary from either California Medical Facility at
Vacaville or San Quentin. During this time, surgical and diagnostic
procedures would be performed to locate centres in the brain which

may have been previously damaged and which could serve as the focus for episodes of violent behaviour. If these areas were located and verified that they were indeed the source of aggressive behaviour, neurosurgery would be performed, directed at the previously found cerebral foci. Finally, if it were found that surgery was indicated the patient would be rehospitalized at the UCSF Medical Center for its performance.

It is estimated that the total effort, including the necessary screening by physicians, the hospitalizations, pay and transportation for correctional officers would amount to $48,000; grant funds required would be $36,000 with the Department of Corrections providing the twenty-five per cent in kind match.

Very sincerely,
R. K. PROCUNIER

*

*Vacaville: Lobotomies, Shock Therapy, and Torture for
'Violent' California Prisoners*
[Good Times/Liberation News Service]

VACAVILLE, Calif. – California State prison authorities are just now putting the finishing touches on an intensive psychiatric prison centre at the Vacaville State Mental Facility to control 'the aggressive, destructive, political inmate'.

The new faculty will house up to eighty prisoners and will open in late January or early February. The prisoners will be taken from the maximum security adjustment centres at Soledad, Folsom, and San Quentin. Psychiatrists will administer 'aversion therapy' to inmates considered 'the most violent'.

The therapy may include electrical and insulin shock, fever treatments, sodium pentothal (truth serum) interviews, Anectine (a death-simulating drug), anti-testosterone injections (to neutralize sex hormones), electrode brain implants, and lobotomies.

According to a letter that was ripped off recently, R. K. Procunier, California Chief of the Department of Corrections, wrote on 8 September to Robert Lawson, Executive Officer of the California Council on Criminal Justice [about the intended lobotomy programme. The complete letter is printed as preceding article – Ed.].

The outlines of the new Vacaville facility have been leaking out to the Press for the past few months, but detailed information was not available until 19 November, when the Department of Corrections held a 'think session' at the University of California at Davis. The meeting was to get support among the psychiatric profession.

Fortunately Dr Edward Opton, Jr, a Berkeley research psychologist with a strong liberal orientation, was invited. Opton contacted the Medical Committee for Human Rights to get the shocking information presented at the conference out to the public.

According to Dr Opton's notes from the meeting, the Vacaville centre has become necessary in the eyes of prison administrators because of the catastrophic failure of the relatively new adjustment centres demonstrated by George Jackson's 'escape'/ murder from the San Quentin AC. Adjustment centres are maximum security prisons.

Prison administrators, far from understanding the real causes of prisoner violence – a reaction to the highly repressive life they are forced to live, inside the adjustment centres – seem to blame it on 'some sort of organic agitator', according to Dr Opton's notes.

The meeting was led by Dr George Bach-y-Rita, the head research psychiatrist at the new unit. He mentioned a few of the treatments his personnel would experiment with. One would be the anti-testosterone injections to counteract sex drive and supposedly reduce the tensions a prisoner feels 'without the negative side effects in terms of poor self-image that direct castration creates'.

Dr Bach-y-Rita also feels that about ten per cent of the adjustment centre inmates would benefit from partial frontal lobotomies in which sections of the brain controlling motivation and drive would be cut out.

This method usually leaves the patient a passive vegetable capable of only simple tasks. Another experimental technique would be to implant electrodes in the brain to control behaviour directly.

But the basic method to be used on most of the prisoners will be 'aversion therapy'. Aversion therapy is aimed at making the prisoner sick or terrified every time he gets involved in violence. It works like this :

The patient is strapped into a chair in front of a movie screen. While he is shown movies of violence and sex, he is tortured. He may be given shocks, or drugs to make him feel nauseous or like he is dying. His eyes are clamped open so that he can't turn away from the screen.

The process is repeated daily until the man is deeply conditioned in his reactions. Supposedly then when the reformed prisoner tries to commit violence, his new drive takes over and makes him helpless. Aversion therapy using the death-simulating drug Anectine has recently been reported in the treatment of homosexuals at California's Atascadero State Hospital.

You don't have to worry, though, according to the administrators, because the Vacaville treatments will be voluntary. 'If they don't want to take the drug they don't have to,' says Dr L. J. Pope, warden of the facility. 'If they want to stay coo-coo and stay locked up all their lives that's all right with us.'

At the end of December, the Department of Corrections bowed to mounting public and professional pressure and publicly tabled plans for brain surgery on violent inmates at the new Vacaville facility.

Director of prison planning and development Walter Barkdull was making no promises, though he said that the brain surgery proposal 'hasn't been abandoned, but it's certainly been put into a dormant state'.

Deputy Chief of the Department of Corrections added, 'Although the brain surgery part of the programme is shelved, the rest of the programme will go forward after the first of the year.'

13. Radical Psychiatry in Italy: 'Love is Not Enough'

Donata Mebane-Francescato and Susan Jones

An oriental fable tells of a man who was entered by a serpent while he was asleep. The serpent settled in the man's stomach and took over control of his life so that the man no longer belonged to himself. One day, after a long period of domination, the serpent finally left; but the man no longer knew what to do with his freedom. He had become so used to submitting his will to that of the serpent, his wishes and impulses to those of the beast, that he had lost the capacity to wish, to strive, or to act autonomously. Instead of freedom he found only the 'emptiness of the void', for the departure of the serpent had taken with it the man's new essence – the adaptive fruit of his occupation. He was left with the awesome task of reclaiming, little by little, the former human content of his life.

It is hardly surprising that a sensitive psychiatrist would see in this fable a parable of the condition of the mentally ill. What is impressive is that Dr Franco Basaglia, an Italian psychiatrist and author of *L'Istituzione Negata* (The Institution Denied), should see in the insidious serpent an analogy with the entire institutional, oppressive, political fabric of Western society: through the same actions of prevarication and violence by which the serpent destroyed the man, our system breeds 'mental illness' by forcing the unwary individual to incorporate and submit to the very enemy who destroys him. And, warns Basaglia, *all* of us who participate in society are slaves of the serpent, and if we do not struggle to destroy or vomit it, we will lose all hope of regaining our human dignity.

Although Italy is far from being in the *avant-garde* of the mental health revolution, *L'Istituzione Negata* documents an exemplary attempt by its radical author not only to reverse the

conventional pattern of institutional treatment of the mentally
ill, but even more significantly, to see beyond the preliminary
internal changes to a global, critical awareness of our social
situation.

Basaglia's convictions grew out of his personal experience as
director of the Provincial Psychiatric Hospital of Gorizia, a large,
state institution located on the border between Italy and Yugo-
slavia. When he took over the directorship in 1961, he was confronted with the typical atmosphere of a lower class, custodial
institution: locked wards; a rigid daily schedule constructed
more for the benefit of the attendants than for the patients; a
bedtime hour of six o'clock; and such customary procedures as
tying the patients to their beds at night. One of the long-term
inmates explained, 'When someone died, a bell would ring; and
we all used to wish the bell would toll for us, for life held no
hope.'

Faced with what he termed a 'tragic nuthouse reality', Basaglia
started by questioning all the institutional givens; and 'depsychiatrization' became his *leitmotif*. By depsychiatrization he
meant a single-minded attempt to eschew any preconceived system of thinking or acting and to begin instead on undefined,
uncoded terrain. Not only did he refuse to accept that his patients
were irretrievably sick people and that his psychiatric role was
that of a paternalistic custodian, but he defied as well the man-
date of society which had put them both in their positions. He
felt that the institutionalized mentally ill were ill first of all
because they were deprived of their human rights and then excluded and abandoned by everybody.

In Basaglia's eyes, the level of dehumanization attained by
his patients was not so much a symptom of their illness but
rather the brutal consequence of the continual violence and
humiliation that institutional life had heaped upon them. He
saw them as victims of the same power imbalance which had
made them the refuse of society outside the institution walls. Violence, said Basaglia, is the prerogative exercised by those who
hold the knife against those who are irrevocably without power
– in every institution, be it the family, the school, the factory,
the university or the hospital, there is a neat division of roles

between those who hold power and those who don't; and this leads to the exclusion and humiliation of the powerless.

Basaglia felt that mental illness could not begin to be understood until these environmental conditions were entirely changed. Having defined the problem as one of the unequal and oppressive power relationship, he set out to change the oppressive conditions in his own institution. And more important, he began a determined campaign to make the patients aware of their oppression, both within the hospital and in the society outside from which they had come. There were simple physical changes: opening up the nine wards; eliminating all uniforms both for the more than 150 doctors, nurses, and social workers and for the 500 patients; replacing the 'Warning – Do Not Enter' sign at the entrance with an invitation to visitors to feel welcome at any time; and permanently opening the gates to the park which housed the hospital wards, church, and factory.

He then tossed out the use of all psychiatric labels, encouraging people to relate to one another as human beings rather than as disease prototypes. All forms of traditional therapy were replaced by a series of group meetings at a variety of levels, from intimate groups to plenary community meetings of patients and staff. In none of these groups was there a traditional therapy emphasis; rather they were a focus for 'consciousness raising' much in the manner of the meetings of the Women's Movement. An effort was made to involve the patients in planning and decisions on the daily operation, programmes, and activities of the hospital; and more significant, there was a continuous push toward politicizing the situation – making the patients aware of their oppressed position, of the wrongs perpetrated on them outside the hospital walls.

Basaglia has compared his work to that being done by Maxwell Jones in England: the techniques of the two therapeutic communities are very similar, but the goals are quite different. He feels that in England there is less conscious effort being aimed at drawing political parallels from within the institution to the outside world, less attention given to promoting awareness of the power structure of society. And to Basaglia, political awareness is the central issue – awareness that the mentally ill

are the objects of social violence. The violence directed against
them is twofold: first, violence used to remove the patient for-
cibly from social contact, and the more subtle violence used
before institutionalization, when the patient was a person without social or economic power, a failure in a system that seeks to
remove its contradictions from the public eye.

In Basaglia's view, psychiatrists have been used by the system
as technicians – its hirelings, whose job it is to take care of the
rejects, deviants, and failures, keeping them out of sight so that
the system would not have to confront the injustices and inequi-
ties which promote these deviances. Psychiatrists, sociologists,
psychologists, and social workers have become the new administrators of the violence of the power structure. In the measure
that they soothe conflicts, break down resistance, and 'solve' the
problems created by situational realities, they perpetuate the
global violence by convincing the individual to accommodate to
the oppressive conditions.

Basaglia's solution is to refuse to administer the therapeutic
act when it serves only to mitigate the reaction of the excluded
against the excluder. And to do this, therapists have to become
aware of their own exclusion from real power, even when they
serve as the technicians of this power. In his mind, therapy is an
encounter between equals, and the less equal the power distri-
bution, the less possibility there is of a therapeutic encounter.
Thus he makes an important distinction between private
therapy, where the client has a modicum of power in that he can
freely enter into or terminate the relationship, and the situation
of the institutionalized patient who has no freedom of choice in
either his treatment or its administrator.

Ideally, therapy is a political act; and it becomes so to the
degree that it tends to integrate an ongoing crisis back into the
roots from which the crisis sprang, giving the individual an
awareness of the personal and social conditions which provoked
his crisis. The first step toward liberation is to help the patient
regain his sense of existential freedom and responsibility, his
right to a full human life. To accomplish this monumental task,
the therapeutic community is the preferred vehicle; but it, too,
runs the risk of becoming just another tool in the hands of the

power structure, another gimmick for controlling the deviants and victims of the system. For this reason the therapeutic community must be only a transitional step toward the full assumption of political awareness and personal responsibility. Changing the traditional authority and power structure and experimenting with new roles within the institution can throw into dazzling relief the difference between this new reality and the oppression awaiting the patient in the world outside. Unless this new awareness can be carried beyond the hospital walls to greater engagement against the oppressive elements of the society at large, its efforts are to no avail. 'Love' in the sense of therapeutic isolation and protection is not enough – it is necessary to change the basic social institutions which give rise to the need for therapy.

Unfortunately the next global step to take is not clear to Basaglia; Italy, especially, is not ready for a social, political revolution. He concludes, somewhat pessimistically, that all radical therapists can do is to resist being co-opted and to keep alive, in themselves and in their patients, the vital awareness of the oppression and violence to which we all fall prey.

The path Basaglia indicates is certainly an uneasy and tortuous one. On one hand, there is the continual danger of becoming involuted in our change efforts, of becoming sold on one technique or approach through which we have experienced some success; and to be tempted to repeat this same pattern at the expense of exploring new flexible pathways with a wider impact on society at large.

On the other hand we are faced with a more subtle and insidious problem: the 'so what' syndrome, those feelings of disillusionment and defeat which arise when we contemplate the paucity of our resources and the magnitude of the task. The serpent within and without is so powerful as to make the struggle toward a more human, loving, just society seem hopeless.

Basaglia's conclusions seem to illustrate this second crisis point. He has achieved a great deal within a limited setting (he has rehabilitated fifty per cent of so-called hopeless cases) and now the possibilities of his having a great influence on the rest of Italian society look dismal, so confusion and the temptation to despair grow powerful. It would be a big waste if this feeling of impotence were to keep Basaglia and the rest of us from continuing the search.

In our lifetime, we will probably not see the total personal, social, and political changes we want; however, to go on struggling we must have the hope that small contributions do have a cumulative effect, that we together as people can have a voice in shaping a better future. In the words of Camus:

> I know that the great tragedies of history often fascinate men with approaching horror. Paralysed, they cannot make up their minds to do anything but wait. So they wait, and one day the Gorgon devours them. But I should like to convince you that the spell can be broken, that there is only an ILLUSION OF IMPOTENCE, that strength of heart, intelligence and courage are enough to stop fate and sometimes reverse it. One has merely to will this, not blindly, but with a firm and reasoned will.

14. A Mental Patient's Liberation Project: Statement and Bill of Rights

New York Mental Patients' Liberation Front

We, of the Mental Patients' Liberation Project, are former mental patients. We've all been labelled schizophrenic, manic depressive, psychotic, and neurotic – labels that have degraded us, made us feel inferior. Now we're beginning to get together – beginning to see that these labels are not true but have been thrown at us because we have refused to conform – refused to adjust to a society where to be normal is to be an unquestioning robot, without emotion and creativity. As ex-mental patients we know what it's like to be locked up in mental institutions for this refusal; we know what it's like to be treated as an object – to be made to feel less of a person than 'normal' people on the outside. We've all felt the boredom, the regimentation, the inhumane physical and psychological abuses of institutional life – life on the inside. We are now beginning to realize that we are no longer alone in these feelings – that we are all brothers and sisters. Now for the first time we're beginning to fight for ourselves – fight for our personal liberty. We, of the Mental Patients' Liberation Project, want to work to change the conditions we have experienced. We have drawn up a Bill of Rights for Mental Patients – rights that we unquestioningly should have but rights that have been refused to us. Because these rights are not now legally ours we are now going to fight to make them a reality.

Mental Patients' Bill of Rights

We are ex-mental patients. We have been subjected to brutalization in mental hospitals and by the psychiatric profession. In almost every state of the union, a mental patient has fewer *de facto* rights than a murderer condemned to die or to life imprisonment. As human beings, you are entitled to basic human rights that are taken for granted by the general population. You are entitled to protection by and recourse to the law. The purpose of the Mental Patients' Liberation Project is to help those who are still institutionalized. This Bill of Rights was prepared by those at the first meeting of MPLP held on 13 June 1971 at the Washington Square Methodist Church. If you know someone in a mental hospital, give him/her a copy of these rights. If you are in a hospital and need legal help, try to find someone to call the Dolphin Center.

1. You are a human being and are entitled to be treated as such with as much decency and respect as is accorded to any other human being.

2. You are an American citizen and are entitled to every right established by the Declaration of Independence and guaranteed by the Constitution of the United States of America.

3. You have the right to the integrity of your own mind and the integrity of your own body.

4. Treatment and medication can be administered only with your consent, you have the right to demand to know all relevant information regarding said treatment and/or medication.

5. You have the right to have access to your own legal and medical counsel.

6. You have the right to refuse to work in a mental hospital and/or to choose what work you shall do and you have the right to receive the minimum wage for such work as is set by the state labour laws.

7. You have the right to decent medical attention when you feel you need it just as any other human being has that right.

8. You have the right to uncensored communication by phone, letter, and in person with whomever you wish and at any time you wish.

9. You have the right not to be treated like a criminal: not to be locked up against your will; not to be committed involuntarily; not to be fingerprinted or 'mugged' (photographed).

10. You have the right to decent living conditions. You're paying for it and the taxpayers are paying for it.

11. You have the right to retain your own personal property. No one has the right to confiscate what is legally yours, no matter what reason is given. That is commonly known as theft.

12. You have the right to bring grievance against those who have mistreated you and the right to counsel and a court hearing. You are entitled to protection by the law against retaliation.

13. You have the right to refuse to be a guinea pig for experimental drugs and treatments and to refuse to be used as learning material for students. You have the right to demand reimbursement if you are so used.

14. You have the right not to have your character questioned or defamed.

15. You have the right to request an alternative to legal commitment or incarceration in a mental hospital.

The Mental Patients' Liberation Project plans to set up neighbourhood crisis centres as alternatives to incarceration and voluntary commitment to hospitals. We plan to set up a legal aid society for those whose rights are taken away and/or abused. Although our immediate aim is to help those currently in hospitals, we are also interested in helping those who are suffering from job discrimination, discriminatory school admissions' policies, and discrimination and abuse at the hands of the psychiatric profession. Call the number listed below if you are interested in our group or if you need legal assistance.

Please contact us if there is any specific condition you would like us to work against:

New York Mental Patients' Liberation Project
56 East 45th Street
New York, N.Y. 10003

15. Psychology as a Social Problem: An Investigation into the Society for the Psychological Study of Social Issues (SPSSI)

Lanny Beckman

Editorial Introduction

There is a misconception that the Society for the Psychological Study of Social Issues (SPSSI) began as a radical organization and was later either co-opted or turned to the right on its own. To provide some background for the following article and letter by Lanny Beckman, we have checked out the situation thoroughly, including reading much material from all issues of SPSSI's publication, the Journal of Social Issues (JSI), *which began in 1945.*

Beginning in 1936, SPSSI was no more than a group of psychologists who considered themselves applied psychologists: this included a large number of industrial psychologists, people who were attempting to 'cool out' workers in large factories so that the machinery of US capitalism would run more smoothly, insuring greater profit to the bosses. Gardner Murphy, Gordon Allport, and Kurt Lewin were among the prominent 'heavies' in the early days of SPSSI. Lewin was at MIT with his Research Centre for Group Dynamics, a precursor of modern-day think-tanks, which specialize in working out systems of repression to be used by the liberals. A 1947 issue of JSI spoke of the importance of industrial psychologists helping solve the 'morale problem in young textile workers'. A year later a whole issue was devoted to industrial psychology, supplying important information on how to squeeze more out of workers while making it look like a beneficial programme for them.

In the McCarthy era, SPSSI played 'cold warrior' along with the majority of the intellectual/academic community. Ernest Melby, in a 1953 JSI article, wrote:

By now there can be no question in informed minds where the university faculties stand with regard to Communism. They are as opposed to Communism as Senator McCarthy. They have been opposing it longer and more effectively, partially because many of them are older and also because they saw the danger of all totalitarian threats long before he did.

So, the psychology 'radicals' were taking a harder line on communism than the reactionary McCarthy! It goes without saying that SPSSI supported Melby's position, given that the article was published in a special issue on the subject and given that there was no criticism of the article by the editors. Four years later SPSSI picked up on the 'yellow peril', printing a special issue on 'brainwashing' in China.

What about the turbulent 1960s – did SPSSI side with the black and anti-war movements? Not at all! In 1966 JSI had a special issue on 'Misconception and the Vietnamese War'. One of the contributors was Ralph White who had worked for the United States Information Service, a government propaganda and counter-insurgency outfit. White wrote how wrong it was for the Viet Cong to kill the puppet administrators of the Saigon régime, and felt that:

All in all, it seems clear that if democracy is defined as individual freedom, the Viet Cong (like the government of North Viet Nam) permits even less of it than the post-Diem military governments in the South have permitted, and in that sense is less democratic.

Continuing its pro-imperialist position, in 1968 JSI printed an issue on 'Social Psychology of Developing Countries'. The articles investigated all sorts of nonsense psychological classifications without mentioning that US imperialism was the main factor in the material and psychological oppression of the peoples of the 'developing countries'.

If imperialists were welcome in the ranks of SPSSI, so were racists. Arthur Jensen, famed for his racist IQ studies, was an editorial consultant for a 1970 JSI number, JSI always couches its politics in psychological double-talk, like a 1969 article on 'Motivation and Academic Achievement of Negro Americans', which dealt with testing models which had no bearing at all on the reality of racism in this country. Student rebellion received similar treatment. A 1969 issue on 'Alienated Youth' contained no articles by alienated youth, only articles by rich professionals who make their money investigating alienated youth. Likewise the special issue of last year on 'The New Left and the Old', in which academics (rather than movement people) wrote phony articles about things which movement people feel are integral to their lives. Nathan Hackman, one of the contributors to that issue, is a labour relations analyst and past member of the US Wage Stabilization Board, a professional position which immediately defines him as a strikebreaker. SPSSI's myopic view went so far as to have Armand Mause, editor of the issue, speak of The Village Voice as a movement publication and C. Wright Mills as a movement 'personality' Of course, the black, women's, gay, latino, and other liberation movements were totally neglected.

Other recent issues of JSI have included 'Socialization, the Law, and Society,' without having any articles by prisoners or about prison revolts or political prisoners. Another 1971 issue, on drug use, included an article by Herman Kahn of the Hudson Institute, a major counter-insurgency planner for South-east Asia.

None of this is surprising, given SPSSI's role as 'liberal' front for the atrocities of the American Psychological Association.* SPSSI invited S. I. Hayakawa, past SPSSI Council member and notorious for his repression of the San Francisco State College revolt, as a special speaker at the 1970 American Psychological Association convention. And who did they trump up to cool things down when radicals threatened disruption – none

---

* We speak of atrocities in the sense of the American Psychological Association being the primary professional organization of all types of US psychologists, who do everything from counter-insurgency work and military psychology to more everyday rip-off therapy. SPSSI, as a division of the APA, attempts to play the role of running interference for the repressive psychology establishment.

other than soft-spoken members of Psychologists for Social Action (PSA) who happened to be SPSSI members. In fact, a large number of PSA members are SPSSI members too!

It is often a waste of time to do exposés of the psychology establishment. But when misconceptions are rampant, as in reference to SPSSI, it is incumbent upon us to present exposés. Part of this is a demand for self-criticism by supposed radicals on the SPSSI Council – namely Marc Pilisuk and Richard Flacks. Another part of it is to clarify our position so that we will not fall prey to the faulty and repressive methodology and practice of groups like SPSSI.

Lanny Beckman, near the completion of his doctorate, and a long-time SPSSI member, writes here of why he quit both graduate school and SPSSI. His feelings, from being in the middle of the shit, give us much important information about SPSSI as well as North American psychology in general.

*

The Society for the Psychological Study of Social Issues is made up mainly of social psychologists. It is the liberal face of the reactionary sloth of social science. The members have a number of things in common. They are concerned about social problems. They want to apply their 'expertise' to the solution of social problems. They earn over $10,000 a year – which enables them to spend a lot of time thinking about social problems and making 'responsible' pronouncements about social action.

In case you don't get the point: social problems are their bread and butter. In case you still don't get the point: SPSSI is a *liberal* organization. It's *concerned*. It doesn't do anything and that makes it all the more concerned. As long as nothing changes, SPSSI will be in business. As long as there are social problems like 'Negroes' and poor people to be concerned about and to study, those five-figure salaries will just keep rolling in.

When you get right down to it though, SPSSI doesn't really see 'Negroes' as constituting a social problem. It sees them as constituting a subject matter. I mean, SPSSI is made up of academics, and academics gotta publish or they might wind up being subject matter themselves.

In its periodical, the *Journal of Social Issues* (JSI), SPSSI publishes thought-provoking agitational articles with catchy titles like 'The SRS Model as a Predictor of Negro Responsiveness to Reinforcement'. The author's summary of this almost randomly chosen article pretty well captures the sort of 'expertise' that SPSSI endeavours to apply to social problems. (Note: If you can actually make it through the entire summary, step up your programme of self-criticism.)

An attempt was made to demonstrate the relevance of an inter-personally oriented incongruity model – Baron's SRS theory – to understand Negro responsiveness to social reinforcement. Based on the SRS model it was hypothesized that Negroes would find a low rate of approval from a white authority figure, at least under certain conditions, more appropriate and preferred than a high rate of approval. The results of a series of studies carried out with disadvantaged Negro youth suggest that this proposition is relevant to under-standing how Negro self-evaluation and task performance is affected by social reinforcement parameters such as type, source, and fre-quency of reinforcement. The role of such research in broadening the focus of the SRS model from a monistic to a multidimensional conception is also discussed.

The political implications of this viewpoint are blatantly obvious. It is important for students with growing political con-sciousness to bear in mind that the foregoing summary typifies the most progressive attitude in mainstream psychology. It is also important to see that it is the kind of repressive horseshit that lies behind tempting platitudes about 'social action' and 'the social scientist's responsibility as a citizen'.

I got out of the social sciences by the skin of my teeth – a couple of months from a Ph.D. In the letter below, I bid fare-well to the arid field of academic psychology and to the pious little corner occupied by SPSSI. I submit the letter to the *Radical Therapist* in the hope that it might deter students from pursuing the illusion that the tools of social science offer any real solution to the myriad problems proliferated by Amerikan imperialism.

Newsletter Editor
Society for the Psychological Study
   of Social Issues
Post Office Box 1248
Ann Arbor, Michigan 48106

Dear Sir:

I am writing to cancel my membership and journal subscription. This is concurrent with my decision to drop out of psychology. It has taken me a long time and a lot of hard work to become a drop-out, but looking back, I feel that it's all been worth it. The decision to quit was not an easy one; I too like the security and fat salary that goes along with having a Ph.D., but there comes a time when you must say no to the bullshit.

I ask you not to dismiss this too easily. I've been around the field for quite a while – six years as a graduate student – and have a pretty good understanding of what constitutes academic psychology. I've received consistently high marks and all of the (misguided) praise that they engender. I have read hundreds of mainstream psychological journals and texts, have passed my doctoral comprehensives, written the first draft of my dissertation and have only a couple of months to complete all requirements. I do not view my decision to quit as either fanatical or foolhardy, but as the first sensible and honest action I've taken since entering the field as a graduate student in 1964.

After almost a decade of formal study, I would like to take this opportunity to summarize my feelings about psychology in general and S P S S I in particular.

Psychology, as defined in North American universities, is a spiritual wasteland. Well, of course, what has spirituality to do with the objective study of behaviour? But then, what has spirituality to do with the desolate quality of life in America? I see the two issues as inherently related. Psychology is the study of alienated man, but lacks the recognition that it is so. Psychology is the product of alienated men, men so removed from the meaning of their humanity that they believe that rigour, control, experimentation and statistics constitute vehicles toward understanding human life. Academic psychology is a reflection of American alienation. It explains nothing about the human condition, but *is* itself a symptom of a poisoned culture and, like that culture, requires explanation and radical change.

Should the world survive the evils in which social science plays its part, historians will look back on the dinosaur of American imperialism and see psychology as a tiny ganglion in its toe. And they will be amazed that for a century, a group of men and women, who pretentiously called themselves Doctors, were so blind as actually to believe that the methods of science could illuminate anything of the human heart.

Well, these criticisms apply equally to fields such as contemporary philosophy, but where psychology differs is in the fact that it is also an intellectual wasteland. The level of intelligence one finds in mainstream publications is astonishingly banal. Psychology is an object of ridicule among intellectuals. How often I have felt embarrassment when a friend has glanced through one of my books and shaken his head at the pathetic simple-mindedness aggrandized by inflated psychological jargon. The best minds in the field are third-rate thinkers.

What a tragedy that students who bring to their freshman course the naïve and healthy desire to study the 'meaning of life' are exposed to the ignorance and reactionary platitudes that parade under the banner of psychology. The best students continue to leave the field. I take this to be a hopeful sign. The liberal rejoinder that the student ought not to reject, say the experimental method, until he has familiarized himself with it is nonsense. Wasting several years familiarizing oneself with the valueless is wasting several years. One function of a teacher (to use an obsolete term) is to encourage students to avoid what is worthless. The psychologist who does so, however, finds himself out of a job. It is my conclusion that psychology has nothing to teach and will eventually find itself without students.

As far as SPSSI goes, I find it in many ways the most objectionable branch of the psychological establishment. If anything, its intellectual impoverishment is even greater than the other branches. It's a tight race, however, and I wouldn't want to argue the point.

From a political – or as you would have it, 'social action' – point of view, SPSSI brings into sharpest relief the bankruptcy of the liberal position. Your chickenshit reformism, your 'Activists' Corner', your rational consideration as to whether military psychology promotes human welfare (how can men and women of reputed intelligence even entertain such an insane proposition?) – all of these typify the fraudulent and comfortable concerns of over-paid professionals living in a world filled with misery and oppression.

'SPSSI,' you say, 'provides an important avenue through which social scientists can apply their knowledge and insights to some of the critical social problems of today.' I believe that social scientists possess no special expertise to solve social problems. Your record in military, educational, industrial, and marketing psychology leaves little doubt that your expertise serves only to create and perpetuate social problems. It's no coincidence that social science has been used by the powerful to make their schools, factories, and wars run more efficiently. The biases underlying positivist methodology co-ordinate perfectly with the needs of the ruling class: the separation of subject and object; the concern with external, measurable behaviour; the pre-occupation with method rather than content; the need to manipulate, control, and predict. Again, it's no coincidence that terms like 'manipulate' and 'control' are desirable in the lexicon of social science and pejorative in the vocabulary of social ethics.

The myth that scientific methodology is value neutral, and that therefore social scientists can beneficially apply their knowledge to social problems, is false. To be sure, most SPSSI members would agree that regrettably much applied research in the social sciences has been used to reinforce rather than alleviate problems. But then, they would go on, that is not the fault of the methodology; no, that's the fault of the application of the methodology. For methods are abstract tools; it's up to us how we use them, etc., etc.

I reject that line of reasoning. I don't believe in the separability of method and application. Both evolve interdependently in a context of specific political and economic realities. Who controls the funds to support what research? Mainly, as we all know, government, military, industry and its tax-exempt foundations foot the bill for research which sharpens the tools of 'value-neutral' methodology. And, as most of us know, they do so because that methodology, when applied, serves their interests. Workers produce more; consumers buy more; inhabitants are made more docile in concentration camps called paci-fication centres.

The entire network of research projects is strictly controlled econ-omically. There is no academic freedom. That's another fake myth that SPSSI fights so tenaciously to uphold. And there are no data. The world isn't given to us: it's created. The belief in data is one more piece of the positivist pie baked up by SPSSI, science, and the established powers. As Laing says, the things gathered in research are *capta*, the things which have been seized.

And SPSSI seizes at every turn the things which betray its avowed intention of mitigating social problems. You study blacks, the poor, hippies, radicals, delinquents, the emotionally disturbed – all the groups your government tells you are problems. The oppressed *are* problems; they threaten vested interests; they have to be under-stood and boiled into the putrid soup of American culture. And SPSSI is there, Johnny-on-the-spot, to study them, to understand them, to help the system accommodate them.

Hopefully, the giant machine, which you strive so sanctimoniously and ineffectively to lubricate, will one day grind to a halt. [*We're not so sure that S P S S I's lubrication is so ineffective and the machine will have to be halted by the people* — *the* Radical Therapist.] And then your most catastrophic expectation will have come true: there will be no research funds with which to study social problems. Or worse yet, there may not even be any social problems.

My conclusion after four years as an undergraduate and six years as a graduate student is that academic psychology offers me no knowledge or insights about the social world in which I live. Rather, it consistently beclouds any understanding.

I have always disliked the pomposity with which psychologists have named their ignorance science. The situation reaches absurd proportions, however, when SPSSI couples that pomposity with pious resolutions about social action. Logical arguments aside, my visceral reaction against SPSSI is provoked mainly by the relentless strain of self-righteousness that runs through everything you publish.

You are a group of men and women earning hugely inflated salaries, while in its name retarding social progress. Consider whether you would be willing to take a cut of $10,000 a year to see the 'social problem' with which you are professionally concerned disappear. If your answer is no, I advise you to return to the less hypocritical lie of doing socially irrelevant research. If the answer is yes, I encourage you to sacrifice the remaining thousands of dollars, get out of the field, and join forces with 'your' oppressed group to change the conditions responsible for its misery.*

I would like you to print this letter intact as I believe that it is

* There are other possible choices which I have not mentioned. The most important of these would be to remain in the university and to work for genuine social change *there*, i.e., in the social sciences themselves. As I state in the title of this article, psychology is itself a 'social problem' and not a tool for solving other problems. This is a fact which most psychologists fail to recognize. This failure leads 'concerned' psychologists to apply their energies towards helping external groups, without realizing that the very structure of the psychological establishment militates against effecting real change in these external areas. To make a point which is more than merely an analogy, progressive whites had to realize that the black problem was really a white problem. Psychologists must also realize that the problem is theirs. The solution lies, not in studying 'Negro Responsiveness to Reinforcement from a White Authority Figure', but in studying — and working to change — the psychologist's responsiveness to reinforcement from research-funding agencies. [*Further communication from author* — *the* Radical Therapist.]

relevant to the entire SPSSI enterprise, that it speaks to a wide cross-section of your membership, and that it articulates that sliver of doubt which pricks the liberal conscience now and then (especially late at night). If you are offended by the obscenities, you may change 'bullshit' in paragraph one to 'hypocrisy' and 'chickenshit' in paragraph nine to 'cowardly'.

III. Women, Men and Children

16. Letter to Her Psychiatrist

Nadine Miller

4 June 1970

Taking this vacation was the best thing that I could have done, and should have done a long time ago. It is not only the change of location that has been helpful, but also the change of routine, the time and space to think without pressure, and being with people I trust. The past week has been a really new high – a whole different perspective is visible to me. Whereas, before I could only think that the city and all that goes with it was destroying much of my feeling for life, and distorting my ability to think, I now know that it is true. I feel that so many more things enter the area of the possible. I know that it is against my survival instinct to live amongst the daily perversions which one has in the city. For the second time in my life, I feel in touch with my body. I have spent many hours thinking about decisions I had to make before I go back to the city, and this letter is only part of a number of positions I have made.

I know that I have made the decision to stop therapy a number of times, and each time I was not really sure of the reason, but was led by a feeling – a feeling that said therapy was not in my best interest, and might even be working against me. At those times I could not articulate the reason, although I used certain situations as the excuse for ending therapy. What I realize now is that it is true I could not discuss certain things with you; how could I trust you? I tried to force myself to think of you as untouched or unaffected by your position, sex, class, privileges, and prejudices. I was operating under a false premise, namely that we could have an honest, open exchange of ideas. Instead I have had to guess where you stand from things you imply, rather than have real feedback on which to defend my accusations. I also see that there are very real reasons why you would want to withhold information from me, and also channel things into a direction which would and did work against me as a woman.

Therapy acts to enforce the whole male structure, and ultimately forces women into dependence upon an area which, founded and dominated by men, has been used against women. Let me explain. You, by virtue of your title, set yourself up as the source of knowledge. You have something that I want. As a woman, forced to accept the whole male structure, I accept the idea that I have a problem, rather than realizing that I as a woman am forced to function in a male supremacist structure and that I cannot function as a human being when I am constantly being knocked down, forced to have meaningless relationships with men because I am afraid of the consequences if I don't, forced to submit to a life of educational tracking – and then told I am sick when I refuse to put up with any more of the shit. I am tired of being told I have a basic insecurity, a mother complex, a father complex. I am tired of thinking of myself as Crazy – a nice way to make sure I never throw off the oppression – a way to keep women dependent upon the oppressors.

Men make the definitions of crazy or not crazy, they then set themselves up as the saviours. They have the 'answer'. Of course they don't tell you (the patient) what they know. How else could they keep you dependent. Let's get down to the real facts. You have said that my involvement with Women's Liberation was an outlet for my hostility against men. I was made to feel that it was just another part of therapy. Instead of hitting a punching bag, I joined Women's Liberation. If I did not share the pain of many women, I would begin to feel that I have a unique problem. I read books (written by men) in which I am told that I am maladjusted, cannot accept authority, sexually deviant, etc., etc.

I was lucky enough to realize that my hostility towards men was real, and was not an individual problem. You bet I had reasons to hate men – you not being the least. From age three I was dragged to shrink after shrink because I was 'too aggressive'. Meaning I was not acting as a little girl should. I hit boys and talked back. I hated my father for treating my mother so badly, and hated my mother for not defending herself (at the time I thought she had a choice). When I talked to you about the Collective, you made me feel it was an 'escape', whatever that means. I mean, why should I live alone, work nine till five, five days a week? You call wanting to live with others, wanting to share living responsibilities, an escape. You think I am running away from my problems. Well, God damn it – I am tired of thinking that it is *my* problem, rather than a political problem.

When I accuse you of using your maleness, and class against me, you say I am hostile – as if there is no basis for my feeling that way. You refuse to accept the fact that I prefer a relationship with a woman than with a man. You insist that there are 'good' men around. If you use yourself as an example, well I am even more convinced that there are none. When we talked about me wanting to keep my baby, all you could say was how difficult it would be for me to get married, continue my schooling, meet other people (men). Did you ever think that maybe I didn't want to get married? Did you ever think that a Collective could be an alternative? Did you ever think of how I could do it, or did you only say, 'I have a patient who tried and has a messed-up kid.'

You see, there are very real reasons why you would want me to think certain things. I mean, what would happen if all women began to realize that they were not sick or crazy but reacting to very real problems, shared by many other women. Sure I hate sex with men. It has never been good. I don't come because I am made numb, used as a machine. You have said that I pick these kinds of men. What shit! There aren't any others around. I mean it takes a long time to raise a man's consciousness – and I have given up. I have been wrong in thinking that you know more about me than I know about myself. That is the same line men always use, 'You're too emotional.'

Even a female psychiatrist falls into the same trap. She also accepts the male structure (and there are many reasons why she does), so that I would not go to a female psychiatrist. The whole psychological thing is based on the premise that there are *individual* problems rather than a social problem which is political.

I have reached the point where I know there is only one solution for me as a woman – unity with other women and ultimately a revolution. I have also identified my oppressors. No, it is not society (that is too general). My oppressors are not institutions. My oppressors are *men* – and all the superstructures which are set up by men: I refuse to allow *men to define* me anymore. I refuse to support a system which works against me and my sisters.

One other thing. The $28.00 which I owe you will be given to the Women's Centre as a donation. Since you used your privileges to exploit me, I feel it is only fair (if there is such a thing) for me to take your money and give it to the same people you have made money from.

Let it also be understood, that when I have done things like this which were in my best interest, you resorted to calling me crazy rather than dealing with my feelings. By thinking of me as crazy, you exempted yourself from all responsibility. Well, this time it won't work. If you cannot call me crazy then you will just be angry. I really don't care what you do. I know where things are at. For once I have told it like it is. . .

All Power to Women.

17. Therapist Turned Woman

Pat Webbink

I feel a conflict as a therapist, between wanting to be real and at the same time hiding behind my pedigrees and playing an uptight shrink role. Sometimes I feel fragmented, trying to be 'distant, competent, and strong' when I may feel loving, sad, angry, frightened. If I try to help others to be comfortable with their human needs I must be comfortable with my own. Some of the training I've had is especially difficult to unlearn because it reinforces culturally learned fears of openness and intimacy. Do I dare let it all hang out? I thought I would try in a protected atmosphere and so I decided to put in my two days at the fall meeting of the Association for Humanistic Psychology. I hoped that there I would meet others who were also trying to find truth and change in a traditionally uptight profession.

I walked into the Washington Hilton Hotel. A bunch of 'professionals' who had taken off jackets, ties and mini skirts at the American Psychological Association convention had changed into bermuda shorts and hot pants and had emerged as the Association for Humanistic Psychologists. What resulted was a pitiful display of people trying to release their ids for professional masks. And I was there – lady shrink seeking meaningful change in a rigid profession.

'Power to the Person' was the engaging title for the conference; better stated it was 'Power to the Penis'. Not only was the male domination as heavy as it is in straight conventions, but here the rhetoric of humanism and liberation were permission for quick lays. Anywhere one turned, there were strangers pawing one another. Not to conform was 'unhumanistic'. What was even more baffling was that there probably were some very real interactions taking place, but it was impossible to tell how genuine people were. There was so much phoniness, that a person seeking genuine contact got lost in the crowd.

My first meeting was on 'Risking My Craziness – Letting Go'. The description attracted my attention: *The ability to experience and be my craziness is extremely threatening. My controls become greater and greater until my controls are out of control, and I become what I fear. This experimental session will explore methods for experimenting with one's ability to let go, to risk his craziness, and to enter the twilight zone of his existence.*

Several hundred people were patiently waiting for the meeting to begin. Five pricks came running out screeching 'Let's clap for ourselves.' Before I had a chance to question what's so special about us that we should clap for ourselves, the audience passively obeyed and began clapping, yelling and shouting for joy. Did they really feel this? I got up. 'Why isn't there a woman on your programme?' I got a blank stare for a reply – 'Are you crazy, lady? One of those libbers, eh?'

We were then told to get on our hands and knees and play like snakes or cars in a traffic jam. Picture several hundred screaming, pushing humanist psychotherapists on the floor hissing at each other, 'authentic', 'real', 'in touch'. Then we were told to be baby kittens. A man came up to me and had the nerve to play 'mating dog'. I did have to give him credit for having the guts to be blatantly sexist rather than conformist, as everyone else was being.

The meeting turned into a humanistic hug session – male strangers having a high from the superficial meeting of bodies, feeling that they had engaged in meaningful emotional communication. No wonder the convention is called human-is-tic, that is playing at being human. They will return to their jobs with a renewed sense of hope, with the courage to brave the next year of boredom. I was told by one therapist that for him the convention was a refuelling job. I guess if one needs this kind of fantasy, one creates it.

The convention was a carnival. I travelled from session to session hearing that each Man had the Enlightened Answer. Each had his own ego trip to share with you – why he was a better theRapist than anyone else, how people came to him from miles around after exhausting all paths of salvation. Occasionally there was a mumble of false modesty. 'I find myself making mistakes.' To add to the mystique, everybody had an unpronounceable name for His therapy: 'The transpersonal, bioenergetics, orthomolecular approach, hyperemperia-experiences beyond hypnosis, rolfing.' A little of this, a pinch of that; borrowed techniques of massage, touch, yoga, astrology, Zen, hypnosis, Buddhist meditation, hypnosis and drama were glorified into The Therapy.

I moved into the lobby to escape all of those men walking around as if something was poking them up the ass. I heard 'Step right up. Join the Women's Caucus table' (next to a stylishly bearded stocky man who was doing his thing – liberating us hussies).

The meeting that evening was open to men and women; the afternoon's solicitors were seated behind a table, while the rest of us peons were gathered around them. Clearly the agenda was closed. We arrived to discover that we were to correct and comment on a group of resolutions which had been drafted by this 'liberated' group the night before. Having the honour of deciding if the commas were in the right place, gave us a real feeling of communal democracy.

The woman who read the resolution repeatedly stated that although they had complaints, the Association for Humanistic Psychology was nicer to women than other organizations and that as women we should be very grateful. As she read through one of the wordy announcements, she told us that we should work to make the resolutions concise because that's what men like and we were submitting our pleas to an all-male board.

Several of us finally walked out to discuss the issues which were vital to us – not commas or pleasing the guys – but how we as women could work to free ourselves and our sisters from the oppressions which we all are fighting. We shared what we were doing in different cities. There was a much needed feeling of sharing and communicating.

One woman was organizing her campus doing consciousness-raising exercises, which helped women to become aware of their feelings about themselves, their sisters and their dependence on men. I thought about my work and I told how the women I work with and I are growing together, are beginning to take equal responsibility in our group for expressing our feelings and being sensitive to each other.

When I feel I've communicated with someone in a very beautiful way, I try not to accept that as a qualification for 'guruship', like my brother therapists at the humanist bash. When I walk out of a therapy hour caught up in my own magnificence and humming 'Jesus Christ Superstar', I stop and remind myself that I'm still the same ol' imperfect being who runs from closeness, finds it hard to cry, and oppresses others.

A woman seeker (a better word than patient) after several months in therapy called to say that she did not want to continue. She reluctantly agreed to come in and talk about it. I felt powerless, scared of losing someone I cared about. I wanted to keep her. The only thing I could think of doing was to indirectly manipulate her into staying. I thought of making some esoteric interpretations about her 'resistance', using scare tactics such as suggesting that it would be self-destructive for her to leave.

As the day approached, I found myself thinking about her, feeling very uncomfortable with my planned strategy. Then at 3 a.m. one morning, my defences were down and I began to cry and to face my fears of losing her, of being rejected, abandoned. As I came closer to my feelings, I became closer to hers and to her need for freedom, which she had never been allowed at home. I thought of the way her parents would have mystified her by saying they were meeting her needs when they were really meeting their own.

I felt a real sense of inner liberation. When she arrived the next day, I told her about the process I had been going through. I reached over to her and said, 'You are free to leave. I really mean that.' Without a lot of explanation between us, she and I knew that a new type of relationship was possible between us. Now we are able to relate to each other on a much deeper level. Sometimes we laugh, cry, hug and kiss.

Unfortunately, by accepting my title as psychologist, I imply that my actions are in the name of authority, that if I am effective it is because I am a 'professional'. How ironic! Because, when you and I touch, it is often in spite of my professional 'training' and not because of it. As a professional, I was taught to share little of myself, to remain distant and objective. There are some realistic reasons for this. As a professional, I am more legally accountable, and vulnerable for my activities. Also, because of the fact that people often project strong demands of perfection onto the therapist, they can become irrationally infuriated at me. That's scarey. It gets lonely up there on the pedestal, and I'm sick of playing phoney games which alienate me from myself and from others. I want to put my feet in the water – no matter how polluted – and groove on that sense of community and sisterhood that I had never found before I became involved in the women's movement. I want to share my new-found meaning to life with other women.

Yet, I want to resist the temptation to become the instant humanistically humanist, the liberated lady shrink, the heavy in the movement.

We have a beautiful movement. Let's not run it into the ground by becoming defensive, rigid adherents. We must not claim, as do our humanistic friends, that we have The Answer. There isn't any. We do not need to hide out in the Women's Movement with our problems. We should gain strength from the movement for our personal liberation and to help us free our sisters.

Our strength comes in the courage to be open, to admit the painful confusion of not knowing it all. We cannot counter all objections, we can only know that although we haven't got The Answer, we sure as hell are on the right path.

I hope we'll work to create a centre for women where we can go when we need to be with sisters, night or day. It should be a place where we can freak out if need be, and know we are in a safe and loving atmosphere, a place where our vague feelings of dissatisfaction with the boxes we've been put in for so many years become clarified, where we begin to see why women are plagued with feelings of being ugly, stupid, worthless, inadequate, a place where angry reactions are not ridiculed, or used as evidence of our 'abnormality', and a place where we can question society's oppression without being labelled as sick, hostile, castrating bitches, libbies afflicted with penis envy.

18. The Myth of the Vaginal Orgasm

Anne Koedt

Whenever female orgasm and frigidity is discussed, a false distinction is made between the vaginal and the clitoral orgasm. Frigidity has generally been defined by men as the failure of women to have vaginal orgasms. Actually the vagina is not a highly sensitive area and is not constructed to achieve orgasm. It is the clitoris which is the centre of sexual sensitivity and which is the female equivalent of the penis.

I think this explains a great many things: first of all, the fact that the so-called frigidity rate among women is phenomenally high. Rather than tracing female frigidity to false assumptions about female anatomy, our 'experts' have declared frigidity a psychological problem of women. Those women who complained about it were recommended psychiatrists, so that they might discover their 'problem' – diagnosed generally as a failure to adjust to their role as women.

The facts of female anatomy and sexual response tell a different story. There is only one area for sexual climax, although there are many areas for sexual arousal; that area is the clitoris. All orgasms are extensions of sensation from this area. Since the clitoris is not necessarily stimulated sufficiently in the conventional sexual positions, we are left 'frigid'.

Aside from physical stimulation, which is the common cause of orgasm for most people, there is also stimulation through primarily mental processes. Some women, for example, may achieve orgasm through sexual fantasies, or through fetishes. However, while the stimulation may be psychological, the orgasm manifests itself physically. Thus, while the cause is psychological, the *effect* is still physical, and the orgasm necessarily takes place in the sexual organ equipped for sexual climax – the clitoris. The orgasm experience may also differ in degree of intensity – some more localized, and some more diffuse and sensitive. But they are all clitoral orgasms.

All this leads to some interesting questions about conventional sex and our role in it. Men have orgasms essentially by friction with the vagina, not the clitoral area, which is external and not able to cause friction the way penetration does. Women have thus been defined sexually in terms of what pleases men; our own biology has not been properly analysed. Instead, we are fed the myth of the liberated woman and her vaginal orgasm – an orgasm which in fact does not exist.

What we must do is redefine our sexuality. We must discard the 'normal' concepts of sex and create new guidelines which take into account mutual sexual enjoyment. While the idea of mutual enjoyment is liberally applauded in marriage manuals, it is not followed to its logical conclusion. We must begin to demand that if certain sexual positions now defined as 'standard' are not mutually conducive to orgasm, they no longer be defined as standard. New techniques must be used or devised which transform this particular aspect of our current sexual exploitation.

Freud – a Father of the Vaginal Orgasm

Freud contended that the clitoral orgasm was adolescent, and that upon puberty, when women began having intercourse with men, women should transfer the centre of orgasm to the vagina. The vagina, it was assumed, was able to produce a parallel, but more mature, orgasm than the clitoris. Much work was done to elaborate on this theory, but little was done to challenge the basic assumptions.

To fully appreciate this incredible invention, perhaps Freud's general attitude about women should first be recalled. Mary Ellman, in *Thinking About Women*, summed it up this way:

Everything in Freud's patronizing and fearful attitude toward women follows from their lack of a penis, but it is only in his essay *The Psychology of Women* that Freud makes explicit ... the deprecations of women which are implicit in his work. He then prescribes for them the abandonment of the life of the mind, which will interfere with their sexual function. When the psychoanalysed patient is male, the analyst sets himself the task of developing the man's capacities; but with women patients, the job is to resign them to the limits of their sexuality. As Mr Rieff puts it, for Freud, 'Analysis cannot encourage in women new energies for success and achievement, but only teach them the lesson of rational resignation.'

It was Freud's feelings about women's secondary and inferior relationship to men that formed the basis for his theories on female sexuality.

Once having laid down the law about the nature of our sexuality, Freud not so strangely discovered a tremendous problem of frigidity in women. His recommended cure for a woman who was frigid was psychiatric care. She was suffering from failure to mentally adjust to her 'natural' role as a woman. Frank S. Caprio, a contemporary follower of these ideas, states:

. . . whenever a woman is incapable of achieving an orgasm via coitus, provided her husband is an adequate partner, and prefers clitoral stimulation to any other form of sexual activity, she can be regarded as suffering from frigidity and requires psychiatric assistance. [*The Sexually Adequate Female*, p. 64.]

The explanation given was that women were envious of men – 'renunciation of womanhood'. Thus it was diagnosed as an anti-male phenomenon.

It is important to emphasize that Freud did not base his theory upon a study of woman's anatomy, but rather upon his assumptions of woman as an inferior appendage to man, and her consequent social and psychological role. In their attempts to deal with the ensuing problem of mass frigidity, Freudians created elaborate mental gymnastics. Marie Bonaparte, in *Female Sexuality*, goes so far as to suggest surgery to help women back on their rightful path. Having discovered a strange connection between the nonfrigid woman and the location of the clitoris near the vagina,

it then occurred to me that where, in certain women, this gap was excessive, and clitoral fixation obdurate, a clitoridal-vaginal reconciliation might be effected by surgical means, which would then benefit the normal erotic function. Professor Halban, of Vienna, as much a biologist as surgeon, became interested in the problem and worked out a simple operative technique. In this, the suspensory ligament of the clitoris was severed and the clitoris secured to the underlying structures, thus fixing it in a lower position, with eventual reduction of the labia minora. [p. 148.]

But the severest damage was not in the area of surgery, where Freudians ran around absurdly trying to change female anatomy to fit their basic assumptions. The worst damage was done to the mental health of women, who either suffered silently with self-blame, or flocked to the psychiatrists looking desperately for the hidden and terrible repression that kept them from their vaginal destiny.

Lack of Evidence?

One may perhaps at first claim that these are unknown and unexplored areas, but upon closer examination this is certainly not true today, nor was it true even in the past. For example, men have known that women suffered from frigidity often during intercourse. So the problem was there. Also, there is much specific evidence. Men knew that the clitoris was and is the essential organ for masturbation, whether in children or adult women. So obviously women made it clear where *they* thought their sexuality was located. Men also seem suspiciously aware of the clitoral powers during 'foreplay', when they want to arouse women and produce the necessary lubrication for penetration. Foreplay is a concept created for male purposes, but works to the disadvantage of many women, since as soon as the woman is aroused the man changes to vaginal stimulation, leaving her both aroused and unsatisfied.

It has also been known that women need no anaesthesia inside the vagina during surgery, thus pointing to the fact that the vagina is in fact not a highly sensitive area.

Today, with extensive knowledge of anatomy, with Kinsey, and Masters and Johnson, to mention just a few sources, there is no ignorance on the subject. There are, however, social reasons why this knowledge has not been popularized. We are living in a male society which has not sought change in women's role.

Anatomical Evidence

Rather than starting with what women *ought* to feel, it would seem logical to start out with the anatomical facts regarding the clitoris and vagina.

THE CLITORIS is a small equivalent of the penis, except for the fact that the urethra does not go through it as in the man's penis. Its erection is similar to the male erection, and the head of the clitoris has the same type of structure and function as the head of the penis. G. Lombard Kelly, in *Sexual Feeling in Married Men and Women*, says:

> The head of the clitoris is also composed of erectile tissue, and it possesses a very sensitive epithelium or surface covering, supplied with special nerve endings called genital corpuscles, which are peculiarly adapted for sensory stimulation that under proper mental conditions terminates in the sexual orgasm. No other part of the female generative tract has such corpuscles. [Pocket Books, p. 35.]

The clitoris has no other function than that of sexual pleasure.

THE VAGINA – Its functions are related to the reproductive function. Principally, (1) menstruation, (2) receive penis, (3) hold semen, and (4) birth passage. The interior of the vagina, which according to the defenders of the vaginally caused orgasm is the centre and producer of the orgasm, is

> like nearly all other internal body structures poorly supplied with end organs of touch. The internal entodermal origin of the lining of the vagina makes it similar in this respect to the rectum and other parts of the digestive tract. [Kinsey, *Sexual Behaviour in the Human Female*, p. 580: Pocket Books edn.]

The degree of insensitivity inside the vagina is so high that 'among the women who were tested in our gynecologic sample, less than 14 per cent were at all conscious that they had been touched'. [Kinsey, p. 580.]

Even the importance of the vagina as an *erotic* centre (as opposed to an orgasmic centre) has been found to be minor.

OTHER AREAS – Labia minora and the vestibule of the vagina. These two sensitive areas may trigger off a clitoral orgasm. Because they can be effectively stimulated during 'normal' coitus, though infrequent, this kind of stimulation is incorrectly thought to be vaginal orgasm. However, it is important to distinguish between areas which can stimulate the clitoris, incapable of producing the orgasm themselves, and the clitoris:

Regardless of what means of excitation is used to bring the individual to the state of sexual climax, the sensation is perceived by the genital corpuscles and is localized where they are situated: in the head of the clitoris or penis. [Kelly, p. 49.]

PSYCHOLOGICALLY STIMULATED ORGASM – Aside from the above mentioned direct and indirect stimulations of the clitoris, there is a third way an orgasm may be triggered. This is through mental (cortical) stimulation, where the imagination stimulates the brain, which in turn stimulates the genital corpuscles of the glands to set off an orgasm.

Women Who Say They Have Vaginal Orgasms

CONFUSION – Because of the lack of knowledge of their own anatomy, some women accept the idea that an orgasm felt during 'normal' intercourse was vaginally caused. This confusion is caused by a combination of two factors. One, failing to locate the centre of the orgasm, and two, by a desire to fit her experience to the male-defined idea of sexual normalcy. Considering that women know little about their anatomy, it is easy to be confused.

DECEPTION – The vast majority of women who pretend vaginal orgasm to their men are faking it to, as Ti-Grace Atkinson says, 'get the job'. In a new best-selling Danish book, *I Accuse* (my own translation), Mette Ejlersen specifically deals with this common problem, which she calls the 'sex comedy'. This comedy has many causes. First of all, the man brings a great deal of pressure to bear on the woman, because he considers his ability as a lover at stake. So as not to offend his ego, the woman will comply with the prescribed role and go through simulated ecstasy. In some of the other Danish women mentioned, women who were left frigid were turned off to sex, and pretended vaginal orgasm to hurry up the sex act. Others admitted that they had faked vaginal orgasm to catch a man. In one case, the woman pretended vaginal orgasm to get him to leave his first wife, who admitted being vaginally frigid. Later she was forced to continue the deception, since obviously she couldn't tell him to stimulate her clitorally.

Many more women were simply afraid to establish their right to equal enjoyment, seeing the sexual act as being primarily for the man's benefit, and any pleasure that the woman got as an added extra.

Other women, with just enough ego to reject the man's idea that they needed psychiatric care, refused to admit their frigidity. They wouldn't accept self-blame, but they didn't know how to solve the problem, not knowing the physiological facts about themselves. So they were left in a peculiar limbo.

Again, perhaps one of the most infuriating and damaging results of this whole charade has been that women who were perfectly healthy sexually were taught that they were not. So in addition to being sexually deprived, these women were told to blame themselves when they deserved no blame. Looking for a cure to a problem that has none can lead a woman on an endless path of self-hatred and insecurity. For she is told by her analyst that not even in her one role allowed in a male society – the role of a woman – is she successful. She is put on the defensive, with phony data as evidence that she better try to be even more feminine, think more feminine, and reject her envy of men. That is, shuffle even harder, baby.

Why Men Maintain The Myth

1. SEXUAL PENETRATION IS PREFERRED – The best stimulant for the penis is the woman's vagina. It supplies the necessary

friction and lubrication. From a strictly technical point of view this position offers the best physical conditions, even though the man may try other positions for variation.

2. THE INVISIBLE WOMAN – One of the elements of male chauvinism is the refusal or inability to see women as total, separate human beings. Rather, men have chosen to define women only in terms of how they benefited men's lives. Sexually, a woman was not seen as an individual wanting to share equally in the sexual act, any more than she was seen as a person with independent desires when she did anything else in society. Thus, it was easy to make up what was convenient about women; for on top of that, society has been a function of male interests, and women were not organized to form even a vocal opposition to the male experts.

3. THE PENIS AS EPITOME OF MASCULINITY – Men define their lives greatly in terms of masculinity. It is a *universal*, as opposed to racial, ego boosting, which is localized by the geography of racial mixtures.

The essence of male chauvinism is not the practical, economic services women supply. It is the psychological superiority. This kind of negative definition of self, rather than positive definition based upon one's own achievements and development, has of course chained the victim and the oppressor both. But by far the most brutalized of the two is the victim.

An analogy is racism, where the white racist compensates his feelings of unworthiness by creating an image of the black man (it is primarily a male struggle) as biologically inferior to him. Because of his power in a white male power structure, the white man can socially enforce this mythical division.

To the extent that men try to rationalize and justify male superiority through physical differentiation, masculinity may be symbolized by being the *most* muscular, the most hairy, with the deepest voice and the biggest penis. Women, on the other hand, are approved of (i.e., called feminine) if they are weak, petite, shave their legs, have high soft voices and no penis.

Since the clitoris is almost identical to the penis, one finds a great deal of evidence of men in various societies either trying to ignore the clitoris and emphasize the vagina (as did Freud), or, as in some places in the Mideast, actually performing clitoridectomy. Freud saw this ancient and still practised custom as a way of further 'feminizing' the female by removing this cardinal vestige of her masculinity. It should be noted also that a big clitoris is considered ugly and masculine. Some cultures engage in the practice of pouring a chemical on the clitoris to make it shrivel up into proper size.

It seems clear to me that men in fact fear the clitoris as a threat to their masculinity.

4. SEXUALLY EXPENDABLE MALE – Men fear that they will become sexually expendable if the clitoris is substituted for the vagina as the centre of pleasure for women. Actually this has a great deal of validity if one considers *only* the anatomy. The position of the penis inside the vagina, while perfect for reproduction, does not necessarily stimulate an orgasm in women because the clitoris is located externally and higher up. Women must rely upon indirect stimulation in the 'normal' position.

Lesbian sexuality could make an excellent case, based upon anatomical data, for the extinction of the male organ. Albert Ellis says something to the effect that a man without a penis can make a woman an excellent lover.

Considering that the vagina is very desirable from a man's point of view, purely on physical grounds, one begins to see the dilemma for men. And it forces us as well to discard many 'physical' arguments explaining why women go to bed with men. What is left, it seems to me, are primarily psychological reasons why women select men at the exclusion of women as sexual partners.

5. CONTROL OF WOMEN – One reason given to explain the Mideastern practice of clitoridectomy is that it will keep the women from straying. By removing the sexual organ capable of orgasm, it must be assumed that her sexual drive will diminish. Considering how men look upon their women as property, particularly in very backward nations, we should begin to consider a great deal more why it is not in the men's interest to have women totally free sexually. The double standard, as practised for example in Latin America, is set up to keep the woman as

total property of the husband, while he is free to have affairs as he wishes.

6. LESBIANISM AND BISEXUALITY – Aside from the strictly anatomical reasons why women might equally seek other women as lovers, there is a fear on men's part that women will seek the company of other women on a full, human basis. The establishment of clitoral orgasm as fact would threaten the heterosexual *institution*. For it would indicate that sexual pleasure was obtainable from either men *or* women, thus making heterosexuality not an absolute, but an option. It would thus open up the whole question of *human* sexual relationships beyond the confines of the present male-female role system.

Bibliography

MARIE BONAPARTE, *Female Sexuality* (Grove Press).

FRANK S. CAPRIO, *The Sexually Adequate Female* (Fawcett Gold Medal Books).

METTE EJLERSEN, *I Accuse (Jeg Anklager)*, Chr. Erichsens Forlag (Danish).

ALBERT ELLIS, *Sex Without Guilt* (Grove Press).

MARY ELLMAN, *Thinking About Women* (Macmillan).

G. LOMBARD KELLY, *Sexual Feelings in Married Men and Women* (Pocket Books).

ALFRED C. KINSEY, *Sexual Behaviour in the Human Female* (Pocket Books).

MASTERS and JOHNSON, *Human Sexual Response* (Interscience).

Also see:

INGE and STEN HEGELER, *The ABZ of Love* (Spearman).

19. Marriage and Psychotherapy

Phyllis Chesler

Many American women enter individual psychoanalysis or psychotherapy just as they enter marriage: with a sense of urgency and desperation, and without questioning their own motives. This is not surprising. Both psychotherapy and marriage are the two major socially approved institutions for women, especially for middle-class women. There is some evidence that single and divorced women seek psychiatric help more often than people in other groups – as if not being married is experienced as an 'illness' which psychotherapy can cure (Gurin, 1965; Bart, 1968; Chesler, 1970). Both psychotherapy and marriage isolate women from each other; both institutions emphasize individual rather than or before collective solutions to a woman's problems. Both institutions may be viewed as redramatizations of a little girl's relation to her father in a male-dominated society. Both institutions are based on a woman's helplessness and dependence on a 'stronger' male or female authority figure – as husband or psychotherapist. Most women, as well as most men, seem to prefer men as 'doctors', just as they prefer male children rather than or before female children. For example, in analysing the records of a middle-class clinic population, I have found that preference for a male rather than a female therapist is voluntarily stated twice as often by both male and female patients.

Both psychotherapy and marriage may be viewed as a way of socially controlling and oppressing women. At the same time, both institutions may be viewed as the two safest havens for women, in a society that offers them no others. Psychotherapy and marriage are ways in which a woman can safely express (and politically de-fuse) her anger and unhappiness – by experiencing them as a form of emotional 'illness'. Many women experience headaches, terrible fatigue, chronic depression, frigidity, and an overwhelming sense of inferiority. (In Freud's Vienna this was all called 'hysteria'.) Each woman as patient, thinks these symptoms are unique and are her own fault. She is 'neurotic' – rather than economically and psychologically oppressed. She wants from a psychotherapist what she wants – and often can't get – from a husband: attention, understanding, merciful relief, a *personal solution* – in the arms of the 'right' husband, on the couch of the 'right' therapist. In a complicated way, the institutions of marriage and psychotherapy not only mirror each other: therapy is a way of shoring up the marriage institution by substituting for it, by supplementing it, by encouraging an intrapsychic rather than a political vision. Specifically, the institution of psychotherapy may be used by many women as a way of keeping a bad marriage together, or as a way of terminating it in order to form a 'good' marriage. Some women may use psychotherapy as a way to learn how to 'catch' a husband – by practising with a male therapist. Seventy-one out of 105 women patients at a middle-class clinic were single; forty-eight preferred male therapists. (It is interesting that forty-three out of seventy-one male patients were also single; however, only eight of them volunteered a preference for a female therapist.) It seems likely that women probably spend more time during a therapy session talking about their husbands or boyfriends – or lack of them – than they do talking about their lack of an independent identity or their superficial relations to other women.

Both the institution of psychotherapy and of marriage encourage women to talk – often endlessly – rather than to act (except in their socially prearranged roles as passive 'woman' or 'patient'). In marriage, the talking is usually of an indirect nature. Open expressions of rage are too dangerous and ineffective for the isolated and economically dependent women. (Often, such 'kitchen' declarations end in tears, self-blame, and in the husband graciously agreeing with his wife that she was 'not herself'.) Even control of a simple – but serious – conversation is usually impossible for most wives when several men, including their husbands, are present. The 'wife'-woman talk to each other, or they listen silently while the men talk. Very rarely, if ever, do men listen silently to a group of women talking. Even if there are a number of women talking, and only one man present, he will question the women, perhaps patiently, perhaps not, but always in order to ultimately control the conversation, and always from a 'superior' position.

In psychotherapy, the 'patient'-woman is encouraged – in fact *directed* to talk, and by a therapist who is at least expected to be, or is perceived as 'superior' or objective. The traditional therapist may be viewed as ultimately controlling what the patient says – through a subtle system of rewards (attention, 'interpretations', etc.). In a sense, the treatment monologue or dialogue is taking place in a 'laboratory'. At its best, such conversation cannot be successfully transferred by the woman – acting by herself alone – to those people in her office, on the streets, or in her bedroom, who directly profit from her oppression. (She would be laughed at, viewed as 'silly' or 'crazy', and if she persisted, would be out of a job – as secretary or wife.) Psychotherapeutic 'talking' is indirect in the sense that it does not involve the woman in a verbal confrontation with the significant people in her life. It is indirect also in that words – *any* words – are permitted, so long as certain actions of consequence are avoided. (Such as not paying one's bill, or having – or refusing to have – sexual relations with one's therapist.)

The traditional psychoanalytic theories about women are at best, confused and incomplete, and at worst, false. However, what takes place in therapy may be more determined by the therapist's personality and ideas, and by the patient's expectations, than by any psychoanalytic 'theory'. Both husbands (beginning with Adam) and psychotherapists (beginning with Freud and including most *female* psychotherapists) tend to view women as children. For example, in a recent study by Broverman *et al.*, on clinicians' judgements of what is 'normal, adult behaviour', what is male behaviour, and what is female behaviour, both male and female clinicians correlated masculine rather than feminine behaviour with what they considered to be 'normal', and 'adult'. Specifically, women were viewed as more emotional, more concerned about their appearance, less objective, less independent, less adventurous, more easily influenced, less aggressive, less competitive, more excitable in minor crises, than were men. And these traits were not considered 'normal' or 'adult'. Obviously, the ethic of mental health is a masculine one in our society. Two sociologists writing in 1968 (Phillips and Segal) suggest that women seek psychiatric help (as well as medical help) more often than men because the social role of 'woman' allows her to display emotional and physical distress more easily than men:

> Sensitive or emotional behaviour is more tolerated in women, to the point of aberration, while self-assertive, aggressive, vigorous physical demonstrations are more tolerated among men . . . our argument is simply that it is more culturally appropriate and acceptable for women to be expressive about their difficulties.

And women can 'express' themselves away – in both marriage and in psychotherapy.

Many psychoanalytic concepts and values were and are re-volutionary and liberating ones. What I've been objecting to throughout this paper is the way in which these concepts have been institutionalized. For most women, the psychotherapeutic encounter is just one more instance of an unequal relationship, just one more instance of a power relationship in which she is submissive and the authority figure is dominant. I wonder how well such a structure can encourage independence – or healthy dependence – in a woman? I wonder what a woman can learn from a male therapist (however well-intentioned) whose own values are sexist, who has been conditioned to view women as inferior, as threatening, as childish, as castrating, as *alien* to himself? How free from the dictates of a sexist society can a female as *patient* be with a *male* therapist? And if therapy could, theoretically, be used to overcome such oppressive sex-role stereotyping, why should the female patient pay money for it – rather than her male therapist – who presumably would be learning to relate to women in a nonsexist way? (And who may in fact, be enjoying a psychological 'service' from his female patient, namely being able to feel superior to, or in control of, his own forbidden longings for dependence, emotionality, etc. – longings he has been trained to project onto women as a *caste*;

projections which he can experience most safely with a woman who is a patient – rather than with a wife or a girlfriend or a mother.) How much can a male therapist empathize with a female patient? In Masters and Johnson's recently published *Human Sexual Inadequacy,* they state that their research supported unequivocally the

premise that no man will ever fully understand a woman's sexual function or dysfunction ... [and the same is true for women] ... it helps immeasurably for a distressed, relatively inarticulate or emotionally unstable wife to have available a female cotherapist to interpret what she is saying and even what she is attempting unsuccessfully to express to the uncomprehending husband and often to the male cotherapist as well.

I would go one step further here and ask: and what if the female cotherapist is male-oriented, is élitist, is as much a sexist as a male therapist? What if the female therapist has never realized that she is oppressed – *as a woman?* What if the female therapist views marriage and children as 'fulfilment' for all women – other than herself?

Obviously, if 'mental illness' does exist, it is not effectively or humanely cured or even isolated in psychiatric hospitals, or in private therapy. If it doesn't exist, psychiatric hospitals and private therapy function as political prisons – for the aged, the young, the unmarried, the poor, the black, and the female.

What practical suggestions can be made following such an analysis of what the institution of psychotherapy has in common with the institution of marriage?

1. Therapists, male and female, must learn to recognize the stereotypes about women that they share, the unconscious power strategies that are typically in play, and the often stifling nature of the therapeutic interaction.
2. Women patients should seek women clinicians who are feminists, i.e., who understand female problems and the broad social conditions that have produced them.
3. All women – both patients and clinicians – should join some aspects of the Women's Liberation Movement.

4. All-female therapeutic communities should be established, both in urban and rural settings. Perhaps only a feminist 'crash pad' would free women from economic as well as psychological dependence on male structures.

Bibliography

1. BART, PAULINE B., 'Social Structure and Vocabularies of Discomfort: What Happened to Female Hysteria?' *Journal of Health and Social Behavior*, Vol. 9, No. 3, 1968.
2. BROVERMAN, I. K., BROVERMAN, D. M., CLARKSON, R., ROSENKRANTZ, P., VOGEL, S., 'Sex Role Stereotypes and Clinical Judgments of Mental Health', *Journal of Consulting Psychology*, 1969.
3. CHESLER, P. 'Women as Psychiatric and Psychotherapeutic Patients', *Journal of Marriage and the Family*, November 1971, Vol. 33, No. 4.
4. GURIN, G., *et al.*, *Americans View Their Mental Health*, New York, Basic Books, 1960.
5. HOLLINGSHEAD, A. B., and REDLICH, F. C., *Social Class and Mental Illness*, New York, John Wiley, 1958.
6. MASTERS, W. H. and JOHNSON, V. E. *Human Sexual Inadequacy*, Little Brown and Co., Boston, 1970.
7. PHILLIPS, P. L. and SEGAL, B. E., 'Sexual Status and Psychiatric Symptoms,' *American Sociological Review*, Feb. 1969.
8. SZASZ, T., *The Myth of Mental Illness*, Hoeber-Harper, 1961.

20. Lesbianism

Martha Shelley

If hostility to men causes lesbianism, then it seems to me that in a male-dominated society lesbianism is a sign of mental health.

The psychiatrists have also forgotten that lesbianism involves love between women. Isn't love between equals healthier than sucking-up to an oppressor? And when they claim we aren't capable of loving men, even if we want to – I ask you, straight man, are you capable of loving another man so deeply that you aren't afraid of his body or afraid to put your body in his hands? Are you really capable of loving women, or is your sexuality just another expression of your hostility? Is it an act of love or sexual conquest? An act of sexual imperialism?

I do not mean to condemn all males. I have found some beautiful, loving men among the revolutionaries, among the hippies, and the male homosexuals. But the average man – including the average student male radical – wants a passive sex-object-cum-domestic-cum-baby-nurse to clean up after him while he does all the fun things and bosses her around – while he plays either big-shot executive or Che Guevara – and he is my oppressor and my enemy.

Lesbianism is one road to freedom – freedom from oppression by men.

To see lesbianism in this context – as a mode of living neither better nor worse than others, as one which offers its own opportunities – one must abandon the notion that deviance from the norm arises from personal illness.

It is generally accepted that America is a 'sick society'. There is an inevitable corollary to this statement, which has not been generally accepted: that people within our society are all crippled by virtue of being forced to conform to certain norms.

(Those who conform most easily can be seen as either the most healthy, because adaptable, or most sick, because least spirited.) The black is struggling to free himself not only from white oppression, but from the sickness of self-contempt and the sick roles he has been forced to play. Women are struggling to liberate their minds from sick sexual roles. It is clear that the self-abasing, suffering, shuffling black is not someone with a personal neurosis, but society's victim – and someone who has been forced to learn certain techniques for survival. Few people understand that the same is true of the self-abnegating passive housewife. Fewer understand this truth about the homosexual.

These techniques of survival help us meet certain needs, at the expense of others.

For women, as for other groups, there are several American norms. All of them have their rewards – and their penalties. The nice girl next door, virginal until her marriage – the Miss America type – is rewarded with community respect and respectability. She loses her individuality and her freedom to become a toothpaste smile and a chastity belt. The career woman gains independence and a larger margin of freedom – *if* she is willing to work twice as hard as a man for less pay, and *if* she can cope with emotional strains similar to those that beset the black intellectual surrounded by white colleagues. The starlet, call girl, or bunny whose source of income is directly related to her image as a sex object gains some financial independence and freedom from housework. She doesn't have to work as hard as the career woman, but she pays through psychological degradation as a sex object, and through the insecurity of knowing that her career – based on youthful good looks – is short-lived.

The lesbian, through her ability to obtain love and sexual satisfaction from other women, is freed of dependence on men for love, sex, and money. She does not have to do menial chores for them (at least at home), nor cater to their egos, nor submit to hasty and inept sexual encounters. She is freed from fear of unwanted pregnancy and the pains of childbirth, and from the drudgery of child-raising.

On the other hand, she pays three penalties. The rewards of child-raising are denied her. This is a great loss for some women, but not for others. Few women abandon their children, as compared with the multitudes of men who abandon both wives and children. Few men take much interest in the process of child-raising. One suspects that it might not be much fun for the average person, and so the men leave it to the women.

The lesbian must compete with men in the job market, facing the same job and salary discrimination as her straight sister. On the other hand, she has more of a chance of success since her career is not interrupted by childbirth.

Finally, she faces the most severe contempt and ridicule that society can heap on a woman.

A year ago, when Women's Liberation picketed the 1968 Miss America Pageant, the most terrible epithet heaped on our straight sisters was 'lesbian'. The sisters faced hostile audiences who called them 'commies', 'tramps', 'bathless', etc., and they faced these labels with equanimity; but they broke into tears when they were called lesbians. When a woman showed up at a feminist meeting and announced that she was a lesbian, many women avoided her. Others told her to keep her mouth shut, for fear that she would endanger the cause. They felt that men could be persuaded to accept some measure of equality for women – as long as these women would parade their devotion to heterosexuality and motherhood.

A woman who is totally independent of men – who obtains love, sex, and self-esteem from other women – is a terrible threat to male supremacy. She doesn't need them, and therefore they have very little power over her.

I have met many, many feminists who were not lesbians – but I have never met a lesbian who was not a feminist. Straight women by the millions have been sold the belief that they must subordinate themselves to men, accept less pay for equal work, and do all the shitwork around the house. I have met straight women who would die to preserve their chains. I have never met a lesbian who believed that she was innately less rational or capable than a man; who swallowed one word of the 'woman's role' horseshit.

Lesbians, because they are not afraid of being abandoned by men, are less reluctant to express hostility towards the male class

– the oppressors of women. Hostility towards your oppressor is healthy – but the guardians of modern morality, the psychiatrists, have interpreted this hostility as an illness, and they say this illness causes and is lesbianism.

21. Vietnam: A Feminist Analysis

Boston Lesbian Feminists

[This speech was written by Lesbian Feminists Hollibaugh, von Bretzel, Crichton and Lindbloom, and was given on 6 May 1972, at a large anti-war rally in Boston.

All publicity prior to the rally listed an all-male roster of speakers. Women were contacted at the last minute and were then met with blatant sexism. A crowd-pleasing rock concert mentality was more than reluctant to put women speakers on the platform. We were not announced until after many people had left and then only because women in the audience shouted for a woman speaker.]

'The subject of feminism is very ordinary; it's the question of male domination that makes everybody angry.'

I am speaking today about the politics of rape. There is a national phenomenon in this country that promotes myths about sex and violence that are recreated in imperialist wars against Third World countries. Rape is an act of aggression in which the victim is denied her self determination. It is an act of violence which always carries with it the threat of death. And finally, rape is a form of mass terrorism, for the victims of rape are chosen indiscriminately, but our male dominated culture tells us that it is women who cause rape by being immoral or in the wrong place at the wrong time – in essence, by behaving as though we were free.

For years the male theorists of the anti-war movement have spoken about the reasons America is involved in Vietnam: the imperialist search for profits in the war in Vietnam, and the American corporate need for a war to maintain a stable domestic economy.

This analysis of the war, while correct, has never gone far enough. It has been unable to explain the unprecedented sadism which is the overriding characteristic of this war. What is the rationale for the obsession we find in the universities, corporations and military institutions of AmeriKa, with increasingly hideous and perverse methods of torture and death as applied to the people of another race and land?

Through the years, scientists and professors have been inventing things like flechette pellets – tiny steel arrows with larger fins at one end – which enter the body enlarging the wound and lodge in the blood vessels – they're designed to shred the internal organs; white phosphorus, a more sophisticated version of napalm, that usually has to burn its way down to the bone before going out. The 'area-denial' programme where they flood whole areas with hundreds and thousands of mines designed to look like leaves or animal droppings and to make the area totally uninhabitable for humans. Thousands of square miles of territory in Indochina are now flooded with little mines which are manufactured for the sole purpose of blowing off a foot. They can't blow up a truck or anything else; they are only designed to make passage impossible. While white white-collar boys sit in their labs inventing these atrocities, the army recruits from its male youth the manpower to prove the potency of its weaponry on the battlefield.

The result is Total War, primarily against the civilian population. The civilians are usually the ones that are in and around the villages; they can't keep on the move all the time because they have families and belongings and homes. They are the ones who signal the weapons, the ones who are the main casualties.

A 23-month-old baby is senselessly electro-shocked into unconsciousness.

Where does this come from in the AmeriKan psyche? These perversions are the products of the mentality of rape. The mentality that produces the kind of war they continue to fight starts at home. Let's run down a few unknown facts about rape – about male sexual violence.

Susan Griffin, in an article called 'The Politics of Rape', found that official crime statistics tell women: forcible rape is the most frequently committed violent crime in AmeriKa.

Now let's once and for all smash the white male propaganda that says most crimes of rape are committed by black men on white women. Historically and statistically this is a lie. 90 per cent of all incidences of rape do not cross racial lines – these crimes of sexual violence are usually committed by men against women of their own race.

Another myth: the rapist is a lonely creep who sees a woman without male protection and is suddenly overpowered by his innate craving for sex. BULLSHIT.

83 per cent of rapes by men in twos are premeditated.

90 per cent of all group rapes are premeditated.

58 per cent of single rapes are premeditated. Rape is not a crime of passion; it is an act of aggression. An undeclared war against women.

Another myth: that men who rape women are pathological, as distinct from your basic average run-of-the-mill male. Amir's study called 'Patterns in Forcible Rape' says men who rape are not abnormal. Amir writes 'studies indicate that *sex offenders do not constitute a psychopathological type*; nor are they as a group invariably more disturbed than the control groups to which they are compared.' Allen Taylor – a parole officer who has worked with rapists in prison facilities – stated the question in plainer language: 'Those men were the most normal men there. They had a lot of hangups, that men walking out on the street have.'

Let's just examine two more aspects of rape – keeping in mind that all these things about rape are symptoms of a male dominated culture which feeds on the combination of sex and violence. The myth that some men protect you and some men rape you is false. First of all, the rapist is an average man. But secondly every man in this society gets male benefits from the existence of rape. These armchair rapists have their potency and masculinity vicariously confirmed through rape – witness the number of pages given over to violent sex crimes in men's adventure magazines.

Another way all men have their power enhanced by rape, is the need then put into women for protection – the ancient chivalry racket, men protecting women from other men. It's not unlike the protection relationships which the Mafia established with small businesses.

And finally, it is a fact that the most excessive degrees of violence occur in group rape. Far from discouraging or curbing violence upon women, the presence of other men may in fact encourage sadism, and even cause the behaviour. Men egg each other on. . .

What does all this have to do with Vietnam?

What starts as the socialization of male sexual violence in this culture is used by corporate and military interests to train a vicious, killing army – in the labs, and on the battlefields. Examples of the inseparability of sex and violence in the male are endless. In basic training the following chant is used to teach the distinction between a rifle, which is a weapon, and a gun, which is a cock. 'This is my rifle, this is my gun. One is for killing, one is for fun.' With such training it is not surprising that a major in Vietnam is quoted as saying 'Don't let the news media fool you. These kids are maybe 18 or 19 – but they are beautiful killers – just beautiful. . .'

What is routine conduct at home is routine conduct abroad. Acts of male domination and violence are the cornerstones of society in the United States. Here in the states we are torn with conflicts of race, class and sex. When we transport these conflicts overseas they show up in the army, in the highest echelons of the Thieu government, and in the destruction of culture in Saigon. *And underpinning it all is the assumption of AmeriKa's absolute right to rule where AmeriKa will.*

The passion with which we perpetuate this war: war crimes no longer war crimes but genocide; violence promoted to contain a war we have no hope of winning.

I. F. Stone said last week there is a possibility Nixon would finally use nuclear weapons to blow Vietnam to bits rather than be caught with his pants down at the Moscow summit conference: Genocide of a whole people in order to save male face. *This is the height of war insanity.*

We are faced with an imperative. Without a feminist analysis we will never confront some of the deepest motivations behind the waging of aggressive wars.

The same men and power structure who victimize women are engaged in the act of raping Vietnam, raping Black people, and the very earth we live upon. Rape is a classic act of domination where the emotions of hatred, contempt, and the desire to break or violate personality takes place. This breaking of the personality characterizes modern life itself. No simple reforms can eliminate rape.

As the symbolic expression of the white male hierarchy, *rape is the ultimate act of our civilization,* one which, Valerie Solanis warns, 'is in danger of humping itself to death'.

22. Surviving Psychotherapy

Christopher Z. Hobson

Through such actions as the disruption of last summer's American Psychiatric Association convention, the Gay Liberation movement has focused attention on psychiatrists' treatment of homosexuality. Some writers have criticized Freudian and neo-Freudian theories of homosexuality; others have exposed barbaric clinical practices such as the use of electroshock 'therapy'. Little has been written, however, about the experience of psychotherapy.

My own experiences were not dramatic: I never had shock treatment, I never even encountered the gay analogue of the hair-raisingly male-chauvinist statements reported by some Women's Liberation activists who have had psychotherapy.

My therapists – there were three over the years – were all intelligent, somewhat sensitive men. I cannot even claim that they tried to convince me that homosexuality was an illness: product of an orthodox upbringing, I was convinced before I ever consulted them. All I can claim is that their treatment contributed nothing to my awareness of myself and even retarded it; that this was connected to their view of homosexuality as an illness; that my self-understanding eventually grew from quite different sources.

I first applied the term 'homosexual' to myself when I was fourteen. If I wasn't then an irreversible homosexual, I was fast becoming one: almost all my sexual inclinations were towards males, virtually none toward females. I sought psychotherapy when I was seventeen, basically because I desperately wanted to be heterosexual. I was in therapy in my last year in high school and for four years in college. Nothing changed – though I did gain insight into various personal and especially family relationships. For two years after college I was a teacher; then I was fired for a homosexual affair with a student. Beginning graduate school, I began therapy again and continued for five years on a once-weekly basis.

In my teens I tried actively not to be homosexual. Even when I stopped trying, at twenty-two, I didn't accept being gay – I merely decided to express it *until something changed*, because I realized that in trying not to love men, I was losing the ability to love at all. Not until I was twenty-five did I begin to see homosexuality as something that shouldn't be despised, and not until I was twenty-eight – only one year ago – did I 'come out' in the sense of beginning to live openly as a homosexual. Only then, moreover, did I actively step into gay life and begin to meet other gay people. During those fourteen years, I had almost no sexual contacts and was, naturally, unhappy, frustrated, and confused. If my entry into gay life seems unusually late, I am convinced this isn't so: while manning a Gay Liberation telephone in recent months, I have talked to many more like myself.

During those fourteen years of waste and unnecessary grief, my psychotherapists exposed none of what was really wrong. Please note: this means *what I now believe was really wrong*. Biased, yes – but true in my experience; I will stand on my judgement and on that standard so regularly invoked by psychotherapists themselves, success. In my opinion, I am healthier now.

I was not the happy homosexual who doesn't enter Dr Socarides' office (and doesn't enter his statistics). There I was – in my teens, guilty about masturbation (my only form of sexual expression) and about homosexuality; occasionally thinking of suicide; drawn into passionate friendship with 'straight' males and either guilty about the sexual element or blind to it; infrequently but regularly revealing the truth (in conversation, in the most nonsexual way) and sometimes, very infrequently, making tentative sexual advances – usually rejected. In later years, fewer self-revelations (I had control of myself now, achieved with the aid of my therapists: I never told anyone unless it was necessary) and more frequent advances.

In therapy, I looked for the factors which had caused my homosexuality. It did not occur to me that no one asked what caused heterosexuality, or that the two questions stood on a par. None of my psychotherapists ever pointed this out. When discussing my urge to self-revelation, my therapists and I explored the dynamics of this 'Dostoevskian' manifestation – guilt, eagerness for punishment combined with eagerness for acceptance, etc. All of this, I must make clear, was true – I *was* guilty, eager for punishment, and eager for acceptance. But while exploring this (and, as I mentioned, helping me master the urge) *none of my therapists exposed to me the simple, blinding underlying truth that in a society which condemns homosexuality and hence forces it to be secret, the homosexual will wish to break out of the secrecy by telling someone, and hence, that the urge itself was not sick at all.* I had to figure this out for myself, at twenty-eight. Still less did any of my therapists ask why I *told* my friends rather than making sexual advances, or explore with me the question why I didn't seek gay society where I could make advances without risk.

My other psychotherapeutic experiences, or non-experiences, were like this. Twice while in therapy, I met homosexual acquaintances with whom the possibility of a real relationship existed, and shunned them. A therapist might usefully have explored why I was so guilty, even urged me to overcome this guilt; instead, these occurrences became evidence that I did not really want to be homosexual (which we already knew) and *since my not wanting to be gay was implicitly a sign (perhaps my only sign) of health, these occurrences were not examined critically.* Similarly, my therapists spent much time trying to discover why my relationships with straight friends were so passionate – rather than asking me why I formed these passionate relationships *with straights.* Similarly, after the homosexual affair which lost me my teaching job – a very warm relationship which continues, intermittently, to this day – I brought to my next therapist the datum that while in bed with my lover, I felt completely harmonious and 'natural', not 'sick' at all and not even guilty. Although this contradicted the very basis of the feeling which led me to psychotherapy, my therapist never took the initiative in exploring this contradiction.

This all might be thought to result from the 'non-directive' quality of psychotherapy, or some psychotherapy. But elsewhere, my therapists *were* 'directive'. Very late, actually while I was 'coming out' through Gay Liberation, I had a sexual affair with a woman (also, a warm one, interrupted only by circumstances). To this my therapist's response was positive: with a little smile, 'Well, I see *something* has "come out".' The therapist's cues revealed clearly enough the idea of a repressed heterosexuality which *should* be 'brought out', and though Freudian theory assumes an inborn bisexuality (an assumption I don't share, not regarding *any* particular form of sexuality as inborn), this theory assumes that repressed *homo*sexuality *shouldn't* be brought out, but should be sublimated. Thus psychotherapy in my case was directive indeed.

Rather than from 'non-direction' the omissions of my therapists seem to me to have resulted from their assumption that I was, by definition, sick – that homosexuality (but not heterosexuality) is a pathology. It did not occur to them to 'direct' me in ways which might raise in my mind the idea that I was *not* sick. But how can I complain of this? Didn't I know this was their theory, and didn't I myself share the assumptions?

The point is simply that the therapists *failed to help me understand my situation* – to overcome my own *lack* of understanding. Even from a viewpoint assuming homosexuality to be a pathology, it would remain true, I think, that my urge to self-revelation was *in fact* related to my *social* isolation as a homosexual. But my therapists never helped me to understand this. Even from the viewpoint that homosexuality if 'incurable' should be accepted, it might have made sense for me to explore the possible relationships with my two gay college friends. But my therapists never tried to make me focus on this. Similarly, if I hadn't already been moving away from psychotherapy, after my heterosexual affiair (if it had occurred at all) my therapist would have encouraged me to mull over that experience, to try to captivate my heterosexual impulses, and to waste another ten years on top of the fourteen I had wasted already.

Basically, the therapists' theory made them incapable of viewing my situation as I now view it. If I understand it, their view was that the conflicts in my mind about accepting homosexuality indicated a very strong heterosexual impulse being checked subconsciously. In my view today, they indicated a very strong socially conditioned rejection of being gay, combined with certain patterns – such as the tendency to be attracted to straight men – which were related to the inability to think of myself as gay and which created impossible (and, I would now add, unnecessary) conflicts between my sexual impulses and my need for ordinary friendship. (Only in the last year has this conflict become unnecessary: until now, gay people have had either to repress their gay nature while with straight friends, or to make their entire social life among gay people. I wonder how many therapists, exploring this conflict with thousands of gay patients, have tried to expose the *socially conditioned* nature of this conflict.) In short, psychotherapy could not help me to understand my situation because it did not – and given its theoretical basis, *could* not – encourage me to think of my conflicts as resulting from social conditions.

How did I come to do so? Although therapy helped me understand many side issues, my understanding of being gay comes from social movements. My first step towards health – oh yes, I was sick: I was unable to view myself as I was – came when I was twenty-two, in my determination to find love where I could. This step of simple self-preservation, never suggested by any psychotherapist, left me still viewing myself as an inferior creature. The first suggestion that homosexuals were unhappy not because we were sick but because we were oppressed, came from an acquaintance, who *not* coincidentally was a revolutionary socialist, who influenced me as I got deeply into the student radical movement at the late and lucky age of twenty-five.

My first real understanding of my oppression, however, came as the women's liberation movement grew. Some of my closest acquaintances were very active in it. The critique of the social stigmas attached to being a woman, of the myths of female personality type, of the role of social factors in producing the *real* personality disfigurations women suffered – and most of all, of the treatment of all this by psychiatry as personal neurosis demanding personal therapy rather than as social oppression demanding a collective struggle – all this seemed true of myself as

well. Further, my fear and dislike of women, which my therapists and I had spent much time discussing, began to change as
I saw – from the movement, not from my therapists – that I was
not expected (any longer) to relate to women primarily sexually,
something I had always felt unable to do. Simultaneously I
began seeing women and myself as human beings.

Finally gay liberation ... but it shouldn't be necessary to describe how this changed my view of myself. It did, however,
change the direction and content of my life.

My break with psychotherapy came gradually. Women's
liberation made me take seriously the critique of psychiatric
theory as regards women, but this was tangential to my own
therapy. Very late, relations with my therapist became strained
when, discussing my mother and her ambitions for me, he referred to her using me as 'her penis'. I saw that what women's
liberationists had been saying was true: my mother's ambitious
and successful life, in which she had always had to struggle
against the limits placed on her as a woman, was to my therapist
a manifestation of the desire for a penis rather than a rebellion
against constraints which warred against her great abilities. Had
it not been for the women's movement, I might have accepted
this view – and found a new, apparently analytical way to despise
my mother, rather than coming to understand her.

Instead, I asked myself how this theory, which regarded
women so barbarically, regarded me. And I asked my therapist.
His reply, which covered several sessions and touched on both
women and homosexuals, was roughly that homosexuality could
be regarded as a pathology (and heterosexuality could not) because in this society (he said 'culture') the norm for the family
was that of a male occupying a dominant position, a female in a
subordinate position, and the reproduction of these roles in the
young. We agreed that in terms of these roles both an 'aggressive' woman, such as my mother, and a homosexual child were
deviant cases. We differed in that he insisted that this deviance
be viewed simply in terms of its psychic determinants, a position
which I maintained, and he denied, was equivalent to refusing
to question the psychic costs of the dominant pattern. I insisted

that if no positive value were placed on the dominant pattern, then the deviant manifestation had to be viewed not as a psychopathology, but as a manifestation of a pattern which might in the absence of social pressures, be as fulfilling or more fulfilling than the dominant one, but which was socially disapproved. Thus a woman or a homosexual should be encouraged to see social norms *as part of his or her 'problems'*. This my therapist denied.

In the midst of this argument I travelled to another city. Since I was now active in Gay Liberation, I asked the person I was going to see to ask around if a Gay Liberation group existed there. None did, but as a result of his queries, I was telephoned at his house by a man who said he was gay, asked about Gay Liberation, but refused to come to see us. He also refused to give his last name, but he told me his profession – psychologist.

It was clear to me that a profession whose homosexual members had to conceal themselves could not adequately counsel homosexuals. Returning home, I related the incident to my therapist. His reply was that my caller had been a psychologist, not a psychoanalyst. Suppose he had been a psychoanalyst? My therapist replied that there were no homosexual psychoanalysts. In fact, he repeated this three times, as I literally could not believe he had said it. Some psychoanalysts occasionally 'decompensated' and became active homosexuals, he said – but they 'stopped being psychoanalysts'.

You and I both know, dear reader, that this isn't true. At most, it may be true that psychoanalysts publicly identified as gay are forced to give up practice. But my therapist had claimed much more, and the conclusion I was forced to draw was that *his theoretical outlook had so stereotyped his perceptions that he was incapable of correctly perceiving reality*.

This particular incident made me terminate therapy, but in fact I had been moving in that direction for years – every step I took toward living my life as a homosexual, towards being less concealing towards being, finally, openly and proudly gay, was a step towards ending a 'therapy' which encouraged none of this. Even during the few weeks in which I was making the decision to contact Gay Liberation, my therapist, while not actively discouraging this step, cautioned me about it – it was another of my comrades in the Revolutionary movement who, viewing my condition as one of oppression, urged me toward this step.

I, of course, chose on the basis of my inclinations, and I have only my life to offer as evidence that my choice was correct. The last year has been, not just one of the happiest of my life, but one of the *few* happy years of my life. I do not mean I have found bliss – quite the contrary: I have enough problems to convince me that my happiness is not founded on thin ice. I do not believe that this happiness would have been predicted by my therapists. (Similarly the experience of several Gay Liberation activists, who 'came out' as homosexuals for the first time *after* several years of well-adjusted heterosexual life, would not have been predicted by psychoanalytic theory.) And all over the United States there are thousands in psychotherapy, and millions more under the pervasive social influence of psychiatric dogma, who never will make this step until they are reached, not by doctors, but by the winds of social protest. As Trotsky said of his comrade Adolf Yoffe, several years in analysis and later an outstanding Bolshevik diplomat, 'The revolution healed Yoffe better than the psychoanalysis of all his complexes.'

23. Psychiatry and Homosexuality: New 'Cures'

Louis Landerson/Liberation News Service

Psychosurgery, as defined by Dr Peter Breggin, constitutes 'a deadening operation that involves deliberate, irreversible damaging of an individual's brain for the purpose of altering behaviour that others have deemed undesirable'.

Among the victims of this operation are depressed middle-aged women, drug addicts, and very young children. It has also been reported as a method of 'treatment' for homosexuality.

An article in *Medical World News* reports that Dr Robert G. Heath claims success in a limited number of male homosexuals by turning 'repugnant feelings towards the opposite sex into pleasurable feelings by means of electrical stimulation (through implanted electrodes) of the septal region of the brain'.

Though not as widespread as surgery, aversive conditioning therapy is fast becoming standard in the repertoire of the 'New Psychiatrists'. The medium used to induce the conditioned response varies from drugs to electricity. The 'Errorless Extinction of Penile Responses', another cure for male homosexuality, consists of wiring the penis of a patient and giving him an electric shock if he responds by erection to photos of naked males.

As the pharmaceutical industry grinds out new and more effective drugs, these are rapidly being absorbed into aversive conditioning therapy programmes. Two such drugs are succinylcholine and apomorphine.

Succinylcholine is an economical and time-saving method of controlling aggressive behaviour. It is ordinarily used before electroshock treatment to decrease the danger of physical injury to patients through bone breakage. The general effect is a decidedly unpleasant and fearful sensation. Succinylcholine offers an easily controlled, quick-acting, fear-producing experience during which the senses are intact and the patient is susceptible to suggestion.

Within thirty to forty seconds after injection, the drug causes paralysis of, among other organs, the diaphragm. 'After respiration stopped, negative and positive suggestions spoken in a confident, authoritarian manner were made by a male technician. The negative suggestions concerned the obliteration of unacceptable behaviour such as fighting and stealing. The positive focused upon the patient's becoming involved with the government, taking individual responsibility, and increasing constructive socialization. These suggestions continued throughout the period of apnea (asphyxiation) until the patient could verbally respond to the technician.'

Succinylcholine was administered to ninety male patients at Atascadero State Hospital in California. 'Deviant sexual behaviour' was one of the criteria used for selection of patients. According to Clinical Director Michael Serber, the drug was used 'as a punishment'.

Apomorphine aversion works a little differently but is equally, if not more, appalling. 'With apomorphine aversion,' says Dr Nathaniel McConaghy in the *American Journal of Psychiatry*, 'the subject was initially given a subcutaneous injection of 1·5 mg. of apomorphine. After about eight minutes, he began to feel nauseated. Severe nausea lasting ten minutes without vomiting was aimed for, and the dose was constantly adjusted throughout to maintain this response. One minute before the nausea came on, the patient switched on a slide projector and viewed a slide of a nude or partly nude man. Before the nausea reached its maximum he turned off the projector. Twenty-eight treatments were administered at two-hour intervals over five days.'

Thioridazine is used in a much more direct and less imaginative way to 'cure' homosexuality. According to Dr L. J. Litkey, in an article in the *International Journal of Neuropsychology*, 'The absence of accepted sexual outlets oftens leads to forms of deviant behaviour, notably homosexuality in which the strong take advantage of the weak. Efforts to curb such aberrant behaviour have generally involved restraints, isolation, or sedatives, but none of these has been more than a stop gap.' Litkey suggests thioridazine.

This drug 'was known to be effective' in treatment for premature ejaculation and nocturnal emissions. Because of its effects of 'strong inhibition of sexual preoccupation and activities', Litkey proposed that it would be effective in controlling homosexual activities in men.

Thioridazine was administered to twelve male homosexual inmates of the New Jersey State Hospital in Trenton. Within a week after the administration of this drug (three times daily), the number of reported incidents of 'homosexual acts' greatly decreased. 'Each patient referred spontaneously to a diminished sexual preoccupation and while some of them welcomed the change, others resented it.'

The endless list of atrocities raises some very important ethical and political questions about psychiatry. First, there is the question of the nature of the psychiatrist's work directed towards people in prison, whatever their sexual orientation.

It has become quite the vogue, in certain professional circles, to devise various imaginative techniques for solving the management problems of state and federal institutions by incapacitating in one way or another those incarcerated.

Drs V. Mark and F. Ervin, for example, have received a $108,930 grant from the Justice Department's Law Enforcement Assistance Division for the following purpose: 'The role of neurobiological dysfunction in the violent offender. Specifically, the grantee will determine the incidence of such disorders in a state penitentiary for men; establish their prevalence in a non-incarcerated population; and improve, devise, and test the usefulness of electrophysiological and neurophysiological techniques for the detection of such disorders in routine examinations.' These two doctors would like to see these treatment and diagnostic techniques extended to the population at large. In their book, *Violence and the Brain*, they recommend surgery as a solution to 'unacceptable levels of violence'. Joined by Dr W. Sweet (all three of Boston), they suggest, in a letter to the editor of the *Journal of the American Medical Association* (11 September 1967), that the cause of race riots may be brain dysfunction, and that rather than deal with these riots in a political way, authorities should consider surgery, that is, *psycho*surgery, as a solution.

The federal government is planning a 'Behavioral Research Centre' in Butner, North Carolina. According to the Federal Bureau of Prisons, 'The Centre will serve the United States Bureau of Prisons as a developer of new treatment techniques to effectively modify criminal behaviour. Centre programmes will accept especially selected groups of offenders from other Bureau of Prisons facilities to develop new approaches for correcting various classes of offenders not reached by traditional correction programmes.' The programmes will treat 'patients who constitute a *management problem* [emphasis added] beyond the capacities of other correctional institutions'. Patients are to include 'alcoholic felons, minority groups, overly passive follower types, sexually assaultive inmates, and high security risks'.

The political implications of this new vogue are very clear. Psychiatrists categorize as 'mental illness' those behaviour patterns that have been traditionally associated with oppressed minority groups and political activists; the proposed solutions to problematic behaviour are devised purely with the convenience of correctional institutions in mind.

To speak of voluntary submission to these treatments is based on naïve misunderstanding of conditions in institutions. The pressures of institutional life prevent rational, unbiased, and free personal decisions with regard to official programmes of treatment. These treatment programmes are being used *without the consent of the patient, or with his forced consent*. This is as true for non-homosexuals as for homosexuals.

In prison some homosexual relations occur between consenting individuals; others, which are most publicized, involve violence and at least one unwilling participant. Psychiatric treatment is prescribed for both these groups. To treat members of the first group is to act upon the assumption that homosexuality, regardless of its context, is a sickness.

The fact that we are considering incarcerated persons – for whom misery and abuse have been institutionalized – is in itself a sufficient indictment against the use of any of the treatments described.

Secondly, as a gay man, I am moved to outrage by the inordinate cruelty and insensitivity with which homosexual 'patients' are treated by heterosexual psychiatrists. Dr Litkey speaks about the elimination of homosexual 'pleasurable sensations' in one of his patients. Other articles mention the use of painful electric shocks and drugs which induce severe nausea or terror.

The insidious character of some experiments resides in the unquestioning compliance of patients motivated by self-hatred. There is something inherently evil about helping someone 'repress through punishment' one of his most basic drives, thereby permitting him to lead a 'happy heterosexual life' rather than helping him to come to terms with himself, his homosexuality.

There is something very wrong with a branch of medicine that uses its knowledge to destroy people's humanity, rather than to preserve it.

24. Gay Liberation Manifesto

Carl Wittman

On Orientation

I. WHAT HOMOSEXUALITY IS. Nature leaves undefined the object of sexual desire. The gender of that object is imposed socially. Humans originally made homosexuality taboo because they needed every bit of energy to produce and raise children: survival of species was a priority. With overpopulation and technological change, that taboo continues only to exploit us and enslave us.

As kids we refused to capitulate to demands that we ignore our feelings towards each other. Somewhere we found the strength to resist being indoctrinated, and we should count that among our assets. We have to realize that our loving each other is a good thing, not an unfortunate thing, and that we have a lot to teach straights about sex, love, strength, and resistance.

Homosexuality is *not* a lot of things. It is not a makeshift in the absence of the opposite sex; it is not hatred or rejection of the opposite sex; it is not genetic; it is not the result of broken homes except inasmuch as we could see the sham of AmeriKan marriage. *Homosexuality is the capacity to love someone of the same sex.*

2. BISEXUALITY. Bisexuality is good; it is the capacity to love people of either sex. The reason so few of us are bisexual is because society made such a big stink about homosexuality that we got forced into seeing ourselves as either straight or non-straight. Also, many gays got turned off to the ways men are supposed to act with women and vice versa, which is pretty messed up. Gays will begin to turn on to women when 1) it's something that we do because we want to, and not because we should; and 2) when women's liberation changes the nature of heterosexual relationships.

We continue to call ourselves homosexual, not bisexual, even if we do make it with the opposite sex also, because saying 'Oh, I'm bi' is a cop-out for a gay. We get told it's OK to sleep with guys as long as we sleep with women too, and that's still putting homosexuality down. We'll be gay until everyone has forgotten that it's an issue. Then we'll begin to be complete.

3. HETEROSEXUALITY. Exclusive heterosexuality is messed up. It reflects a fear of people of the same sex, it's anti-homosexual, and it is fraught with frustration. Heterosexual sex is messed up, too: ask women's liberation about what straight guys are like in bed. Sex is aggression for the male chauvinist; sex is obligation for the traditional woman. And among the young, the modern, the hip, it's only a subtle version of the same. For us to become heterosexual in the sense that our straight brothers and sisters are is not a cure, it is a disease.

On Women

1. LESBIANISM. It's been a male-dominated society for too long, and that has warped both men and women. So gay women are going to see things differently from gay men; they are going to feel put down as women, too. Their liberation is tied up with both gay liberation and women's liberation.

This paper speaks from the gay male viewpoint. And although some of the ideas in it may be equally relevant to gay women, it would be arrogant to presume this to be a manifesto for lesbians.

2. MALE CHAUVINISM. All men are infected with male chauvinism – we were brought up that way. It means we assume that women play subordinate roles and are less human than ourselves. (At an early gay liberation meeting, one guy said, 'Why don't we invite women's liberation – they can bring sandwiches and coffee.') It is no wonder that so few gay women have become active in our groups.

Male chauvinism, however, is not central to us. We can junk it much more easily than straight men can. For we understand oppression. We have largely opted out of a system which

oppresses women daily – our egos are not built on putting
women down and having them build us up. Also, living in a
mostly male world we have become used to playing different
roles, doing our own shitwork. And, finally, we have a common
enemy: the big male chauvinists are also the big anti-gays.

But we need to purge male chauvinism, both in behaviour and
in thought among us. 'Chick' equals 'nigger' equals 'queer'.
Think it over.

3. WOMEN'S LIBERATION. They are assuming their equality
and dignity and in doing so are challenging the same things we
are: the roles, the exploitation of minorities by capitalism, the
arrogant smugness of straight white middle-class AmeriKa.
They are our sisters in struggle.

Problems and differences will become clearer when we begin
to work together. One major problem is our own male chauvinism. Another is uptightness and hostility to homosexuality that
many women have – that is the straight in them. A third problem is differing views on sex: sex for them has meant oppression, while for us it has been a symbol of our freedom. We must
come to know and understand each other's style, jargon, and
humour.

On Roles

1. MIMICRY OF STRAIGHT SOCIETY. We are children of
straight society. We still think straight; that is part of our
oppression. One of the worst of straight concepts is inequality.
Straight (also white, English, male, capitalist) thinking views
things in terms of order and comparison. A is before B, B is
after A; one is below two is below three; there is no room for
equality. This idea gets extended to male/female, on top/on
bottom, spouse/not spouse, heterosexual/homosexual, boss/
worker, white/black, and rich/poor. Our social institutions cause
and reflect this verbal hierarchy. This is AmeriKa.

We've lived in these institutions all our lives. Naturally we
mimic the roles. For too long we mimicked these roles to protect ourselves – a survival mechanism. Now we are becoming

free enough to shed the roles which we've picked up from the institutions which have imprisoned us.

'Stop mimicking straights, stop censoring ourselves!'

2. MARRIAGE. Marriage is a prime example of a straight institution fraught with role playing. Traditional marriage is a rotten, oppressive institution. Those of us who have been in heterosexual marriages too often have blamed our gayness on the breakup of the marriage. No. They broke up because marriage is a contract which smothers both people, denies needs, and places impossible demands on both people. And we had the strength, again, to refuse to capitulate to the roles which were demanded of us.

Gay people must stop gauging their self-respect by how well they mimic straight marriages. Gay marriages will have the same problems as straight ones except in burlesque. For the usual legitimacy and pressures which keep straight marriages together are absent, e.g., kids, what parents think, what neighbours say, property inheritance, etc.

To accept that happiness comes through finding a groovy spouse and settling down, showing the world that 'we're just the same as you', is avoiding the real issues and is an expression of self-hatred.

3. ALTERNATIVES TO MARRIAGE. People want to get married for lots of good reasons, although marriage won't often meet those needs or desires. We're all looking for security, a flow of love, and a feeling of belonging and being needed.

These needs can be met through a number of social relationships and living situations. Things we want to get away from are: a) exclusiveness, propertied attitudes towards each other, a mutual pact against the rest of the world; b) promises about the future, which we have no right to make and which prevent us from, or make us feel guilty about, growing; c) inflexible roles, roles which do not reflect us at the moment but are inherited through mimicry and inability to define egalitarian relationships.

We have to define for ourselves a new pluralistic, role-free social structure. It must contain both the freedom and physical space for people to live alone, live together for a while, live together for a long time, either as couples or in larger numbers; and the ability to flow easily from one of these states to another as our needs change.

Liberation for gay people is defining for ourselves how and with whom we live, instead of measuring our relationships by comparison to straight ones, with straight values.

4. GAY STEREOTYPES. The straights' image of the gay world is defined largely by those of us who have violated straight roles. There is a tendency among 'homophile' groups to deplore gays who play visible roles – the queens and the nellies. As liberated gays, we must take a clear stand. 1. Gays who stand out have become our first martyrs. They came out and withstood disapproval before the rest of us did. 2. If they have suffered from being open, it is straight society whom we must indict, not the queen.

5. CLOSET QUEENS. This phrase is becoming analogous to 'Uncle Tom'. To pretend to be straight sexually, or to pretend to be straight socially, is probably the most harmful pattern of behaviour in the ghetto. The married guy who makes it on the side secretly; the guy who will go to bed once but who won't develop any gay relationships; the pretender at work or school who changes the gender of the friend he's talking about; the guy who'll suck cock in the bushes but who won't go to bed.

If we are liberated, we are open with our sexuality. Closet queenery must end. *Come out*.

But: in saying come out, we have to have our heads clear about a few things: a) closet queens are our brothers, and must be defended against attacks by straight people; b) the fear of coming out is not paranoia; the stakes are high: loss of family ties, loss of job, loss of straight friends – these are all reminders that the oppression is not just in our heads. It's real. Each of us must make the steps towards openness at our own speed and on our own impulses. Being open is the foundation of freedom: it has to be built solidly; c) 'closet queen' is a broad term covering a multitude of forms of defence, self-hatred, lack of strength, and habit. We are all closet queens in some ways, and all of us had to come out – very few of us were 'flagrant' at the age of seven! We must afford our brothers and sisters the same patience we afforded ourselves. And while their closet queenery is part of our oppression, it's more a part of theirs. They alone can decide when and how.

On Oppression

It is important to catalogue and understand the different facets of our oppression. There is no future in arguing about degrees of oppression. A lot of 'movement' types come on with a line of shit about homosexuals not being oppressed as much as blacks or Vietnamese or workers or women. We don't happen to fit into their ideas of class or caste. Bull! When people feel oppressed, they act on that feeling. We feel oppressed. Talk about the priority of black liberation or ending imperialism over and above gay liberation is just anti-gay propaganda.

I. PHYSICAL ATTACKS. We are attacked, beaten, castrated, and left dead time and time again. 'Punks', often of minority groups who look around for someone under them socially, feel encouraged to beat up on 'queens' and cops look the other way. That used to be called lynching.

Cops in most cities have harassed our meeting places: bars and baths and parks. They set up entrapment squads. A Berkeley brother was slain by a cop when he tried to split after finding out that the trick who was making advances to him was a cop. Cities set up 'pervert' registration, which if nothing else scares our brothers deeper into the closet.

One of the most vicious slurs on us is the blame for prison 'gang rapes'. These rapes are invariably done by people who consider themselves straight. The victims of these rapes are us and straights who can't defend themselves. The Press campaign to link prison rapes with homosexuality is an attempt to make straights fear and despise us, so they can oppress us more. It's typical of the fucked-up straight mind to think that homosexual sex involves tying a guy down and fucking him. That's aggression, not sex. If that's what sex is for a lot of straight people, that's a problem they have to solve, not us.

2. PSYCHOLOGICAL WARFARE. Right from the beginning

we have been subjected to a barrage of straight propaganda. Since our parents don't know any homosexuals, we grow up thinking that we're alone and different and perverted. Our school friends identify 'queer' with any nonconformist or bad behaviour. Our elementary-school teachers tell us not to talk to strangers or accept rides. Television, billboards, and magazines put forth a false idealization of male/female relationships, and make us wish we were different, wish we were 'in'. In family-living class we're taught how we're supposed to turn out. And all along, the best we hear if anything about homosexuality is that it's an unfortunate problem.

3. SELF-OPPRESSION. As gay liberation grows, we will find our uptight brothers and sisters, particularly those who are making a buck off our ghettos, coming on strong to defend our *status quo*. This is self-oppression: 'Don't rock the boat'; 'Things in San Francisco [or Atlanta] are OK'; 'Gay people just aren't together'; 'I'm not oppressed'. These lines are right out of the mouths of the straight establishment. A large part of our oppression would end if we would stop putting ourselves and our pride down.

4. INSTITUTIONAL. Discrimination against gays is blatant, if we open our eyes. Homosexual relationships are illegal, and even if these laws are not regularly enforced, they encourage and enforce closet queenery. The bulk of the social work/psychiatric field looks upon homosexuality as a problem, and treats us as sick. Employers let it be known that our skills are acceptable only as long as our sexuality is hidden. Big business and government are particularly notorious offenders.

The US Army stands dead centre in a culture founded on male supremacy and anti-homosexualism, and no homosexual should be required to serve. But the Pentagon wants to have it both ways: officially it excludes a homosexual categorically if he is willing to publicly declare his 'sickness', but in the last three years, as any number of gay men know, the army has drafted homosexuals even if they checked the box (obtaining not only another inductee but also useful information about him that might further his exploitation and oppression). For gay men to concern themselves about exclusion from the military is comparable to black people worrying about being denied entrance to the KKK. Once in, homosexuals are oppressed in every conceivable way, and many even have to carry some of these official forms of discrimination and harassment with them when they return to civilian life.

On Sex

1. WHAT SEX IS. It is both creative expression and communication: good when it is either, and better when it is both. Sex can also be aggression, and usually is when those involved do not see each other as equals; and it can also be perfunctory, when we are distracted or preoccupied. These uses spoil what is good about it.

I like to think of good sex in terms of playing musical instruments: with both people on one level seeing the other body as an object capable of creating beauty when they play it well; and on a second level the players communicating through their mutual production and appreciation of beauty. As in good music, you get totally into it – and coming back out of that state of consciousness is like finishing a work of art or coming back from an episode of an acid or mescaline trip. And to press the analogy further: the variety of music is infinite and varied, depending on the capabilities of the players, both as subjects and as objects. Solos, duets, quartets (symphonies, even, if you happen to dig romantic music!), classical, folk, jazz, soul, country, rock and roll, electric or acoustic – got live if you want it, and everything is permitted! The variations in gender, response, and bodies are like different instruments. And perhaps what we have called sexual orientation probably just means that we have not yet learned to turn on to the total range of musical expression.

2. OBJECTIFICATION. In this scheme, people are sexual objects, but they are also subjects, and are human beings who appreciate themselves as object and subject. This use of human bodies as objects is legitimate (not harmful) only when it is reciprocal. If one person is always object and the other subject,

it stifles the human being in both of them. Objectification must also be open and frank. By silence we often assume that sex means commitments: if it does, OK; but if not, say it. (Of course, it's not all that simple: our capabilities for manipulation are unfathomed – all we can do is try.)

Gay liberation people must understand that women have been treated exclusively and dishonestly as sexual objects. A major part of their liberation is to play down sexual objectification and to develop other aspects of themselves which have been smothered so long. We respect this. We also understand that a few liberated women will be appalled or disgusted at the open and prominent place that we put sex in our lives; and while this is a natural response from their experience, they must learn what it means for us.

For us, sexual objectification is a focus of our quest for freedom. It is precisely that which we are not supposed to share with each other. Learning how to be open and good with each other sexually is part of our liberation. And one obvious distinction: objectification of sex for us is something we choose to do among ourselves, while for women it is imposed by their oppressors.

3. ON POSITIONS AND ROLES. Much of our sexuality has been perverted through mimicry of straights and warped from self-hatred. These sexual perversions are basically anti-gay: 'I like to make it with straight guys,' or 'I'm not gay, but I like to be "done".'

This is role playing at its worst; we must transcend these roles. We strive for democratic, mutual, reciprocal sex. This does not mean that we are all mirror images of each other in bed, but that we break away from roles that enslave us. We already do better in bed than straights do, and we can be better to each other than we have been.

A note on exploitation of children: kids can take care of themselves, and are sexual beings way earlier than we'd like to admit. Those of us who began cruising in early adolescence know this, and we were doing the cruising, not being debauched by dirty old men. Scandals such as the one in Boise, Idaho – blaming a 'ring' of homosexuals for perverting their youth – are the fabrications of Press and police and politicians. And as for child molesting, the overwhelming amount is done by straight guys on little girls: it is not particularly a gay problem, and is caused by the frustrations resulting from anti-sex puritanism.

On Coalition

Right now the bulk of our work has to be among ourselves – self-educating, fending off attacks, and building free territory. Thus basically we have to have a gay/straight vision of the world until the oppression of gays is ended.

But not every straight is our enemy. Many of us have mixed identities, and have ties with other liberation movements: women, blacks, other minority groups; we may also have taken on an identity which is vital to us; ecology, dope, ideology. And face it: we can't change AmeriKa alone:

Who do we look to for coalition?

1. WOMEN'S LIBERATION. Summarizing earlier statements, a) they are our closest ally; we must try hard to get together with them; b) a lesbian caucus is probably the best way to attack gay guys' male chauvinism, and challenge the straightness of women's liberation; c) as males we must be sensitive to their developing identities as women, and respect that; if *we* know what *our* freedom is about, *they* certainly know what's best for *them*.

2. BLACK LIBERATION. See Huey P. Newton's statement to the men of the Black Panther Party on Gay Liberation and Women's Liberation (*Bird*, Vol. 3, No. 40). It would be impossible to overestimate the significance of this vanguard position on the potential solidarity between third world liberation and the struggle against male supremacy and sexism by women and gay people. We must support black liberation, particularly when black people are under attack from the system; we must show our black sisters and brothers that we mean business, and we must figure out which our common enemies are: police, city hall, capitalism.

3. CHICANOS. Basically the same situation – trying to overcome mutual animosity and fear, and finding ways to support

them. The extra problem of super-uptightness and machismo among Latin cultures, and the traditional pattern of Mexicans beating up 'queers', can be overcome: we're both oppressed, and by the same people at the top.

4. WHITE RADICALS AND IDEOLOGUES. No country or political/economic system has treated gay people as anything other than *non grata* so far. We know that we are radical, that we are revolutionaries since we know the system we're under now is a direct source of oppression, and it's not a question of getting our share of the pie. The pie is rotten.

We can look forward to coalition and mutual support with radical groups if they are able to transcend their anti-gay and male chauvinist patterns. We support radical and militant demands when they arise, but only as a group; we can't compromise or soft-pedal our gay identity.

Perhaps most fruitful would be to broach with radicals their stifled homosexuality and the issues which arise from challenging sexual roles. Gay people also have a vanguard role to play in defining, establishing, and operating child-care centres.

5. HIP AND STREET PEOPLE. A major dynamic of rising gay liberation sentiment is the hip revolution within the gay community. Emphasis on love, dropping out, being honest, expressing yourself through hair and clothes, and smoking dope are all attributes of this. The gays who are the least vulnerable to attack by the establishment have been the freest to express themselves on gay liberation.

The hip/street culture has led people into a lot of freeing activities: encounter/sensitivity, the quest for reality, freeing territory for the people, ecological consciousness, communes. These are real points of agreement and probably will make it easier for them to get their heads straight about homosexuality, too.

6. HOMOPHILE ORGANIZATIONS. a) reformist or pokey as they sometimes are, they are our brothers. They'll grow as we have grown and grow. Do not attack them in straight or mixed company; b) ignore their attack on us; c) cooperate where cooperation is possible without essential compromise of our identity.

25. The Rights of Children: Recommendations

Summary recommendations of the *Workshop on the Rights of Children*, Berkeley Conference, Revolutionary People's Constitutional Convention, 14–15 November 1970.

1. Our revolutionary children are entrusted with the responsibility for rediscovering the true human nature, perverted by thousands of years of racism, capitalism, so-called communism, sexism, nationalism, and false religion. Forced limitation of their experience, in the name of protection and love, has always been a central part of reactionary repression, especially for the bourgeois class. The destruction of human potential for love by repression in childhood must end now.

Children must be allowed self-regulation, encouraged to relate joyfully to their bodies without shame or sex-role prejudices, and their affectionate-sexual-sensual characters must be allowed full expression without so-called moralistic interference.

Development, self-discovery, and free expression of affection and exploration into revolutionary non-exploitative and non-oppressive new sexual modes of expression cannot occur where there is interference by imperialist Christian so-called moral laws, ridicule, or guilt, or when children are systematically kept ignorant of the varieties of human joy and pleasure in one another. Encouragement of adult-child affectionate exchange, liberation of spontaneous feeling, and rejection of puritan frigidity plays a vital part in the development of a revolutionary teaching, nurturing, and extended family environment.

2. Children are entitled to civil rights and liberties in no way inferior to those accorded to adults. Child-prisoners in the orphanages and so-called reform schools must be liberated and allowed to find their own place in the People's community.

Adults caring for them, communes, and free children's collectives shall be supported without conditions limiting experimentation into new social forms and structures. Non-exploitative variety and choice are at the heart of the revolution.

3. Children are not property. No child shall be forced to stay within any biological family if it does not suit 'co' (see paragraph 5). Children must have the chance to explore alternatives and to choose from a variety of structures, combining what we now call family, school, work and apprenticeship, summer vacation, etc.

The only final judge of the suitability of a particular family or environment for a particular child must be that child.

In this period before the end of repression there will undoubtedly be many situations in which the responsibility and experience of revolutionary adults will force them into some arbitrary limitations on the freedom of children in their care to protect both from reactionary repression. This need should be explained to and understood by the children, and they should be taught from an early age the skills necessary for survival under repression, such as how to lie without embarrassment when interrogated. In every revolutionary family the freedoms of individuals to some extent will be limited by the needs of other members, and the whole group, but we should always struggle to confine these limitations to rationally justified ones which are balanced by the advantages provided by belonging to the group. Like adults, the child should be free to judge that balance for coself and if co desires, co should be free to seek an alternative family group to accept co, on cos terms.

A child's revolt, violence, or thievery shows that the environment is not responsive to his or her needs. Materialist needs are exaggerated by capitalist advertising. The child's needs for people can never be satisfied by the nuclear family alone, but an extended family is necessary. A richness of particular forms is expected in revolutionary society as a value in itself, but also important for testing and trial, since in our present state we are limited in our knowledge of third-world alternative forms (reported to us by Western chauvinist anthropologists) and the full impact of a non-capitalist, ecologically sensitive, and humane technology remains unexplored.

4. The free movement of children in the world, exploration of life styles, city and country, the forms of useful work and labour (true education), will be possible only if children are

economically independent. All children are entitled to their share of guaranteed income, fruit of the labour of all past generations, given to us in the form of the arts, sciences, technology, and capital, the last at present stolen from the people by the institutions of capitalism. The child should control cos food, shelter, and necessities of life. This is important to the individual freedom necessary for the maximum development of individual talents which will finally benefit all humankind.

5. We urge all of our revolutionary brothers and sisters to become aware that the emotional overtones of imperialist language have a strong effect in conditioning children's minds to oppression, instilling Western chauvinism and cultural prejudices. These effects are difficult to overcome in even revolutionary adulthood since they are not ideas which can be corrected, but are feelings, fears, and anxieties which can be overcome only by long struggle. This is prejudice of all kinds.

It is no accident that we have been tricked into using words like fuck, prick, cunt, motherfucker, cocksucker, or asshole as insults. When we use these words as insults we teach our children that bodies are shameful, not beautiful, we make them frightened of their curiosity, and we transmit to them our own inhibitions about non-conventional love expression.

In these recommendations we have tried to eliminate some of the sexism which has become embedded in the language by adopting the suggestions of Mary Orovan of the New York Radical Feminists. In this usage instead of using the masculine personal pronouns like 'he' or 'his', when we really mean children of both sexes, we use the ancient alternative Indo-European root word 'co'. Where sexist language would use 'he', meaning 'he-she', 'co' is used. 'Co' is also used in place of 'him' (for him-her), with the context making the difference clear. The old possessive 'his' (for his-hers) is replaced by 'cos', and 'coself' replaces 'himself'. Humankind replaces mankind. Revolutionary language must reflect revolutionary consciousness and we believe this change is needed now in all communications and newspapers of the people, and is preferable to the awkward grammatical structures resorted to when we avoid the normal sexist usage. In speech we believe revolutionaries should lovingly teach their brothers and sisters the harmfulness of imperialist language, encourage change, and be tolerant of long-established habits which may persist. The consciousness is what is important, not perfect use, and this can often be advanced without raising defensiveness.

We believe these language changes will make an important contribution to the unity of the people, since they reflect and give evidence of the new sensitivity of our brothers and sisters to one another's oppression, and the new consciousness of humankind which is behind the revolution.

26. The Sexual Abuse of Children: A Feminist Point of View

Florence Rush

When I was asked to talk on the sexual abuse of children, I was not certain where the subject would lead. I am a social worker, had worked for the Society for the Prevention of Cruelty to Children, and remembered that the sexual victims brought to my attention were always female children and that the offenders were always male adults. This triggered off other recollections. I had worked some years back in an institution for dependent and neglected girls. I dug up some old notes and discovered that all those in my case-load had been sexually victimized at one time or another, running the gamut from exposure to male exhibitionists, to touching and fondling, to rape, incest and carnal abuse. There was not a single girl who did not have an experience to relate. With my memory set in motion, I went back to when I was twenty and worked in an orphanage one summer between school years. I lived in the institution and was in charge of a summer programme for the girls between seven and fifteen years of age. Soon after I began on the job, I learned that the male director would regularly take some of the girls to his apartment and sexually molest them. One night I returned to the institution late to find the director in the hall entrance where he began to fondle and kiss me. The next day I reported his behaviour plus his other activities to the Board of Directors. I was questioned very carefully and gently asked if I hadn't encouraged him just a teeny bit. I held my ground and the director was fired. Please do not get the wrong impression. I quickly learned that the director was stealing the institution blind but no one could prove this, and I accommodated the Board by offering a perfect solution to their problem. A week later I was dismissed on the pretext that the institution had run out of funds and could no longer pay my salary. As I walked

out the door, the new director, a man, entered. Tearfully the
orphans and I said goodbye, and it appeared to me that these
children and young women were helplessly prepared to face
the same abuse which might be heaped upon them by the new
director.

I said to myself at that time that these were poor children,
who were unprotected and exposed to the evils of poverty. They
came from broken homes, were economically disadvantaged and
this could not happen to a child in a stable family situation. This
line of thinking, however, did not sit right with me and something kept prodding me to remember more. I did remember
more, I remembered myself. I came from a very stable family
which was both culturally and economically advantaged. At the
age of six my mother sent me alone to the friendly family dentist
who did more feeling than drilling. When I told my mother of
my experience, she did not believe me. At the age of ten, I was
molested by the father of a boy I secretly loved and I somehow
connected my secret love with the father's treatment of me and
felt ashamed and guilty. At thirteen, my uncle, my mother's
brother, came to visit from Chicago and wouldn't keep his hands
off me. Again I told my mother and she scolded me for making
up stories. Repeated lack of success did teach me never to report
such incidents again.

At about that same time, I became obsessed with movies. I
loved them, went every time I could, but found I could never
get through a double feature without finding the hand of some
gentleman up my skirt. My girl friend Jane and I worked out a
system. If a man would get 'funny', that is if in the middle of a
great Fred Astaire and Ginger Rogers movie, one of us discovered a strange hand between our legs, it was time to get up
and say in a loud voice, 'I must go home now because my mother
is expecting me.' Jane and I would then change seats and hope
we would be left alone long enough to see the end of the film. It
never occurred to us to holler at the man, hit him or even report
him to the management. It never occurred to us to hold the
man responsible for what he had done. This was our problem,
not his, and we handled it as best we could. In subsequent years,
Jane and I reported regularly to each other on the number of

exposed men we had seen, how we handled attempts to be touched and how we escaped from what might develop into something violent and dangerous. After a while we became rather casual about our experiences, rarely became outraged, but simply tried to develop greater skills in avoiding and extricating ourselves from the sexual aggression of men without embarrassing the offender. This was excellent training and prepared me in later years for the breast grabbers, the bottom pinchers and the body rubbers. The horror, the shame and the humiliation never left me, but until recently I never knew I had the right to be outraged and fight back. I was, after all, trained to be a woman.

After these memories, my thesis for this presentation became clear. *The sexual abuse of children is an early manifestation of male power and oppression of the female.* For myself, I need no statistics or research to prove my point, but to make my presentation credible, I have searched for supportive evidence. There is, significantly, very little material on the subject of sexual abuse generally and particularly as it relates to children. I think I found enough, however, for my purposes today. I will refer to five studies. The first is the one I have chosen as my authority and is the one most sympathetic to child victims of sex crimes. It is entitled 'Protecting the Child Victim of Sex Crimes Committed by Adults' and is put out by the American Humane Association. I found this report to be the least prejudiced, the most scholarly, most humane and most informative as compared to the other studies I referred to. The following statistics, statements and conclusions are drawn from this study which is based on the investigation of 263 child victims of sexual abuse.

1. National statistics on the incidence of sexual offenders against children are wholly unavoidable. The FBI's annual Information Crime Report is concerned with statistics on the offender and not the victim. It does not even carry a breakdown of the total incidence of all crimes against children. What makes an assessment even more difficult, except for rare cases of brutal attack or fatal situations, is that cases of sex offences against children are not generally publicized by the Press.[1]

2. The problem of sexual abuse of children is of unknown

national dimensions but findings strongly point to the probability of an enormous national incidence many times larger than the reported incidence of child abuse (physical abuse other than sexual).

3. By an overwhelming ratio, 97 per cent of offenders were male and ranged in age from seventeen to sixty-eight.

4. Victims were on a ratio of ten girls to one boy. The boys were victims of male homosexuals. The victims ranged in age from infants to under sixteen and the median age was eleven.

5. In 75 per cent of the cases, the offender was known to the child or family such as a father, stepfather, mother's lover, brother, uncle or friend of the family – 25 per cent of the offenders were alleged to be strangers.

6. 60 per cent of the child victims were coerced by direct force, or threat of bodily harm. In 25 per cent the lure was based on the child's loyalty and affection for a friend or relative. 15 per cent were based on tangible lures.

7. Children were subjected to sexual offences of all types varying from indecent exposure to full intercourse, rape and incest. The majority of incest is between fathers and young daughters.

8. Two-thirds of the child victims were found to be emotionally damaged by the occurrence with 14 per cent severely disturbed. Twenty-nine of the victims became pregnant as a result of the offence.

9. In 41 per cent of the cases, the offences were repeated and perpetuated over a period of time ranging from weeks to seven years.

10. All the cases in the study were reported to the police (263). They made 173 arrests and 106 were released on bail; this resulted in bringing the offender back into the community thus again exposing the child victim to danger.

11. More than 1,000 court appearances were required for the 173 cases prosecuted and this resulted in extreme tension and stress for both child and family. 44 per cent of the cases were dismissed for lack of proof.

12. In almost two-thirds of the homes, the parents were found to be inadequate. They were deemed to be failing to provide the

care and protection necessary for their children's welfare. (I will come back to this last point later.)[2]

I will comment now on four other studies. The following quotations and my comments will focus on general and professional attitudes which relentlessly forgive the adult male offender and indicate little concern for the female child victim.* I will refer to the studies as Study Number one, two, three and four. I will identify my source material later to anyone who wishes the information.

Study Number 1

This was an investigation of 1,365 convicted male sex offenders – 868 offenders committed offences against children. The following are direct quotes taken from the study.

> Not only do they (women) commit fewer illegal sexual acts ... but society tends to ignore or tolerate their breaches. Persons hesitate to sign a complaint against a female, police loathe to arrest and juries loathe to convict.
>
> The indifference is justifiable. The average female has a much lower 'sex drive' than the average male, consequently she is least likely to behave in a sexually illegal manner.
>
> If a woman, walking past an apartment, stops to watch a man undressing ... the man is arrested as an exhibitionist.[3]

I thought I would first like to establish the author's attitude towards women. The author feels that the biologically limited woman with her low sex drives is not impelled to commit sex crimes. If she were, however, society would be loath to punish her. On the other hand men, biologically endowed with powerful sex drives, naturally commit sex crimes. Despite his natural propensity towards sex crimes, men are accused of sex crimes which they do not commit. It may be confused, but the author's feelings come through loud and clear. His opinion of women is no secret. Now let us hear what he has to say about children.

* In many of the quotations words and phrases have been deleted only to clarify and emphasize. The deletions did not alter the essential meaning of the quotations.

The horror with which society views the adult who has sexual relations with young children is lessened when one examines the behaviour of other mammals. Sexual activity between adult and immature animals is common and appears to be biologically normal.[4]

Disregard for age, sex and species need not be regarded as biologically pathological; it is precisely what we see in various animals, particularly in monkeys.[5]

I once saw my cat have kittens. After each kitten was born, the mother ate the afterbirth and cleaned her babies with her tongue. I've had three children and am delighted I did not have to follow the example of the mother cat. Maybe monkeys are more like us. I don't know, but it never occurred to me that the behaviour of animals was the norm for human behaviour. The author now explains one kind of sexual offender.

Exhibitionism is an expression of hostility and sadism; a way to frighten and shock. Very few of these people (exhibitionists) consciously feel hostility and on the whole are to be pitied rather than to be feared.[6]

I guess dirty old men need love too. Again the author's logic eludes me, but the contradiction and bias are obvious.

Study Number 2

Here we have an examination of forty-one children and the study attempts to estimate the psychologically harmful effects of sexual assault on children. The author draws heavily on Freudian theories of infant sexuality.

He (Freud) noted that the majority of children could escape from the sexual situation if they wished and he maintained that the silence shown by some children following seduction, could be explained in terms of their own feeling of guilt in yielding to forbidden attraction . . .
The girl will strive to counteract her fear of the bad or sadistic penis by introducing a good one in coitus . . .[7]

Bender and Blau (experts in child study) noted that the most striking feature of sexually assaulted children was their unusually attractive personalities. This was so noticeable that the authors frequently considered the possibility that the child might have been the actual seducer rather than the one innocently seduced.[8]

The myth of childhood innocence seems, in the main, to have been rejected and some degree of participation by the victim group is accepted by all studies.[9]

The suggestion is, therefore, made that the sexual assault of children by adults does not have a particularly detrimental effect on the child's subsequent development . . . The need for affection, which may have well predisposed the child to this form of sexual acting out, will be outgrown.[10]

Isn't it strange how victims are held responsible for offences against them! Our sexuality as women and children is not used to understand us but to psychologically trap us so that, we are told, the woman seeks to be raped and the little girl wants sexual abuse. And while the woman invites rape and the child invites sexual abuse, men are permitted their sexual indulgences, American soldiers rape and kill Vietnamese women and children and the Hell's Angels roam free to raid and rape. The myth of consent – that is the psychiatric and popular use of ill-defined sexual motivation and acting out to explain and condone the victimization of women and children – is unforgivable and shameful.

Study Number 3

This study involved a general investigation into the sexual behaviour of women. Over 4,000 women were studied and 24 per cent of these reported pre-adolescent experiences with an adult male.

But it is difficult to understand why a child, except for its cultural conditioning, should be disturbed by having its genitalia touched or disturbed by seeing the genitalia of another person . . . Some of the more experienced students of juvenile problems have come to believe that the emotional reactions of the parents, police and other adults ... may disturb the child more seriously than the contacts themselves. The current hysteria over sex offenders may well have serious effects on the ability of many children to work out sexual adjustment some years later.[11]

With the usual male arrogance, the author cannot imagine that a sexual assault on a child constitutes a gross and devastating shock and insult, so he blames everyone but the offender. The fact is that sexual offences are barely noticed except in the most violent and sensational instances. Most sex offences are never revealed; when revealed, most are either ignored or not reported; if reported a large percentage are dismissed for lack of proof and when proof is established, many are dropped because of the pressure and humiliation forced on the victim and family by the authorities.

Study Number 4

This study deals with twenty cases of incest and involves the father as offender and daughters as victims. The preponderance of incest cases are between fathers and young daughters. The author, although sympathetic with the victim, still does not deal with the offender, but looks to the mother to control the problem.

There follow several examples of father behaviour described by 13 mothers and, in every instance, corroborated by the child victim; breaking a radio over the mother's head; burning the child with hot irons, chasing the mother out of the house with a gun ... locking mother or children in closets while he sexually abused the child victim ... forcing sexual intercourse with the child in the mother's presence ... etc.[12]

After examining the character of the incest family ... the unavoidable conclusion seems to be that the failure of the mother to protect the child against the contingency of incestuous victimization is a crucial and fruitful area of study ...[13]

Considering the father offender as a possible source of control of incest behaviour seems . . . like considering the fox . . . as guard in the henhouse . . .[14]

The mother is the only possible agent of incest control within the family group.[15]

The father rapes and brutalizes and it turns out to be the mother's fault and responsibility. Has anyone thought of the fantastic notion of getting rid of the father? Let me read you a statement of a fourteen-year-old girl taken down by the police.

I was about nine years old when my father first began to come to my bedroom, which I shared with my two sisters, at night and started to touch my breasts and private parts. This would usually happen in the evening when my mother went to the movies or when she was in the living room and my older sister, Anne, was looking at TV or taking a shower. It was within the same year that my father began to have intercourse with me which is putting his penis into my private parts. This was very painful to me when it started. My father told me this was normal and all girls did this with their fathers. When I said I was going to tell my mother or someone about it, he said that what my mother does not know would not hurt her. Sometimes he would hit me when I would refuse him and at times he would take me in the car and, as we rode, touch my vagina.[16]

This completes my report on the studies. I would like to touch very briefly on the subject of female juvenile delinquency. Although female juveniles have a much lower crime rate than male juveniles, the female is reported to be involved in a larger percentage of sexual offences such as sexual promiscuity, adolescent pregnancy and prostitution. Although these offences are all heterosexual and cannot be indulged without the male, the male is rarely regarded as the offender. When a girl rebels against her family or society, she is usually suspected by her family and the community of being sexually promiscuous and is thought of as either a slut or a whore. The young male offender, however, is associated with crimes against society, property, etc. Here is a statement from a psychoanalytic journal regarding male and female juvenile delinquency, which supports psychiatrically the popular attitudes towards male and female delinquency.

The boy's typical delinquent activities contain elements of keen interest in reality; we recognize his fascination with the struggle waged between himself and people, social institutions and the world of nature. In contrast to this, the adolescent girl ... will ... take revenge on her mother, by whom she feels rejected, by seeking sexual relations ...

In female delinquency, the infantile instinctual organization ... finds bodily outlet in genital activity. The pregenital instinctual aims ... relate her delinquency to perversion. An adolescent boy ... caught in an ambivalent conflict with his father, might defend himself ... by getting drunk, destroying property, or stealing a car ... His actions are ... an attempt at progressive development.[17]

If we get past the psychiatric mumbo-jumbo, we are told that delinquent boys are trying to grow and develop, while delinquent girls take revenge on their mothers and are trapped in perversion by their 'pregenital instinctual aims'.

Earlier, I referred to a statistic, which noted that two-thirds of the families of sexually abused children were inadequate. According to most anthropologists and sociologists, the purpose of the family is the protection of children. From what I have heard, read and seen, it would seem to me that the protectors and the offenders are one and the same. The fact is that families, generally, are given the job of socializing children to fill prescribed roles and thus supply the needs of a power society. My mother's inability to protect me from sexual abuse did not occur because she was worse than any other mother, but because, like all women, she was guilty and repulsed by her own sexuality and taught me to feel the same way. Seventy-five per cent of the sexually abused children are victims of family members or friends. All children suffer at the hands of their family whether the abuse be sexual, physical, or emotional, but children have nowhere to go outside the family. They have no options, no choices and no power. Ingrained in our present family system is the nucleus of male power and domination and no matter how often we witness the devastatingly harmful effects of this arrangement on women and children, the victims are asked to uphold the family and submit to its abuse. Let me read to you from a publication called 'Violence Against Children'. The passage is part of a study on the physical abuse against children in the United States, completed at Brandeis University; Advanced Studies in Social Welfare.

> Most societies, including America ... have not developed absolute cultural and legal sanctions against the use of physical force towards children by adults. Not only is such use of physical force not prohibited, but it is even encouraged by many societies ...
> Children were considered property of their parents in many societies and parents had, thus, absolute power over life and death.[18]

> Children in America ... have always been subjected to a wide range of physical and non-physical abuse by parents and other caretakers ... and indirectly by society as a whole. Such abusive treatment of children seems to be inherent in the basic inequality of physical makeup and social status between adults and children, and ... permissive or even encouraging attitudes toward the use of physical force.[19]

It is assumed that because children are not fully grown, they have not the knowledge, the humanity nor the feeling to know what they want. As women we are treated the same way and children feel as we do, only more so, because they are even more helpless and dependent. It is interesting to note, however, how early and eagerly, male children take on and integrate the attitudes and advantage of male supremacy. I talked one evening to a group of high school students, young men and women about fourteen years of age. When I pointed to the similarities between the oppression of women and children, the male students objected vehemently almost to the point of physical revulsion. Already contaminated, they could not bear to be identified with women. But for those male children who are not yet contaminated and for all the female children who are being abused, manipulated, and prepared for the role of subjugation and exploitation, we must offer help in the light of our own oppression and new feminist understanding. We must begin to study and understand what is happening to children today.

From my personal experience as a woman, as a female child, as a social worker and, after talking to countless women, after reading and researching, and with my deepened understanding and radicalization from my involvement in the women's movement, I have drawn some conclusions regarding the sexual abuse of children.

1. That the sexual abuse of children, who are overwhelmingly female, by sexual offenders, who are overwhelmingly male adults, is part and parcel of the male dominated society which overtly and covertly subjugates women.

2. That the sexual molestation and abuse of female children is not regarded seriously by society, is winked at, rationalized and allowed to continue through a complex of customs and mores which applauds the male's sexual aggression and denies the female's pain, humiliation and outrage.

3. That sexual abuse of children is permitted because it is an unspoken but prominent factor in socializing and preparing the female to accept a subordinate role; to feel guilty, ashamed, and to tolerate, through fear, the power exercised over her by men. That the female's early sexual experiences prepare her to submit in later life to the adult forms of sexual abuse heaped on her by her boy friend, her lover, and her husband. In short, the sexual abuse of female children is a process of education which prepares them to become the sweethearts and wives of America.

4. That the family itself is an instrument of sexual and other forms of child abuse, and that in order to protect children, we must find new ways of rearing them so they may have optimum opportunity to achieve full human growth and potential.

5. That we must begin to think of children's liberation as being the same as women's liberation. The female child and woman are the same person, merely at a different stage of development. The growth from childhood to adulthood is a process not a 'gap' or separation. The female infant, child, woman and old woman are subject to the same evils. The separations are false, provoke hostility and are used to divide us.

In closing, let me read a passage from Shulamith Firestone's book, *The Dialectic of Sex*.

Children, then, are not freer than adults. They are burdened by a wish fantasy in direct proportion to the restraints of their narrow lives; with an unpleasant sense of their own physical inadequacy and ridiculousness; with constant shame about their dependence, economic and otherwise; and humiliation concerning, their natural ignorance of practical affairs. Children are repressed at every waking minute. Childhood is hell.

Except for the ego rewards in having children of one's own, few men show any interest in children ... So it is up to the feminist revolutionaries to do so. We must include the oppression of children in any programme for feminist revolution or we will be subject to the same failing of which we have so often accused men; of not having gone deep enough in our analysis.

There are no children yet able to write their own book or tell their own story. We will have to, one last time, do it for them.[20]

Bibliography

1. VINCENT DE FRANCIS, *Protecting the Child Victim of Sex Crimes* (Denver; The American Humane Association, Children's Division, 1965), pamphlet.

2. VINCENT DE FRANCIS, *Protecting the Child Victim of Sex Crimes Committed by Adults* (Denver; The American Humane Association, Children's Division, 1966), pp. 1–3, 215–233.

3. PAUL GEBHART, *et al.*, *Sex Offenders* (New York; Harper and Row, 1965), pp. 9, 10.

4. ibid., p. 54.

5. ibid., p. 276.

6. ibid., p. 399.

7. LINDY BURTON, *Vulnerable Children* (New York, Schocken Books, 1968), p. 29.

8. ibid., p. 104.

9. ibid., p. 113.

10. ibid., p. 169.

11. ALFRED KINSEY, *et al.*, *Sexual Behavior in the Human Female* (New York; Pocket Books, 1953), p. 121.

12. YVONNE TORMES, *Child Victim of Incest* (Denver; The American Humane Association, Children's Division), pamphlet, p. 27.

13. ibid., p. 32.

14. ibid., p. 33.

15. ibid., p. 35.

16. DE FRANCIS, op. cit., p. 112.

17. PETER BLOS, 'Preoedipal Factors in the Etiology of Female Delinquency', *The Psychoanalytic Study of the Child* (New York; International Universities Press, 1957), Vol. XII, p. 232.

18. DAVID GIL., *Violence Against Children* (Waltham; Harvard University Press, 1970), p. 9.

19. ibid., p. 1.

20. SHULAMITH FIRESTONE, *The Dialectic of Sex* (New York; William Morrow and Company, 1970), pp. 117, 118.

IV. Self Help and Communities

27. Madness and Morals

Morton Schatzman

Thou lovest Truth and Beauty and Righteousness: and I for thy
sake say it is well and seemly to love these things. But in my heart I
laugh at thy love. Yet I would not have thee see my laughter. I would
laugh alone.

My friend, thou art good and cautious and wise: nay, thou art
perfect — and I, too, speak with thee wisely and cautiously. And yet
I am mad. But I mask my madness. I would be mad alone.

My friend, thou art not my friend, but how shall I make thee
understand? My path is not thy path, yet together we walk, hand in
hand — Kahlil Gibran, *The Madman*

There is reason to believe that a society that sees people as
mentally ill, calls them mentally ill and treats them as mentally
ill aggravates *by* those acts the condition it calls mental illness.

People in a group label behaviour which breaks rules of the
group as bad, criminal, malicious, sinful, selfish, immature,
foolish, idiotic, ignorant, and so on. They develop criteria to
judge which behaviour breaks rules and how to label it. They
cannot apply any of these labels to the behaviour of some individuals who persistently break rules. Men in other times and
places ascribed this behaviour to witchcraft, spirit-possession, or
demons. Today men in the industrial nations of the world see
the same behaviour as symptoms of mental illness.

Men in western society have created norms to define which
items in the cosmos must be seen as real or unreal and as inner
or outer. If a man sees as real what they say he should see as
unreal or vice versa, or as inner what they say he should see as
outer or vice versa, and if he argues the validity of his view by a
style of argument which they consider abnormal or does not
argue it at all, they are likely to see him as mentally ill. Western
society appoints psychiatrists as experts to examine some of its

members who break rules to discern if they break those rules for which they can be called mentally ill.

The tradition of scientific medicine teaches a doctor to keep distinct his moral attitude towards diseased persons from his non-moral objective attitude towards their diseases. But the moral views of western society define for a psychiatrist what persons he may diagnose as mentally ill and whom he may treat. A psychiatrist, especially if he works in a mental hospital, is concerned with surveying morals and mediating rules. He must deny this if he wishes to believe that he adheres to the principles of scientific medicine. Although he sees 'pathology' in behaviour which breaks rules, *because* it breaks rules, he does not say so, and usually does not even say that he considers it to break rules. If he works in a mental hospital he imposes rules on patients, rewards obedience and punishes disobedience, and calls these activities treatment. In the more advanced mental hospitals he tutors patients to think, feel and act 'appropriately', and calls this 'therapy'. These manoeuvres confuse many patients and induce them to respond in unusual ways, which the psychiatrist may see as more evidence of their 'mental illness'.

Many mental patients have always understood this situation; now some social scientists, psychologists, and psychiatrists do. Drs Ronald D. Laing, Aaron Esterson, and David Cooper are psychiatrists in England who saw the need to create alternatives to the traditional mental ward. David Cooper (1967) led people on a ward in a mental hospital near London to question their premises and to change many customary practices. Laing, Esterson, and Cooper formed an association that affiliated with several self-governing households in London where people, most of whom had previously been diagnosed as mentally ill, have lived outside the mental-hospital system. These have been more like hippie communes than like the most liberal mental-hospital wards. I shall describe Kingsley Hall, the largest of them, after explaining the rationale for their existence.

Mental Hospitals

Present-day western men presume that their cultural forebears became enlightened around the end of the eighteenth century to a truth to which men had been blind for too long: that madmen are sick men. The modern experience of madness has been governed by the conviction of 'sane' people that madness is really an illness and by their belief that this truth has been firmly proven by advances in scientific knowledge. They have converted the asylums into medical spaces where doctors have assumed the dominant roles. The doctors have based their powers on the presumption that they have scientific understanding of the inmates. This has been a disguise and a pretension, says Michel Foucault (1965), a French philosopher and psychologist. Psychiatric practice in the mental hospitals has been a *moral* tactic, cloaked with the dignity of scientific truth. The asylum, as set up by the doctors, has been from the beginning, Foucault says:

... a structure that formed a kind of microcosm in which were symbolized the massive structures of bourgeois society and its values: Family-Child relations, centred on the theme of paternal authority; Transgression-Punishment relations, centred on the theme of immediate justice; Madness-Disorder relations, centred on the theme of social and moral order. It is from these that the doctor derives his power to cure ... [p. 274].

Philippe Pinel was a doctor whom historians of psychiatry regard as the father of the modern mental hospital, and whom apologists for the *status quo* call the 'liberator of the insane'. In *A Treatise on Insanity* (1806) he suggested how to 'treat' the 'maniac, who under the influence of the most extravagant fury shall be guilty of every extravagance, both of language and action'.

... no more coercion is employed than what is dictated by attention to personal safety. For this purpose the strait-waistcoat will be generally found amply sufficient. Every case of irritation, real or imaginary, is to be carefully avoided. *Improper application for personal liberty, or any other favour* must be received with acquiescence, taken graciously into consideration, and withheld under some plausible pretext, or post-poned to a more convenient opportunity. The utmost vigilance of the *domestic police* will be necessary to engage the exertions of every maniac, especially during his lucid intervals, in some employment, laborious or otherwise, calculated to employ his thoughts and atten-tion. [p. 87; italics added.]

Although he recommended the use of baths and 'pharma-ceutical formulae' like 'antispasmodics' to calm the 'tumult' of mental patients, he said that the fundamental treatment is *'exclusively moral'* (p. 38).

The extreme importance which I attach to the maintenance of *order* and *moderation* in lunatic institutions, and consequently to the physical and moral qualities requisite to be possessed by their gover-nors, is by no means to be wondered at, since it is a fundamental prin-ciple in the treatment of mania to watch over the impetuosities of passion, and to order such arrangement of police and moral treat-ment as are favourable to that degree of excitement which experience approves as conducive to recovery. [p. 99; italics added.]

He said:

The doctrine in ethics of balancing the passions of men by others of equal or superior force, is not less applicable to the practice of medi-cine, than to the science of *politics*, and is probably not the only point of resemblance between the art of *governing* mankind and that of healing their diseases. [p. 228; italics added.]

'The Importance of an Enlightened System of Police for the Internal Management of Lunatic Asylums' is the title of one of the six sections of this book.

The principles of treatment have not changed since Pinel, but the techniques have become more sophisticated. Tranquillizing drugs, electro-convulsive shock and insulin coma maintain 'order' and 'moderation' more effectively than the strait-jackets and antispasmodics did, and psychotherapy and therapeutic-community meetings are more likely to persuade patients to conform than was the moral instruction of the governors of lunatic asylums. The treatment that hospital psychiatrists give is still exclusively moral. Unlike Pinel, they do not say that it is.

Mental hospitals like prisons confine deviant persons, but

they confuse their inmates more, since they do not tell them what rules they have broken, nor even that they have broken rules. The psychiatrist in the mental hospital tries to persuade *himself*, his colleagues in the medical profession, the staff, the patients, the patients' families and friends, and society that he practises medicine, and denies to himself and all others that any persuasion occurs or is even necessary. To frame his activities within a medical model he calls a trial, 'examination'; a judgement, 'diagnosis'; a sentence, 'disposition'; and correction, 'treatment'. If his patients claim they are not ill they challenge his pretensions.

One must admire the ingenuity with which he copes with this contingency. He presumes that a basic 'symptom' of the 'mentally-ill' patient is his failure to know that he is ill. When the patient disagrees with the doctor who says he is ill, the doctor does not tell him that he should not disagree, but that he does not *know* what he is saying, and that he does not, *because* he is ill. He hears the patient's statement that he is not ill as evidence that he is too ill to realize that he is ill, and he tells him so. If a patient feels healthy despite being told by his doctor that he is not, and says so, the doctor may tell him that he is not motivated to regain his health.

The psychiatrist outwits by another twist a person who pretends that he is mentally ill to manoeuvre a social situation for personal gain. The psychiatrist who suspects a person of this 'diagnoses' him to suffer from the 'syndrome' of feigning illness which he considers to be a sickness with a poor prognosis (Ganser's Syndrome). If a man knows what is going on, but pretends that he does not, and knows that he is pretending, the psychiatrist may see him as a man who thinks he knows he is pretending, but as really not pretending, and as pretending to pretend.

Bert Kaplan, an American psychologist, says in his introduction to *The Inner World of Mental Illness* (1964), 'a series of first-person accounts of what it was like' to be 'mentally ill',

One of the salient features of the psychopathologies that are described in this book is that they are opposed to a normality which is intimately related to the major value orientations of western society. It may be asserted therefore that abnormality [psychosis] involves a negative relationship to prevailing social normative prescriptions – perhaps the most extreme and complete form of negation that is possible. This is more than an abstract and logical conclusion. In the jargon of the moment we may call this 'alienation'. In this association of abnormality with a refusal to be bound by things as they are and with the striving to be different, we have what is at bottom a concern with the category of change and transcendence. [p. xi.]

The same is so for many of the 'mentally ill' who have not published their ideas. The disease spins off a runaway feedback loop: those who negate the prevailing social norms are negated by those who uphold them, and the upholders are negated in their negations of the negators by the negators ... not *ad infinitum* but *ad* the ascription of 'mental illness' by the upholders upon the opposers.

When Jeremiah broke an earthen vessel in the Temple courtyard to pronounce and predict the destruction of Jerusalem, the Temple police seized him, beat him, and punished him publicly by putting him in the stocks. They did not, as far as we know, suspect him of mental illness. Recently a young man in the NATO military forces, with a position in a chain of command to push a nuclear-missile 'button', decided to refuse to obey orders related to his job. He told his superiors they should not command any man to do such a job. He was diagnosed as schizophrenic and was hospitalized.

All that is certain about mental illness is that some people assert that other people have it. Epistemologically, mental illness has the status of an explanatory concept or a working hypothesis. No one has proven it to exist as a thing nor has anyone described its attributes with scientific precision and reliability.

Since mental hospitals regulate the behaviour and the biochemistry of their inmates to a degree unequalled elsewhere in the 'free world', patients rebel and resist.* Official psychiatry

* Although many inmates of mental hospitals are there because they deviate from social norms in the way they think, feel, and act, mental hospitals insist they conform to a set of rules that permit a narrower spectrum of thoughts, feelings, and acts than society outside does.

trains the young psychiatrist not to see what is in front of his face when it teaches him to class patients' attempts to protest against their situation as signs and symptoms of illness. He learns to label patients as 'ill' with 'personality disorders' if they make problems for *others* by defying the authority of the hospital or of society. He is taught to see those who openly challenge the rules of others as sick with an 'illness' called 'psychopathy' or 'sociopathy', and those who inhibit their challenge due to a fear of the consequences as 'sick' with 'passive-aggressive personality disorders'. He treats the victims of these 'diseases' with drugs and may insist on bedrest too. He learns to see 'acting-out', 'agitation', 'excitement', and 'withdrawal' as 'symptoms' which disturb his patients and not to see that they may be saying by this behaviour that *he* is disturbing them.

Some doctors in their first year of psychiatric training argue at staff meetings that their patients' responses to their situation in the hospital are valid. I have heard their teachers tell them that they have not yet 'worked through' their own 'adolescent personality crises'.

What I describe here is a special case of what Wittgenstein (1958) called the 'bewitchment of our intelligence by means of language' (p. 47). 'A picture held us captive and we could not get outside it, for it lay in our language and language seemed to repeat it to us inexorably' (p. 48).

Laing says (1971),

> The concept of schizophrenia is a straitjacket that restricts psychiatrists and patients. By taking off this straitjacket we can see what happens. It has been shown, in the field of ethology, that observations on the behaviour of animals in captivity tell us *nothing reliable* about their behaviour in their natural setting. The whole of our present civilization may be a captivity. But the observations upon which psychiatrists and psychologists have drawn in order to build up the prevailing picture of schizophrenia have, almost entirely, been made on human beings in double or even treble captivity [pp. 57–8].

The power to confine people in mental hospitals, involuntarily if necessary, deprive them of civil liberties, define their limits of legal redress, and award to their medical governors licence to formulate and execute rules to regulate their management and treatment derives from the State and is guaranteed by the Law. The confinement of the mentally ill must serve a basic homeostatic function to sustain the social and political order in western society, since so many people are confined and so many work to confine them.*

Here is a schematic version of an actual story. Matthew, aged twenty-three, is from a devout Christian family. When he was twelve his father died; since thirteen he has slept in the same bed as his mother, at her request, because she has feared to sleep alone. He meets a woman of his own age whom he likes and whom he kisses one evening. That night 'vampires' attack him in his sleep. When the nightmares continue, his mother takes him to a G.P. who tells her he shows early signs of mental illness and suggests he go into a hospital before his 'disease' progresses further.

He enters a mental hospital as an in-patient. He says to his psychiatrist the next day, 'Please help me. You are a messenger from God. You will decide my fate: whether I will go to heaven or hell. Do I have any power to influence you? If I confess that I have masturbated, will I help my chances with God or hurt them?' The psychiatrist thinks Matthew is being 'grandiose' and 'overideational', and *therefore* diagnoses him as a paranoid schizophrenic – grandiosity and overideation are 'symptoms' of paranoid schizophrenia. The staff think the 'disease' is due mainly to an inherited constitutional biochemical defect. They believe the 'illness' appears now because the sexual excitement stressed his delicate state. They do not implicate his mother's feelings and behaviour towards him, or his towards her, as pertinent to understanding his 'illness'. They see his mother as nervous about his health but they dismiss this observation as irrelevant. Besides, how can they blame her for her concern, especially since her husband has died from an illness? The

---

* Edwin Lemert, an American sociologist, has observed that when people excommunicate others they develop and perpetuate false beliefs about them. He feels this process plays an important part in the social life of human groups.

hospital is a good place for Matthew: he will have a chance to rest because the rules forbid all sexual contact.

The psychiatrist treats him with a common tranquillizing drug which is thought to have an anti-schizophrenia action. As the dose is raised progressively he develops a new 'symptom': he says he is being poisoned. The common side-effects of this drug occur at the same time: dry mouth, nasal congestion, blurred vision, constipation, drowsiness, stiffness of the muscles of the mouth, and occasional dizziness. The staff realize that the drug is responsible for these effects. Since the doctor has diagnosed him as a paranoid schizophrenic they see his belief that he is being poisoned as a 'progression' of his 'disease', which is occurring *despite* the efficacy of the drug.

The doctor raises the dosage of the drug. Matthew now shows the effects of high dosage: a pill-rolling tremor of both hands, mask-like rigidity of his facial muscles, a stooped posture, and short quick steps when he walks. He reveals to an attendant on the ward that he has phoned the municipal health department to complain that the hospital poisons its inmates, and that he has done this to protect others. He frequently says that he is frightened. The staff now believe his 'disease-process' is worsening.

The doctor adds a second tranquillizing drug, administered by injection. Matthew develops a rash over a large part of his body. He says that the doctors are 'in league with the Devil' to arrange that he burns in Hell for his sins, and that he would 'rather die than suffer eternal damnation'.

The staff see him as 'deteriorating' rapidly despite the best modern treatment. They see his 'illness' as *'unresponsive'* to drug therapy. The doctor orders electro-convulsive shock therapy. Patients often experience this therapy as an assault and always suffer some memory loss, after it. The doctor knows this but he wishes to help Matthew before it is too late.

The staff do not see Matthew's behaviour as a consequence of his experience of *their* behaviour towards him. Here is an outline of some transactions between him and them in which I infer his experience of his situation, and interpret his behaviour as an attempt to cope with *their* behaviour.

Matthew sees that the psychiatrist in his relations with patients is in the role of a powerful master in control of charges. Matthew also sees that the psychiatrist does not see himself as being in this role, but as a doctor treating sick patients, too sick to know what is best for them. Matthew fears the doctor's power, but fears that if he tells him so, he will offend the doctor. A nurse tells Matthew that patients, in order to help themselves, should tell the doctor their important thoughts. What should Matthew do? He fears telling the doctor the truth, but also fearing to disobey the nurse's advice, he fears lying or saying nothing to the doctor. He cannot leave the hospital: the nurse has told him he is ill and belongs there. Also, although he entered the hospital voluntarily, the psychiatrist can confine him involuntarily. Trapped in a perfect double bind, Matthew tells the doctor: 'Please help me. You are God's messenger. You will decide my fate: whether I will go to heaven or hell,' *et seq*. In this way he tells the doctor the truth about how he feels towards him, but in metaphor, thus partially masking his true feelings. His religious upbringing colours the content of what he says; his dilemma imposes the *necessity* to speak in metaphor. He does not realize that these statements lead his doctor to diagnose him as a paranoid schizophrenic.

Although staff 'treat' a patient by frequently telling him that he is 'sick', they usually do not tell him his diagnosis. Nor do the staff tell a patient which data his doctor thinks are pertinent to the diagnosis, or how, or why he thinks the data are pertinent. If a patient asks to know this information, to which all the staff have access, they generally reply evasively.

Matthew is not sure why his doctor has ordered a drug for him. When he asks a nurse why, she tells him he is ill and that the drug will make him feel better. He tells the staff that this cannot be the right drug for him since he had felt well before he took it and now feels ill. His doctor says that the fact that he had felt well before he was given the drug does not prove that he had not been ill then, since mentally-ill patients often do not realize they are ill. The nurses tell him at a ward meeting that he should trust his doctor, since the doctor is trained in this field and he is not, and that mistrust is a symptom of mental illness. He feels confused. He mistrusts those who tell him he was ill when he felt well and that the drug they give him can help him to feel better when it makes him feel ill. He mistrusts them more when they tell him he is ill if he mistrusts them. How can he influence the doctor to change his treatment and conceal that he mistrusts the treatment? He says he is being poisoned. In this way he both conceals and reveals his mistrust. Since he does not know the doctor has diagnosed him as a paranoid schizophrenic and has ordered the drug to treat this disease, he does not realize that by saying he is being poisoned he brings about what he most fears: an increase in drug dosage.

I leave it to the reader to complete the analysis of the story from here to the doctor's decision to administer electro-shock therapy.

I have heard many ex mental-patients tell me of experiences in mental hospitals similar in *structure* to my inferences about this man's experience. I read this story to seven of them; they all confirmed that they had found themselves in predicaments like this one, with which they had found it difficult to cope in a sane way. Mental hospitals entangle all their patients in knots which are so constructed that the patients' struggles to untie them tighten the knots.

The staff's practice of translating interpersonal events within the hospital into terms of medical model bewilders the inmates, many of whom are befuddled already before coming to the hospital. Erving Goffman, the American sociologist who studied the social world inside a large American mental hospital, says (1961):

... whatever else these institutions do, one of their central effects is to sustain the self-conception of the professional staff employed there. Inmates and lower staff levels are involved in a vast supportive action – an elaborate dramatized tribute – that has the effect, if not the purpose, of affirming that a medical-like service is in progress here and that the psychiatric staff is providing it. Something about the weakness of this claim is suggested by the industry required to support it ...

Mental patients can find themselves in a special bind. To get out of the hospital, or to ease their life within it. They must show acceptance of the place accorded them, and the place accorded them is to support the occupational role of those who appear to force this bargain. This *self-alienating moral servitude*, which perhaps helps to account for some inmates becoming *mentally confused*, is achieved by invoking the great tradition of the expert servicing relation, especially its medical variety. [pp. 385–6; italics added.]

The mental hospital confronts hapless wayfarers, gives them conundrums to solve, and punishes them dreadfully if they fall. Shall we not find alternatives to this modern Sphinx before it destroys the unwary among us too?

The Anti-Psychiatry Ward

Dr David Cooper in 1962 began to de-hierarchize one ward within a large mental hospital near London. He wished to 'allow a greater degree of freedom of movement out of the highly artificial staff and patient roles imposed on people by conventional psychiatry'. He called his project an 'experiment in anti-psychiatry'. (For an account of this experiment, see Cooper, 1967, pp. 83–104.)

The staff abolished role-bound behaviour such as organizing patients into activity, supervising their domestic work on the ward and treating them. An 'anti-rule' was set up that patients decide their own leave period, attendance at meetings, and getting out of bed. In response to external administrative pressure, the ward staff partially restored their own role-bound behaviour.

David Cooper sees the result of his 'experiment' to be that 'the limits of institutional change are found to be very closely drawn indeed – even in a progressive mental hospital'. He suggests that 'a step forward means ultimately a step out of the mental hospital into the community' (ibid., p. 104).

Kingsley Hall*

'Kingsley Hall' is the name of a building in the East End of London. It was built about sixty years ago. It is three floors in

* I lived at Kingsley Hall for a year. This description is derived mostly from that experience. I am grateful to the people who lived there when I did and to the sponsors of that project for making my experience possible. I also draw on the experiences of people who lived in the community before me, especially Drs Joseph Berke, R. D. Laing, Jerome Liss, and Leon Redler. The views which I express here are my own, and no one else can be considered responsible for them.

height. About thirteen people can live there comfortably, each with their own room. A large ground-floor hall, a games room, a dining room, a meeting room, two kitchens, and three other rooms – used by the occupants as a meditation room, a chapel, and a dark-room for photography – comprise the common rooms. The roof is open and has a garden.

The building had been used in the past as a community centre for meetings of various kinds, and as a settlement house. It has also served as a place of worship. Mahatma Gandhi stayed at Kingsley Hall when he visited London in 1931.

The community I describe here began in June 1965 and has included over one hundred individuals.* The people in the household have made the rules that govern their life together. The household has comprised a major social experiment.

Lectures in psychiatry, anti-psychiatry, and phenomenology, and seminars and meetings with professional people in many fields have occurred at Kingsley Hall. The community has been a link in a chain of 'counter-culture' centres. Experimental drama groups, social scientists of the New Left, classes from the Antiuniversity of London, leaders of the commune movement, and *avant-garde* poets, artists, musicians, dancers and photographers, have met at Kingsley Hall with the residents. The Free School of London met there for the first time.

The founder-members of the project at Kingsley Hall hoped to fulfil in the community their seed-idea that lost souls may be cured by going mad among people who see madness as a chance to die and be reborn. Laing says in *The Politics of Experience* (1967):

No age in the history of humanity has perhaps so lost touch with this natural *healing* process, that implicates *some* of the people whom we label schizophrenic. No age has so devalued it, no age has imposed such prohibitions and deterrences against it, as our own. Instead of the mental hospital, a sort of re-servicing factory for human breakdowns, we need a place where people who have travelled further, and consequently, may be more lost than psychiatrists and other sane

* From 1 June 1965 to November 1968 one hundred and nine people lived in Kingsley Hall for periods of three days or more.

people, can find their way *further* into inner space and time, and back again. Instead of the *degradation* ceremonial of psychiatric examination, diagnosis and prognostication, we need, for those who are ready for it (in psychiatric terminology often those who are about to go into a schizophrenic breakdown), an initiation ceremonial, through which the person will be guided with full social encouragement and sanction into inner space and time. Psychiatrically, this would appear as ex-patients helping future patients to go mad. [p. 105.]

When Freud returned to his patients' earliest memories (and his own) he found traumas that he saw had led them (and him) to repress regions of their (and his) being. He revealed feelings and energy that had been buried and 'bound' together with the forgotten memories of events that had occurred in childhood and infancy. Freud urged his patients to remember their pasts, and to recover their lost feelings, in order to make themselves whole again. He also said he knew of acts of men who had lived before recorded history that survived as 'unconscious' memories in the minds of all living human beings and influenced their behaviour. He did not urge his patients to go back to that time, long before their births, to cure themselves.

Human societies in diverse times and places have relied upon a method of 'psychotherapy' which western man has forgotten and suppressed: the return to Chaos. To cure himself 'archaic' and 'primitive' man goes back beyond the experience of his personal past, beyond the experiences of his ancestors, beyond history, beyond prehistory, beyond the time of this world to enter a mythical, eternal time that precedes all origins. He disintegrates, or is disintegrated, as a person who exists in historical, egoic time; he undergoes psychic chaos, which 'he' experiences as contemporaneous with the amorphous Being whose interior was ruptured by the cosmogony. His rebirth into existence repeats the creation of Cosmos out of Chaos.

Several 'returns' of this sort have occurred at Kingsley Hall. It is too early to know whether cures by this method are feasible in western culture, even among an enclave of people who will permit them to occur. The 'rebirth' of Mary Barnes may encourage those who wish to explore this further.

Mary Barnes is forty-five years old. She came to live at

Kingsley Hall in 1965. She has written an account for me of her experiences; here are some excerpts.

From the age of seventeen years until the time of forty-two years when I came here my time was spent mainly in hospitals. One year was in a mental hospital as a patient. All the rest of the time was on the 'staff side' of several hospitals. I was a Sister, later a Tutor. Kingsley Hall is where I have experienced real healing ... Through the experience of a schizophrenic breakdown twelve years before I came here, I knew what I wanted: to go down, *back to before I was born* and to come up again.

She felt she needed to return to the point where she had taken a wrong turn, and to come back again by another path.

In the mental hospital I had got stuck in my madness. Mostly I was in the pads [padded cell] ... No one knew why – least of all me.

She got out of the hospital and 'somehow I kept out of hospitals as a patient'. Eventually, she came to R. D. Laing. He told her he was looking for a place where it would be possible for her to live through the experiences she sought, but he did not know when he would find one. She chose to 'hold on' until he did. Nineteen months passed before Kingsley Hall became available; she held on during that time. After moving into Kingsley Hall she began to go a long way back.

At first so great was my fear I forgot what I had come for ... Quite suddenly I remembered, 'I've come here to have a breakdown, to go back to before I was born and come up again.'

For several weeks she continued to work at her job at a hospital, which was an hour away. She worked during the day and 'regressed' at Kingsley Hall in the evening. Then she wrote a letter of resignation to the hospital.

Life soon became quite fantastic. Every night at Kingsley Hall I tore off my clothes, feeling I had to be naked. Lay on the floor with my shits and water, smeared the walls with faeces. Was wild and noisy about the house or sitting in a heap on the kitchen floor. Half-aware that I was going mad, there was the terror that I might not know what I was doing, away, outside of Kingsley Hall.

Her resignation at the hospital was accepted.

The tempo was increasing. Down, down, oh God, would I never break.

The others found it difficult to live with her when she smeared faeces on her body and on the walls of her room. Her room was next to the kitchen and the odour diffused through the wall. Should they permit her to do this? Does a person have a right to a 'smell space' that extends beyond the four walls of his or her room?

She stopped eating solid foods and had to be fed milk from a bottle. People took turns feeding her. She stopped talking and lay still in bed for long periods.

In bed I kept my eyes shut so I didn't see people but I heard them... Touch was all important... Sometimes my body had seemed apart, a leg or an arm across the room. The wall became hollow and I seemed to go into it as into a big hole. Vividly aware of people, I was physically isolated in my room, my womb...

That was three years ago.

Eventually, I 'came up' – was 'reborn'. I wanted new clothes, nothing black, the colour I used to wear... I was coming out of the web, working free. Coming to know I was a separate, distinct person.

She has 'come up' again in the views of those who know her. When she was 'down' she began to paint, which she had never done before 1965. To make her first paintings she smeared faeces with her fingers on the walls of her room. Since 1967 she has painted with oils on canvases although she still uses her fingers. She has sold many paintings and has had public exhibitions. She also has written some poems and short stories. Here is a story which she wrote called *The Hollow Tree*.

There was once a tree in the forest who felt very sad and lonely for her trunk was hollow and her head was lost in mist.
Sometimes the mist seemed so thick that her head felt divided from her trunk.
To the other trees, she appeared quite strong, but rather aloof, for no wind ever sent her branches to them.

She felt if she bent she would break, yet she grew so tired of standing straight.

So it was with relief that in a mighty storm she was thrown to the ground. The tree was split, her branches scattered, her roots torn up, and her bark was charred and blackened. She felt stunned, and though her head was clear of the mist, she felt her sap dry as she felt her deadness revealed when the hollow of her trunk was open to the sky.

The other trees looked down and gasped, and didn't quite know whether to turn their branches politely away or whether to try to cover her emptiness and blackness with their green and brown.

The tree moaned for her own life and feared to be suffocated by theirs. She felt she wanted to lay bare and open to the wind, and the rain, and the sun, and that in time she would grow up again, full and brown, from the ground.

So it was that with the wetness of the rain she put down new roots, and by the warmth of the sun she stretched forth new wood.

In the wind her branches bent to other trees, and as their leaves rustled and whispered in the dark, and in the light, the tree felt loved, and laughed with life.

Not everyone who lives at Kingsley Hall desires or *needs* to undergo an experiential drama of this magnitude. Many wish to be free from the well-intentioned misguided harassment of their families or mental hospitals or both. They want to live in a haven where they can simply be, or be *tzu-jan*, translated as 'of itself so', 'spontaneously', 'expanding from within'.

To discover the intelligibility of a social situation one must undergo an experience that is constitutive and regulative of it and that is constituted and regulated by the experiences of each of the others in the situation. Information about the *experience* of living at Kingsley Hall is revealed only to observers living within the building. I asked my fellow-residents at Kingsley Hall to discuss with me their experiences there. Here is what four people said to me.*

* In December 1968 I told each person living in the building that I planned to write about Kingsley Hall and that I wished to include his or her view of his experience there. Everyone talked about his experience to me, alone. I wrote down what each person said verbatim. I chose to present these excerpts because they represent views that are generally shared.

1. My first experience at Kingsley Hall was that I was taking a role very different from any other role I'd ever taken: instead of being always looking at other people ... um ... like father figures ... I think I was mainly in the position where I was told what to do and somehow expected this ... looking for some sort of guidance, I suppose. And then initially when I came here *I* seemed to be the one who was arranging things and making decisions — arranging things and taking quite an active part. . .

I think one of the best things here is that one *doesn't have to be right.* . . Being here, anything goes — sort of. I think of a word — an 'acceptance' of people as they are which I've never found anywhere else. . . Here one can make a kind of contact — a kind of understanding — it's easy to make some sort of contact without words, whereas outside one is limited to making certain sorts of sentences. There is something very unique about it. . . You're not bogged down by conventionalities of having to be polite or make statements which are regarded as conventional forms of politeness, things like: 'Come and sit by the fire' and 'Have you had a good day?' and the other person is expected to go through what sort of a day he's had. . . Here people don't do that. One feels under no obligation to do that. I think it's more honest. People aren't afraid if they don't particularly like the person — they're not afraid not to be friendly.

*　　　*　　　*

2. You have to decide here what you want to do because no one is around to tell you what you should be doing. Like most places I've been in there was always a reason I had to go out — or go to lectures at the university. If I didn't, someone would drag me out or say, 'Are you ill?' Now, no one is telling me I ought to come out and be mixing with people. I can decide if I want to leave my room. There is no external structure, or authority, or formality to fall back on to decide if you ought to do something — it's really up to you. . .

There are little things for me like playing the piano. I'm very unmusical. I can't play an instrument. I've never played an instrument I didn't know in front of anyone. I find here I can do this: bash around and make noise. I don't feel absurd. I can dance too. I never could dance in front of people before. Here, it's just O.K. And also, for the first time since childhood, maybe in my life, I can really play with another person. . .

*　　　*　　　*

3. The main thing about my family and mental hospitals as opposed

Madness and Morals 221

to Kingsley Hall is that here a number of divergent people come together to meet and to try to live out a life with one another where
they can live out their differences – have rows, disagree intently, decide
to do things in ways that will offend others – and still for them to be
tolerated, and for people doing this gradually to become aware of
other people and their inter-effects upon one another. I'm convinced
this *doesn't happen in a mental hospital*: I know it doesn't.

There, in mental hospitals, it's very difficult to relate to people at
all in any sense other than the part they want you to play – so you've
got to learn what rules they want you to carry out in their scheme of
things: whereas here you find various people and you can open up
to them and talk, and relate, and build up understanding. Not where
one person tells another what he should want, how he should dress
and eat. . . One of the things between Kingsley Hall – between a free
situation – and a bound situation is that here a person can do something and isn't made to conform his behaviour in relation to a model
of what others think is right and wrong.

*   *   *

4. One becomes here increasingly sensitive to the importance to
people who maintain those very deluded mystiques of where it's at –
who keep cheating themselves. When I'd be at home it would seem
quite important that the table would be set in a certain way and that
one ate one's sweet with a fork – and how in all those little things
the justification is claimed to be just solely: that this form of behaviour is right because it exists. . .

I was always taught that work was a 'good thing' because it was,
just because it was work – and 'everybody worked, didn't they?' I feel
that it is of course necessary to do work of some kind in order to keep
myself alive. However, I don't believe any more in the very complicated mystique surrounding the necessity for work – I mean point-
less and unfulfilling work – which has nothing to do with this fundamental physical necessity.

I've discovered this here because here I find that many people question things with a greater honesty. People with obvious honesty question many things that one has been taking to be unconditionally true
and valid. . . I feel that this very situation which makes *retreat from
social reality* – well, external reality – possible, in fact eventually,
paradoxically, makes facing *reality in general* almost *unavoidable*.

*

The people who live near Kingsley Hall never let those who live

inside the building forget that the inside is inside an outside that
has a different view of what is True and what is Real, where
the source of Light is, and who is in Exile and who is in the
Kingdom. At half-past eleven one Friday night, four men who
had been drinking in a nearby pub broke into the building and
shouted that we were 'looneys', 'drug addicts', 'lay-abouts', and
'perverts', who 'stank' and were 'desecrating' a community shrine
by our 'foul' behaviour. A lady in a nearby shop called us 'a
bunch of nutters and homosexuals'. The neighbourhood children
continued the eighteenth-century French custom of weekend
visits to the lunatic asylum to view the inmates: they frequently
entered the building by self-invitation just to look around and
giggle. Boys broke with stones the windows facing the street so
many times that we decided to freeze one winter rather than
spend money to repair them again. Children unscrewed the
front-door bell, smashed the front door with an axe, and several
times put dogs' faeces on the floor of the ground-floor hall.

The disagreement between the people who live in the building and those who do not is about morals. All people decide
which thoughts, feelings, acts, persons, and groups of persons
to call right or wrong, good or bad, clean or dirty, true or false,
real or unreal, sane or insane, and so on. Western society inter-
rogates people or groups of people to learn if they assign to
particular thoughts, feelings, acts, persons, and groups of persons
the labels it believes they ought to. Those who live at Kingsley
Hall often do not apply the labels 'correctly' and know it. If
people in western society do not, do they have a right to live
outside a mental hospital? Those who live at Kingsley Hall
affirm that they do. Not all who live outside the building agree.

When residents behave in ways that are considered strange,
they alarm some people outside the building. A man, aged
twenty-eight, who lived at Kingsley Hall, would walk into
neighbourhood pubs and coffee shops and, without saying a
word to anyone, would pick up glasses from tables or counters,
drink the contents and walk out. If a door to a house was left
open he would enter and sit on a chair in the drawing-room until
someone of the house would see him. Then he would get up
and walk out quietly. He never said anything to threaten anyone

and he never touched anyone, but he unnerved people. People would approach him in the street to offer the unsolicited advice that he would 'feel better' if he were in a mental hospital. One resident kept people in the house next door awake at night by playing his record player as loudly as he could. He was experiencing his body as 'numb' and found he could give it 'life' if he played music loudly. He did not wish to disturb anyone; when those whom he disturbed complained, he stopped, and apologized.

The residents of Kingsley Hall have tried several times to begin a dialogue with people in the neighbourhood. We have felt that the children when they harassed us were refracting upon us their parents' fears and resentments of us. Once, the people at Kingsley Hall invited several hundred people in the neighbourhood to a tea to discuss with them why they lived together and to answer any questions. Only about twelve people showed up and by the time they left they still did not seem to have grasped the purpose of the community.

Some neighbourhood groups, for instance an 'Old People's' group and a boys' club, which had been meeting previously in the large ground-floor hall, continued to meet there. One of the residents sometimes played his guitar and sang to the 'Old People'. When I lived there we let the hall one afternoon a week for a few shillings to a ballet class of about twenty girls and their teacher. These services by the community created more *rapport* with people who lived outside than any teach-ins would have, but the children never ceased their hostilities.

People who live, work, or play together make rules to govern which parts of one's body one may bring into contiguity with which parts of the bodies of others. To know which rule applies in a specific case one must know the sex of the persons, their age, their marital status, their feelings towards each other, whether each has consented, whether those who are nearest and dearest to them have consented, how visible to others is the relation, and so on. People forbid each other to talk about some of these rules and even to know that they exist, although they punish those who break them. No mental-hospital ward permits a male psychiatrist to insert his penis into the anus of a male patient, although I doubt whether many people in mental hospitals are aware of such a rule or mention it ever at therapeutic-community meetings. Talk about the existence of such a rule would, I believe, be against the rules of mental hospitals, and talk about these latter rules would violate some other set of rules that are never talked about. 'It' may be what some male patients want most although they may be 'treated' if they say so. 'It' never occurs, and no one thinks much about why it does not, because it is unthinkable in a mental hospital to consider the topic as one about which one might think.

At Kingsley Hall no rule prevents the discovery of any secret rules, which may be forbidding some sexual acts and permitting others. No rule stops anyone from saying: 'We in the building are behaving *as if* there were a regulation that prohibited all A people from doing x, y, or z with all B people. Why are we?' This is important, since studies of families of schizophrenics show that these families confuse their children by making rules that forbid the awareness of other rules. The parents of schizophrenics punish their children when they disobey the first-order rules of the family, and when they show that they know they exist – a knowledge which violates rules of the second-order.

The rules of Kingsley Hall force no one to work to earn money if he does not wish to, nor do they oblige anyone not to work. Everyone pays rent-money into a communal fund. A person's ability to pay and the solvency of the 'cash-box' determine the amount one pays. The community uses the money in the communal fund to pay for food, heating, electricity, repairs and maintenance of all the rooms in the building, and any other items which they choose to buy. People can, and do, 'turn night into day' and do not get out of bed at all if they do not wish to. A resident who tried to compel another resident to do anything for what he presumed to be the other's good would violate the rules of the group.

If someone wishes to live at Kingsley Hall he must meet some or all of the residents first. Sometimes they invite him to stay for an evening meal or a weekend. The residents ask those people to join the community whom they like or whom they feel would benefit at Kingsley Hall or both. The residents con-

sider it best for a balance to exist between those who are free
to deal with ordinary social and economic needs – to shop for
food, wash dishes, scrub floors, clean toilets, stoke the furnace,
repair broken fuses, and pay the bills – and those who cannot or
choose not to be, and wish to work upon themselves. The men
who seek the priceless Pearl in the depths of the ocean may
drown if no one is topside to monitor their oxygen supply. They
need others to look after their physical requirements.

No one who lives at Kingsley Hall sees those who perform
work upon the external material world as 'staff', and those who
do not as 'patients'. No caste system forbids people to move
freely from one sub-group to another, as it does in mental
hospitals. No locus of institutional power subordinates everyone, by an inert sovereign right, to a command-obedience structure that forces those at the 'top' to force those they command
to force others, to force others, etc., to limit the freedom of those
at the 'bottom' for whose limitation of freedom the institution
exists. No organization, no ossified apparatus, imposes upon anyone the need to administrate others: to distribute communal
tasks, to allocate responsibilities, and to make rules. Each person
at Kingsley Hall may choose to assume the obligations of a
reciprocal bond with another person, or other people, or the
group. He pledges to do so or dissolves his pledge by an initiative that originates in his own interior.

Some visitors are curious to know which of the residents had
been labelled 'schizophrenic' by hospital psychiatrists before
they came to live at Kingsley Hall, and which of the residents
had previously worked as staff at mental hospitals as psychiatrists, nurses, or social workers. Their wrong guesses can be
amusing. Guests, in staff positions at mental hospitals, sometimes suppose that those who had previously been labelled
'schizophrenic' are really doctors and nurses, and vice versa.

Where is the machinery for decision-making? How are issues
discussed, clarified, classified? How are agreements reached and
implemented? The community answers these questions differently at different times. Gatherings are most frequent at meals
around the table or wherever people sit when they eat. People
sometimes bring up issues at dinner. An issue might be that

nothing 'important' is being discussed. Matters of the life and death of the soul are more 'important' than whether anyone shops, cooks, or cleans, but someone must do these things. Who? But why should anyone live at Kingsley Hall if 'only' to concern himself about things like that? People sometimes agree to meet at regular intervals, at set times, just to share what they have on their minds. But can a genuine meeting be scheduled? The most common occasion for a meeting is when some people feel the need to come together to talk about a specific matter.

*

When I came to live at Kingsley Hall, several people were meditating together daily from 6 to 7 a.m. Later, some of us gathered for a couple of hours early each morning to discuss our dreams of the night before. We asked each other: 'Do different people weave their dreams out of "day-residues" that derive from the same events? Do we live out with each other during the day our dreams of the night before? Or of the next night? Can we stop assigning to each other roles to play in our dream-scripts during the sleep we sleep when we suppose we are awake?' People symbolized Kingsley Hall in their dreams as a 'rocket-ship in space', a 'make-shift camp in an Israeli desert', a 'children's house', a 'chalet for skiers on a mountainside', a 'Jacob's ladder', and a 'Sinbad's roc'.

Situations that are permitted to unfold at Kingsley Hall would not be allowed to progress so far in other social contexts. Joseph, aged twenty, came to live at Kingsley Hall after three years in mental hospitals. He revealed that 'voices' were 'plotting' against him. 'They' were regarding his thoughts as bad, and 'they' were talking to each other about the need to condemn and punish him. He had to be careful, since 'they' were seeing his belief that they were plotting against him as a bad thought.

He was not sure if he was imagining the voices or if he was overhearing a real plot. If the voices were 'real' they must be using extraordinary means to discover his thoughts – how else could the voices know them? And they must be communicating with each other by unusual means – how else could he hear them and not see them? Maybe they were using 'aerial control'.

If so, where was their apparatus? He cut some of the electric wires in the building and disconnected the telephone receiver to see if that would stop the voices. He also broke into other residents' rooms to search for concealed communication apparatus.

One morning he told me that the night before he had experienced 'the most dreadful thing a human being could imagine'. A 'fire' had burned him to ashes and the pain had been unbearable.

In the next few days he began to knock on the door of girls' rooms in the building late at night to awaken them for a cigarette or to light his cigarette. During the day he would come to their windows and stare at them silently. He would also threaten to set fires and to burn down the building.

People met daily to discuss his behaviour. We invited him to the meetings, and sometimes he came. He always left after a few minutes to dash around the building because he suspected that the visible meeting was a decoy to distract his attention from the 'real' meeting held secretly elsewhere. Was it possible to talk about him without making true in a sense his belief that 'voices' were talking about him? Could we dissolve the 'plot' if he saw our efforts to dissolve it as part of the plot? We revealed *our* predicament to him. Did his behaviour serve some purpose for us? We were coming together more often to talk to each other because of him than we had been before. Had he elected himself to be our scapegoat, for *our* sake?

Once, while we met to talk about his behaviour and to decide what our limits of tolerance should be, he put his mattress on the roof and poured methylated spirits on it. He was going to set it on fire, but a resident saw him and stopped him. The roof is made of cement, so no fire he set there could have spread. Still, he had frightened us. He could set a fire that would spread when none of us were awake. He could endanger our life as a community if the neighbours or the police and fire departments learned we were allowing a man who had been threatening to set fires to live at large – out of jail or mental hospital.

What did his behaviour mean? Was it worth the nuisance or the risk to us to let him live with us while we tried to find out?

What would happen to him if we told him to leave? If we, who wished to understand him and to find a way to live with him, could not, could anyone? We chose to attempt a *modus vivendi* with him a little longer.

Sexual frustration might underlie some of his behaviour. His body had been 'on fire'. He intruded on girls while they slept to ask them to 'light' his 'cigarette'. He felt communication was going on inside other people's rooms from which he was excluded. He looked at girls through their windows. Perhaps his thoughts that the 'voices' were regarding as bad were sexual ones. We confronted him with a sexual translation of his behaviour. Girls told him that he had asked them to light his cigarettes because he lacked enough courage to ask them to make love. Men told him that he had not been able to douse the fire in his body, because he had felt forbidden to masturbate and fuck. His threats to set fires stopped. We revealed to him that he had put our patience to a severe test and that he had approached our threshold of tolerance. We found, by frequently confronting him with our feelings towards him, we could cool the intensity of the situation, though we could not eliminate it.

I am aware of clinical and juridical arguments in favour of imposing clear limits to forbid behaviour of this sort soon after it begins. I am also aware of how much everyone can learn that is new if difficult situations are allowed to unfold. There is no proof that the traditional and customary responses of people to rule-breaking are the most enlightened of all possible ways. Joseph said that he had never realized before coming to Kingsley Hall that people had sent him to mental hospital in the past because his behaviour frightened them. He had been too frightened himself, he said, to be free to see that he had frightened them, and they had not told it to him.

*

Another resident said to me:

Those who live here see Kingsley Hall each in his own way... In common to all who live here ... is a bafflement or refusal as to fulfilment of 'identity' ... the problem is for each to discover some inner need — and to find a way to trust it... It is in honour of this that Kingsley Hall is: a place, simply, where some may encounter selves long forgotten or distorted. . .

Does Kingsley Hall succeed? An irrelevant question: it does no harm, it does no 'cure'. *It* stands silent, peopled by real ghosts; so silent that given time, given luck, they may hear their own hearts beat and elucidate the rhythm.

Postscript

I wrote this article in the spring of 1969. The community discussed here no longer exists at Kingsley Hall. In May 1970 the five-year lease on the building expired.

Some of the people who formerly lived at Kingsley Hall have, under Dr Leon Redler's leadership, set up new households similar in aim and style. Dr Joseph Berke and I, together with friends and colleagues, have created the Arbours Association, registered as a charity in the United Kingdom, in order to provide people in emotional distress help and places to live outside mental hospitals. We have sponsored a few households, now ongoing, and recently have opened a 'crisis centre'. The crisis centre offers accommodation and intensive help for limited periods, in a non-medical setting, to individuals, couples, and families within or between whom a crisis is occurring. It is a unique experiment.

Bibliography

BARNES M., and BERKE, J. (1971), *Mary Barnes: Two Accounts of a Journey Through Madness* (Penguin Books).

COOPER, D. (1967), *Psychiatry and Anti-Psychiatry* (Tavistock Publications).

FOUCAULT, M. (1965), *Madness and Civilization, A History of Insanity in the Age of Reason*, translated by Richard Howard (Tavistock Publications).

GILBRAN, K. (1963), *The Madman, His Parables and Poems* (Heinemann).

GOFFMAN, E. (1961), *Asylums, Essays on the Social Situations of Mental Patients and Other Inmates* (Penguin Books, 1968).

KAPLAN, B. (ed.) (1964), *The Inner World of Mental Illness* (New York and London: Harper and Row).

LAING, R. D. (1967), *The Politics of Experience* (Penguin Books).

LAING, R. D. (1971), *The Politics of the Family* (Tavistock Publications).

PINEL, P. (1806), *A Treatise on Insanity*, first published as *Traité médico-philosophique sur l'aliénation mentale, ou la manie*, 1801, translated by D. D. Davis and published in England (New York: Hafner, 1962).

SCHATZMAN, M. (1973), *Soul Murder: Persecution in the Family* (Allen Lane The Penguin Press).

WITTGENSTEIN, L. (1958), *Philosophical Investigations*, translated by G. E. M. Anscombe (Blackwell).

28. 'Anti-psychiatry'

An Interview with Joseph Berke

Could you tell us a little about yourself?

I've been in London for over eight years. I do psychotherapy and family therapy and am a founder member of the Arbours Housing Association. This is a mental-health charity. It has set up households where people in emotional distress can go for help and to live, as an alternative to mental hospital. One of our households is a crisis intervention centre. We have a team of therapists who can go to people's homes to help individuals, families or even communes during periods of exceptional crisis, such as when someone is 'freaking out', a family is coming apart, etc. Persons who need intensive help, or simply need to get away from it all, can stay at the centre.

You're specifically interested in schizophrenia?

Well, in the whole range of psychological experience of which schizophrenia itself is a very important part. The term itself is important. I emphasize it's a term rather than a condition; and this is an important part of our work, showing how, in fact, people are invalidated in their own life-styles, their life experience, by this term applied to them. It could be another term, like 'depressive', but to take this particular instance of schizophrenia – it doesn't describe their life experience, it's really a label applied to them by certain other people for usually social reasons.

How do you define insanity then?

That would take several months, and the eventual answer would be inadequate. Insanity is really a social rather than personal fact. It's a social and cultural phenomenon. Experiences which are considered 'normal' in a particular culture or sub-culture may be defined as 'mad' in another cultural setting.

Insanity is synonymous with behaviour or experience that is 'unacceptable' within a given cultural framework.

Could you say something about your association with Dr Laing?

I've known him personally for many years. He's a brilliant thinker as well as a 'good bloke'. The particular reason why I came over here was that many of his ideas overlapped with the conclusions I was beginning to draw about the way psychiatry operates. I wanted the opportunity to work with him. We both saw that the way people are treated, in the usual medical/psychiatric sense, doesn't alleviate their suffering, but usually perpetuates it; that doctors act as societal trustees in order to maintain a particular form of conventional behaviour and experience; that the kind of treatment that is given is a form of emotional strait-jacketing, drugs included. Psychiatrists usually try to get people to forget what's bothering them rather than come to terms with it.

Surely this is basically a question of time, money, staffing. The establishment psychiatrist has become a kind of bogeyman for the underground, like the policeman – I find this rather a paranoid idea.

I don't think you can be paranoid enough about how psychiatrists function, and how mental hospitals function in their ways of dealing with people. One of the most important books in this regard is a study by a sociologist named Erving Goffman, entitled *Asylums*. The book is a study of how a mental hospital functions. Goffman spent several months as a nurse's aide in hospital, which is the proper level for finding out what goes on. The people who run hospitals essentially are nurses and nurses' aides, and only by working on that level can you really find out what goes on in a social and personal sense. Goffman found that instead of helping the person who was admitted as patient, the hospital tended to perpetuate the same kind of 'crazy' family situations and relationships which drove the patient 'mad' in the first place. In other words he showed how and why a mental hospital is a 'maddening' environment.

The important thing is to realize *why* people, especially teen-agers, feel that they are going mad, feel that they can't cope, things like that. Usually, it's because of 'crazy' patterns of rela-tionships in their families. We do a lot of work with families, it's an important part of our researches. Often, we find that a person who is labelled insane is often the sanest member of his or her family.

A kind of scapegoat in other words?

Yes, that's right. The reason why the person will be labelled insane is because he will be trying to escape from the 'crazy' or disturbing relationships – the shared behaviour patterns within the family. Take a teenager, for instance, who is trying to assert his own autonomy, rather than going along with the mores, the rituals of the family. When such a person is taken to a mental hospital, more often than not he is probably very frightened, does not understand what is happening. He is taken to a very strange place with the idea that people are going to help him. But sociologically speaking the same kind of patterns which have invalidated him in the family are then repeated in the hospital. So the hospital environment often helps to drive people mad – especially if they feel they are going there to get out of the binds imposed by the family.

You're switching them from one mad environment to another. But what's the alternative? The notion of cure always seems to get lost in all this. How do you actually treat someone who is suffering?

Usually, two factors are associated with the type of suffering you're talking about – social and/or personal invalidation. The first thing to find out is, what is this person feeling, what is this insanity that the person is worried about. Involved in this is the question of semantics. A great deal of invalidation comes about because people are semantically invalidating themselves – having to do with the emotionally loaded word 'schizophrenic' or 'in-sane' or things like that. Because insanity is a social and cultural definition, a textbook definition; it doesn't explain or even ex-press whatever the person is feeling. It's quite possible to read a textbook of psychiatry and feel one is really crazy, because practically everything that is expressed in a textbook of psychiatry is felt by 'normal' people. The point is, there's no such thing as normal people. We're talking about a cross section of people so the thing to find out is what the insanity is all about, what the experience is all about and to distinguish semantic invalidation from these other forms. Really it's a matter of creating an ambience whereby people can look at what their suffering is all about, and make it intelligible to themselves. Suffering is intolerable when it's unintelligible. It doesn't disappear when it becomes intelligible but it usually becomes tolerable. It allows one to try to get at the root of what it's all about.

A lot of people are trying to find a chemical basis for 'schizophrenia'. Could it be caused by a chemical imbalance in the brain?

No chemical causatory link with a condition called schizophrenia has ever been found. There's no condition called schizophrenia: it's a term of personal and social invalidation. This relates to how the word was coined. Originally, the word was 'dementia praecox', an early invention applied to people whose behaviour seemed to show signs of progressive mental and physical deterioration. They then found out that this deterioration doesn't necessarily occur. You see, there's no such thing as schizophrenia really. It's a hodgepodge term – referring to certain symptoms which doctors can supposedly distinguish in other people during the course of an interview. Laing has told me about a paper written in a German psychiatric journal last year by German psychiatrists who diagnose someone as schizophrenic on the basis of a feeling they themselves get in themselves – a strange feeling they call the 'praecox' feeling. In this instance we can clearly see that the diagnosis of schizophrenia is made because of the problems the doctor has, rather than the patient. That's the first point. The second point is that no physical test has ever been positively correlated with a particular mental condition.

There exists a pink spot urine test, there exists a green spot urine test, there exists an orange spot urine test – all this means is that urine tests of people who are supposed to be schizophrenic come out with certain results after adding certain chemical reagents to it. In a mental hospital a few years ago it was found that the product which was supposed to be associated with schizophrenia had to do with the fact that the patients were given coffee in the morning. So, the x spot was a breakdown product of caffeine. And it goes on and on and on.

The original reason for this situation can be found in the annals of medical history. Consider the experience and behaviour of people who were considered witches or demons, possessed and things like that. These people were usually shut away in dismal dungeons to protect the public. Now at the beginning of the eighteenth century a doctor named Philippe Pinel came along and along with him came a lot of other 'do-gooders'. They tried to stop the inhuman way the so-called 'crazies' were treated. They said, 'Lo and behold, if we state these unfortunate people are *not* possessed by demons but have some kind of *sickness*, like a cold, TB, or something like that – then we can treat them as if they were sick and not as if they were mad.' This is an important difference. Because madness is, more often than not, a moral attribution – you're making a statement of morality. A person is *mad* and *bad*; they're very closely associated together. Now if you can then say a person isn't just bad, possessed by demons, devils, morally bad, but is *sick*, then one can change the attitude of the general public to the person.

Then the doctors, having *a priori* defined deviant behaviour as a medical condition, had to apply medical techniques, in order to understand it. So what did they do? First of all, they dissected the brains of people who died at the mental hospital. They were looking for gross conditions, changes in the brain – these weren't found, either. Next, they tried to study the 'madman's' biochemistry. Nowadays, this approach has become very fashionable. Associations are made to the use of psychedelic drugs, because it has been found that the major psychedelic drugs like LSD or DMT or mescaline or whatever are biochemically similar to certain naturally occurring substances in the body such as adrenalin. The reasoning then goes – schizophrenia is due to faulty biochemistry associated with a hyperproduction of

psychedeliogenic substances. So they began to believe that
adrenalinlike substances in the blood cause 'schizophrenia'. Unfortunately this theory has never been substantiated.

In what is usually called schizophrenia, auditory hallucination
is a common symptom. People hear things being told to them by
somebody else – 'Do this.' 'Do that.' 'Don't do that.' Things like
that. But an interesting observation is that with psychedelic
drugs people *rarely* have auditory hallucinations, most of the
experiences of false perception that take place are *visual*. Moreover, people under the influence of psychedelic drugs rarely
have hallucinations of any kind. Most of what happens is a form
of visual illusion. The difference is quite important. Look at
that large wall there. If there was absolutely nothing there, if it
was absolutely totally white, and we began to see something
there, that would be a hallucination. However the fact is that on
the wall there are various pieces of dirt, kinds of plugs and
sockets, and these changes created in *a priori* objects around
which the mind can distort, change, make small, make large –
these are illusions. Most of the time what happens under
psychedelic drugs is that we have strange visual illusions, either
from this or from an after-effect like when you look at the
window there, close your eyes, and you can still see the window
– this is called an eidetic image. It's through a distortion of
actual real objects on the wall or eidetic images that the illu-
sionary events occur. This is very important because if psychedelic drugs or their biochemical analogues in the blood were
causes of 'mental illness', then the people who took such drugs
would have hallucinations and they would be *auditory* not visual.
In fact it is rare to have hallucinations under LSD. Most of
them are illusions, *visual* illusions.

*Can we switch from chemistry to sex? Wilhelm Reich wrote
about the 'schizoid' as a rigid personality unable to find release,
true orgasmic flow in sex due to various muscular tensions and
armourings. I guess a Reichian would say that the root cause of
'schizophrenia' is sex – in its widest sense – repression as a child,
things like that which finally become located in the actual
musculature of the body. You, on the other hand, tend to empha-*

*size the family unit, the family background or situation. There's
a difference here.*

Well, again it has to do with the term schizopherenia which you
are using as applied to a kind of condition, a situation of fact.
Now I don't use it in that way at all. I never met a 'schizophrenic'. Since I don't choose to attribute certain things to other
people by using this word, it really doesn't have much meaning
for me. In order really to get anywhere, we have to talk about
what *experiences* people have. The point is that the term
'schizoid' is often applied to people who have a kind of dis-
association, a break, a split between the soma and the intellect,
the body and the mind. This means that most of their feelings,
emotions, which really involve both mind and body are split off
into a mind component and a body component. This is often
what people mean by schizoid. Also the term has to do with a
split between the head and the heart, the feelings, the emotions
and the intellect. When Reich was using the word orgasm, he
wasn't really limiting himself to simply a genital experience, he
was really referring to the total emotional, physical, mental experience.

*Yeah. But I get the impression that for Reich and the Reich-
ians the ideal orgasm involved the total surrender of self – a
total commitment to the physical reality of another. Now surely
this is something the so-called schizoid is incapable of making:
he's absolutely terrified of letting go, going out of control. But
it's not much use approaching the individual. That's what
impresses me about the importance you attach to family influences, the family situation. But surely it's more extensive
even than the family – you've got to cure the whole society,
change it.*

This is an important point. In fact we're up against a whole
society which is systematically driving its members mad. Individuals might feel that the problem is in themselves but it isn't.
It's a social problem which is experienced at an individual level.
This is the reason why we shouldn't try to perpetuate the individual suffering, try to trick the individual people into thinking
something is wrong with themselves. In fact it's often very

heartening when people realize that what they're experiencing is shared by a lot of other people. There's a lot of people who in the medical sense might be considered schizoid, schizophrenic, whatever it is, who can have great sex, i.e. orgasm, but still be unhappy in other areas. Again this points to the vacuity, the inadequacy of the terms, schizoid, schizophrenic.

Sure. Let's invent a more humane word. Could you finally say something about your work with Mary Barnes? I understand you're writing a book together. Hers seemed a classic madness, if you'll excuse the phrase.

Well, Mary Barnes is a forty-five-year-old woman, English – she had been working in a hospital, experienced nervous breakdowns in the past, and had been diagnosed as a chronic schizophrenic; extremely regressed in a mental hospital, she had recovered and then she started feeling mad again – what *she* thought was going mad. This she experienced as extreme regression, not wanting to do anything, wanting to become a baby again, things like that. She met Laing about six or seven years ago – she'd heard about him through other people – and asked him if she could come to Kingsley Hall, the proposed new 'antipsychiatric' community. Kingsley Hall opened about 1965 and she was one of the first people to move in.

The point about madness is that it is a term applied to a particular form of experience. In Mary's case the experience was that of a return to an earlier version of herself, a wanting to become a baby again, wanting to return to her roots, almost to the foetus, as a way of dealing with the suffering which she felt as an adult. She wanted to see if she could be reborn again. She had to return almost to the position of a foetus in the womb in order to grow up again. And in fact that was what happened over the past few years at Kingsley Hall. Mary returned to being a baby, she was fed with a bottle, she played with her shit, she was taken care of as a baby, she spent a long time in bed not moving at all and, in doing so, returned to a point which was prior to the time when all the anxiety started. The aim in doing that was to grow up again, without all the anxieties associated with growing up in the first place.

I have had a lot to do with Mary. I was principally responsible for taking care of her immediate needs when I lived at
Kingsley Hall between 1965 and 1966, and also afterwards. This
very process of assistance was an experience, you might say, a
death-rebirth experience for me too. This is the reason why I
admire her courage to do what she did – it was a very courageous,
very frightening thing to do, especially because adults just don't
become babies again.

But Mary's experiences confirmed an idea of Laing's and
other people that an experience of regression, of going back
into oneself, can be a very healing experience. There has been a
book written about this by the Polish psychiatrist Kazimierz
Dubrowski entitled *Positive Disintegration*. This is an important
point then and goes back to what we were saying about mental
hospitals. A great deal of what might be called by a psychiatrist
'regression' is a person's natural attempt at self-healing. Our
work and what we consider the proper 'work' of the therapist is
to help a person along the road of his or her disintegrative
experience – provide the essential services; food, a warm place, a
nice atmosphere, and let the breakdown and recovery happen
without interference. Then the return trip – the integrative phase
– will be a very healing experience. The point of mental hospitals
and especially the psychiatrists and nurses and others who work
in them is that they stop this healing process from happening
because of their own fears about what's happening. This personal fear of psychiatrists and nurses about themselves makes
mental hospitals places where healing cannot take place. Therefore these places are not hospitals at all. Truthfully they are
'madhouses', i.e., places where people are driven 'mad', or 'madness' is perpetuated. What we wanted to do was to create an
asylum in the original sense of the word where healing can
happen. Aside from Mary, several other people have had a
similar kind of experience at Kingsley Hall, maybe not as spec-
tacular as she did but just as useful.

Mary and I have written a book together about this entitled,
Mary Barnes: Two Accounts of a Journey Through Madness.
It has recently been published by Penguin Books and consists of
her account of her own experience and her experience with me

and *my* account of my own experience and my experience with her. I say my own experience, because it was as much a profound experience for me as for her.

Thank you.

29. Suggestions for Working with Heavy Strangers and Friends

Kristin Glaser

A 'heavy' person is someone who gives you a gut feeling of 'Oh, God. I don't think I can handle this!' Whether they would be labelled suicidal, hallucinating, needy, or just behaving in strange ways, you feel them as heavy.

'Changes' is a Chicago group of about fifty volunteers who deal regularly with 'heavy' people, strangers and friends alike. The following is an account of what 'Changes' has learned about helping 'heavy' people.

Changes is a 'help network/crisis/phone/struggling to be therapeutic community', located in the Blue Gargoyle coffee shop in the Church of the Disciples of Christ at 5747 S. University Avenue. Some of us are from the University of Chicago: others live and/or work in the community. Our phones are open every evening for rapping, making referrals, and, if we are up to it, we will make a visit, crash people, and give other practical help.

We also spend a lot of time on ourselves. Some Changes people come every night to the office to sit and talk, and meetings are held every Sunday night for training and group stuff. Anyone who calls or comes for help is invited to become part of the Changes community, which tries to make as few distinctions as possible between helper/helpee. 'Being there for someone' is as likely to happen for a regular Changes person in trouble as it is for a new person. There is no required style of relating, but our training emphasizes emphatic listening. Organizationally, we are so flexible that there is often concern whether or not we even exist – people do what they want, and sometimes things don't get done.

Most people who come to Changes, whether to give help or

receive it, are single, relatively together people looking for a community to join. Our usual way of relating to people is *to let* informal listening, caring relationships develop, depending on who happens to be around, who likes whom, etc., and this usually works pretty well. We have learned, though, that some people who come into our community need a very different way of relating.

The following principles were developed through our experience of working with and being worked over by a number of fascinating people who thought they had cancer, only talked Latin, threatened to kill themselves or us, and in other ways opted for the privileges of the insane.

Some Thoughts about Heavy People

1. Some people come and say in plain English, 'Help me with my head,' but very often heavy people don't ask for this in a straight way. Instead, they may ask for a place to stay, or a job. *You* may be able to see their need for change, but *they* don't, and you may feel in a bind because you know you're going to have to deal somehow with their heavy behaviour.

2. Keep in mind that heavy people may have come from another place that tried to make them get help.

3. Some heavy people are old masters at the interaction of 'let's you and me fight about getting help', so if you start giving advice or trying to organize them, you may be giving them an old response that hasn't done them much good. In fact, fighting with others about their 'illness' may be one of the few ways they have to relate. Try to create new ways of relating and avoid the old ways.

4. Many heavy people have become expert at showing how freaky and crazy they are, and some have become highly resourceful at getting people involved with them. Respect this powerful interpersonal skill.

Dealing with Your Own Feelings

Often when people try to deal with a heavy person on an individual basis, one by one they are turned off or worn out by the excessive demands and strange behaviour. You become uncomfortable because you feel you're failing, the heavy person gets more upset because people are turning away, and the situation isn't helpful or productive for anyone.

There are a number of personal issues I usually find I have to deal with. I tend to get uptight because I identify with heavy people in various ways, or I react to them with helplessness followed by anger and depression. Also, I get a strange kick out of someone who is doing crazy things. It's like, 'I can't faint and be superseductive to get attention, but just look at that lady go!' When I catch myself feeling like this, I feel bad. Another problem is feeling guilty about not responding to a heavy man's sexual overtures because of class prejudice. Other people have to deal with their anger at people who are making so many demands ('like babies') and feeling overwhelmed by 'I am responsible to do something for this person'. Another frequent issue is fearing 'I might be like them' or 'somehow they will hurt (contaminate) me'.

In the unstructured Changes community, I've sometimes had trouble because I don't feel like a friend, and I know I'm not the therapist – so what the hell is my role? To avoid feeling like a 'responsible doctor' or a phoney friend, I try to settle on being a community member who is relating with the heavy person. This gives me a standard: I am offering a basic level of caring, concern, and resources that I would probably offer to any person in the group. If the heavy person wants it, a reciprocal relationship is possible. If they don't want to be at the helped end of a one-way relationship, they can be a community person towards me.

Many of these personal reactions to a heavy person can be supportively dealt with by a team, which decides together how everyone will relate with the heavy person. It doesn't matter whether or not the heavy person officially asks for help, because the team also benefits itself by getting together. Ideally, this team is a group of people who know each other well and are comfortable talking about their feelings. In actuality, it is any group of people we can get together.

The Team's Approach

1. The team meets with the heavy person in a relaxed and friendly way, making clear that there is a team in existence and explaining that we like to work around people's needs in groups. To avoid unkept promises or unmet expectations, the team should be very explicit and straight about what it does and doesn't do.

2. When the team is talking with the heavy person, particularly when giving feedback or making plans, at least one team member should take the heavy person's side, making sure he/she is being heard and feelings are being brought out as clearly as possible – even if the team doesn't like what these feelings are.

3. All behaviour is communication of some kind: the team should look very carefully at the heavy person's behaviour. Since communication is a two-way process, we need to look at our own behaviour, too. Instead of seeing craziness as 'in' the heavy person, we should seek the meaning of his/her interpersonal behaviour, by making a 'heavy interaction analysis'. It's essential that this analysis should not put someone in a conceptual box and leave her/him there. Understanding the heavy person's world and needs as a *process* helps the team avoid being trapped by confusion into being rigid or crazy themselves.

The team's analysis might focus on one sequence of communications between two people. For example, 'I got upset when she said that. Why? What was that tapping in me? Did she want me to get angry, or was that a backwards way of wanting me to say hello?' We can also look at the interaction between the heavy person and the whole group.

In one case a woman claimed all sorts of terminal physical illnesses. She would talk very expressively about her complaints and then 'faint' away on the floor, particularly if men were around. We would get very upset and push around trying to revive her in a way that always involved touching her. When we finally realized the pattern we'd gotten into we were able to see her fainting as asking for something from us. We then tried to give her a lot of attention, particularly male attention, when she wasn't talking about her symptoms, and we ignored her when she fainted. The actual situation was much more complicated, of course. The above is an outline of our team's approach.

The team's 'interaction analysis' may be quite wrong, but it provides the basis for a tentative commitment to the heavy person and a plan for acting differently, so the old familiar bad ways don't have to come up as such. Rather than merely having our painful reactions to the heavy person, we can become more active, expanding our interaction. Instead of standing still, waiting to hear the next crazy thing he/she did so we can groan, we can make moves to relate before the crazy things happen.

4. We've found that about five people make a good size team, although others are needed if support is being given around the clock. It's important to divide up responsibilities: who'll help with housing, who'll go to welfare with the person, etc. It's also usually best to have a team coordinator who keeps track of who is doing what and what isn't happening. Team members should have each other's phone numbers, so that help can be reached quickly and easily. Whenever possible, invite the heavy person to the meetings. It may also be productive to have a different heavy person or persons as part of the team.

5. We try to find out if the heavy person has a support network nearby. If there are friends, room-mates, or relatives, it usually helps to try to work with them. Often these people have become scared, bewildered, or just tired and fed up. If we can support them in finding new ways of relating with the heavy person, they are obviously the best bet for the person's long-term support. Also, a lot may be learned from people who know the heavy person. From the friends of a very spacy girl we'd been protecting, we found out that she'd been spacy but able to take care of herself for many years.

6. The team needs to meet frequently, ideally with someone who is experienced with heavy people but not actively involved with this particular person. To avoid feeling bad and wanting to

dump the heavy person, it's essential to keep in touch with our own heavy feelings. As a team, we should constantly review our analysis to see where we're getting stuck. It's easy to get involved in a troubled person's system and find yourself playing a part you didn't intend.

Team Limits

1. The team needs to feel very clearly that it doesn't have to control the heavy person or do anything about her/him 'getting better' – like talking to a therapist, being open about her/his problem, going to a hospital, taking a pill, etc. With some exceptions, the team should not feel responsible for someone's life and welfare. They should not get into control battles about *making* the heavy person do things.

When a situation seems to be heading for a fight, instead of upping the ante of pressure on yourself and the heavy person, try to step sideways. One time on our hotline, a very provocative guy told me he had taken a bunch of pills. Obviously, my next move was supposed to be, 'how many, how long ago, where are you?' and these were things he wouldn't tell me. Instead, I said, 'You must be feeling pretty bad to have done that. Can you tell me what's going on for you?' And we got into a rap about his feelings. About ten minutes later, he was able to back off and say he hadn't taken the pills – yet.

2. The team needs to attend to the heavy person's survival needs. It's pretty hard to get your head together when you aren't sure where your next meal's coming from or where you're staying that night. Sometimes heavy people will resist your efforts to stabilize their living conditions, but we've learned through bad experience that if we keep crashing someone for months, making new arrangements every day, the only result is uproar, a lot of which is due to our own grudginess about limited resources.

If someone is too upset to work, he/she can be put on welfare. Sometimes when heavy people refuse to go on welfare, it indicates their desire that the group support them. Insisting that a heavy person get living security is making the person do something, to which we are generally opposed, but the other side is what the person is making us do by continually coming in for a handout and a place to crash. If we insist on welfare, we should make it clear that it is for *our* good, not theirs. Of course, the person always has the option of splitting.

We also have some very basic limits: we don't want to be shit on, and violence is not acceptable. To keep to these limits, we try to understand behaviour and relate to what's behind it, or by ignoring it, leaving the room, etc. If all else fails, we need to feel comfortable saying, 'I can't be with you when you're like this. There is no way I can be helpful now. I guess you'll have to leave.'

Except in certain suicidal cases, we need to feel comfortable about not being responsible. If there are repeated signs that the person can't make it, sees no way out, and has made previous attempts at suicide, then we need to feel more responsible, or acknowledge that we can't work with the person, if they are someone whose relationship with us can't be trusted as much as their urge for death. We have carried suicidal people, but only when there was one Changes person who was clearly so closely relating with the person that we could absolutely count on a call for help.

We haven't worked out the dimensions of extra responsibility. Obviously, every precaution possible must be taken.

3. Knowing the relationship is free and voluntary on both sides gives everyone a lot of psychological space. People should not have to work with someone they don't like or feel very uncomfortable with. Hopefully, within a non-demanding situation with clear limits, heavy people have maximum flexibility to do what they need to do. And the rest of us should be only as involved as we feel good about. It's always better to have a lot of people involved who each give a little than a few people who feel ripped off and get resentful.

4. No matter how strange, give heavy people credit for having good reasons for their behaviour. Another way of looking for the function of their behaviour is to look for what 'good life thrust might be in their bad way of acting. Then, respond to that life thrust just as if they had acted it out fully and appropriately.

A lot of crummy ways are really only crummy because the right things are being half-done and half-defeated, instead of being fully and freely done. If you respond to the half of it that is happening, that lets it happen more.' (From *The Rap Manual*, written by Gene Gendlin). There are impulses which could be happening while the person is being annoying: if it is appropriate, you could say, 'I'm glad you're reaching for contact with me,' or just respond by giving contact.

If a person asks for something you can't give, tell him/her that, but also that you are glad she/he is in touch with their needs and felt free to ask for them. This is especially important if the need is in the direction of life and growth for the person, such as wanting closeness, sex, or time with you. (*Rap Manual*.)

If you're working with a very freaky person who says one thing that makes sense and then a lot more you can't understand, stick with your one point of contact. 'I really understand it when you say you hated her.' If the person continues to say things that don't make sense, you can repeat that one thing again and again. Also, if someone says something that can't be true ('The Martians took everything from me'), respond to the feeling part ('You feel like you've been fucked over'). (*Rap Manual*.)

Generally, we invite heavy people to share in our community as we would with any new person. They can hang around, work at the coffee shop during the day, and drop in (and work) at the office during the evenings. They are invited to our Sunday night community meetings, which are more formal than our daily meetings. On Sundays if we let them, heavy people are apt to demonstrate how crazy they are by talking constantly about irrelevant things and making the larger meeting very difficult. As very polite folks who tend to ignore heavy people's behaviour, we sometimes increase their disruptiveness. If other members of the group don't handle the situation, someone on the team should respond by listening carefully and reflecting to heavy people those of their feelings that make sense, and also have enough courage to tell heavy people to be quiet when they're making no sense. This reflecting should diminish their need to use crazy methods to make themselves heard.

Sharing your personal life and feelings with heavy people is very helpful: going to the movies, out for coffee, etc. Communicate that you're willing to share your 'normal' life with them – they don't have to be freaky to spend time with you. Be careful, though, that you don't get so caught up in being friends that you forget their need for 'therapeutic' talk, too.

Working with Heavy Friends

It took a near fatality for me to realize that all of these ideas about heavy people apply very much to friends as well as strangers. A casual friend came to see me in a very depressed and confused state, and I kept seeing him alone. It wasn't until he was in the hospital, almost dead from a suicide attempt, that I realized I had ignored all my own past experience when I related with him. There were several ways I had trapped myself and I want to share these as postscripts.

1. It's easy to get caught in a 'snob trip' of thinking your friend is special because she is your friend and able to talk in a rational, intellectual way. If someone is acting dysfunctionally, she should not be cheated of the same good treatment you give others – particularly in the team approach.

2. Avoid letting friends 'really communicate' with you because they can't communicate with their 'traditional shrink'. Something gets messed up if a person communicates in the place where he isn't committed and can't communicate when he is committed. You need to help him/her get the two together to get a working contact with someone or with people generally.

3. When you have an historical relationship with someone, it's essential that you get an outside, experienced opinion because of your own blindness towards your own part in the interaction system.

At Changes, then, we have found that the team 'Heavy Interaction' analysis approach is valuable, because with the team's support you can work towards clearer understanding of what makes sense about a heavy strange person and deal openly with your own reactions of fear, confusion, and prejudice. You are much more apt to have the energy and desire to relate in a real, live way with the heavy person, without backing off and treating them as an 'it'.

30. People's Psychiatry Sheet 1: Handling Psychiatric Emergencies

Michael Glenn

You and your friends can handle many psychiatric emergencies. The crucial elements are *trying* (instead of drawing back), and trusting your own intuition. This sheet is meant as a simple guide, saying no more than common sense, but legitimizing people's efforts to help their sisters and brothers in trouble. Experience is, of course, the best teacher of all.

1. The first thing to do is LISTEN. Don't be in a hurry to give advice. LISTEN first; try to understand what's happening, what the person is feeling. Get into the person's FRAME OF REFERENCE.

Look for a 'handle' to their situation. Try to figure out what's oppressing them, what's making them feel the way they feel. Once you've done that, you can start looking for options, for a way out of the dilemma.

2. You need to be CALM. If you can't be calm, find someone else who can be. As you listen, try to be accepting; don't start laying your trip on them. If they feel something, they have a reason for feeling it; respect their integrity. If you're calm and listening, you can start responding to them, which will help clarify the situation.

3. Understand how people's SELF-ESTEEM can be shot to pieces by crassness, inappropriate humour, or a casual air. Most people in emotional distress are feeling empty and helpless. Try not to make them feel worse about themselves. Look for the genuine assets in them, and in their situation. Try to restore their self-confidence.

4. Follow your hunches and your feelings: they're almost always right. Get in touch with what you feel, then think about it. If you feel sad, chances are the other person feels sad. If you feel scared, chances are the other person is scared too. If you feel angry, chances are the other person is angry too, or manipulating you. If you feel confused, chances are the other person feels confused too. Go ahead and say things like 'I'm really confused by what you say,' or 'You must really feel horrible about all that.' Use feelings, not ideas, as your main guide.

5. Don't be ashamed of being ignorant or feeling helpless. The other person probably feels the same way. Therapy is a human act, not some mysterious mumbo-jumbo: ask questions if you're ignorant; admit it if you feel helpless. Don't pretend to know what you don't. (That's mystifying the other person.)

6. Let the other person tell you in their own way what's wrong. Don't make them follow *your* rules. Don't get them to 'act out their feelings' or do things you learned in some groovy encounter group. This isn't fun and games: if you're trying to help a sister or brother through a trying time, you'd better accept the responsibility that goes with that.

7. People become disturbed in different ways. Some are horribly depressed; some in a state of panic; some violent; some confused and irrational; some incomprehensible. Almost everyone in an emotional crisis is terrified of LOSING CONTROL. They want to feel some kind of support, some kind of protection. Try to give them that.

Try to talk in as quiet a place as possible; if you can see them again, let them know that, and do it. If you can help them deal with their problem without losing control (and humiliating themselves), you are doing good work. (At some future time they may want to relax their control: but they'll do it some place that is protective.)

8. In the same line of thought, if you feel they are out of control, or that they are too much for you to deal with, don't

pretend what you can't do. Decide on bringing someone with more experience to see them, or think about a hospital.

Many people are horrified of mental hospitals. You and your friends should know which hospitals in your area are good and which are atrocious; which shrinks are sympathetic and which are absolute pigs.

If a friend is too disturbed to handle, get them to someone who can help them calm down or to a hospital. It's foolish to take chances with people's lives, especially if they are dangerous to themselves or others.

Don't get hung up on the rhetoric of we-should-all-be-able-to-take-care-of-one-another. Sometimes we simply can't. Then it's good to know what your options are.

9. Tell people what you're doing. Don't mystify them. Don't make phone calls behind their backs, or agree with them when you're planning something else. No matter how flipped out someone is, there's always a part of them that's aware of reality: speak to that part, and they'll respond.

10. If you start feeling bored, try to focus in on the problem. That's where you should be anyway. What's going on? How can you help? How can they help themselves? Do they need a hospital? a shrink? medication? (Although medicines are grossly abused, sometimes they're useful: especially if they can keep a sister or brother out of the hospital.) What is the real problem, and what are their options?

11. A word about DEPRESSIONS... Life in this oppressive society is filled with insults, painful experiences and real losses. Not only is our SELF-ESTEEM smashed time and again. We also have to endure separations from people close to us – friends who leave, who die, who are killed, who go to jail, etc. There's a natural healing-over after such a loss, but it takes time.

Don't expect people not to feel these human feelings. Help them integrate their experience and feelings into themselves.

Often, DEpression is a cover for OPpression. If there's no

'real' loss going on, look for the oppression that's making the other person feel like shit. Help them understand that it's not 'in their heads' but in the real world that such oppression exists.

Help them get in touch with others who share their oppression. Agree with them that they're not bad or crazy. Help them get angry if they deserve to get angry.

12. A word about PARANOIA... Paranoia, as radical therapist Claude Steiner has said, is a state of 'heightened awareness'. Paranoid feelings are almost always justified, at least in part. Don't argue with them; try to see where they're true and what that means for the person.

This society makes all of us suspicious, mistrustful, manipulated: 'paranoid'. Help the paranoid person recognize the truth of their paranoia, and then help them to stop being immobilized or destroyed by their awareness.

13. A word about VIOLENT people... Violent people are often very frightened, and can be calmed down if you protect them and treat them as people, not monsters. Sometimes, though, people are just out of touch. Don't try to be a hero and endanger yourself and others. Do what you can without being foolhardy. Talk straight to someone who's violent; be reasonable, not threatening.

14. We all need to share experience in handling common psychiatric problems. You and your friends can build a list of halfway-houses, decent hospitals, and other therapy resources. If you deal with these problems yourself, you can encourage others to do the same.

15. It's important to remember that the roles of therapist and patient are interchangeable. You may be helping someone today, and being helped tomorrow. That's the way it should be. Our common task is developing our skills, so we can help and strengthen one another and the movement for social change.

31. People's Psychiatry Sheet 2: Common Drug Emergencies

Chuck Robinson

There are three common drug emergencies where your concerned intervention can help someone, and even save their life. These emergencies are freak-outs, overdoses, and chronic drug emergencies.

Freak-outs

Not all psychedelic experiences are positive. There is no way to predict whether or not you or someone else will have a partially bad trip ('bummer') or an extremely negative trip ('freak-out'). When a person is in a mildly frightening place, or is afraid that they may 'bum', they may frown, appear tense, or mention the fact that they are getting scared. A brief 'It'll pass soon, just ride with it. If it gets bad, let me know,' said with relaxed concern, will usually aid the tripper in their search for a more positive space and experience. Extensive questioning, or unreasonable anxiety on your part can make the situation worse. Stay calm, and reassure the person that you will be there if you are needed.

A person can also find themselves in a bad place without warning. The dominant emotions experienced (but not necessarily articulated) during a freak-out are fear and helplessness. Intense fear or disorientation on the part of the tripper allows you to differentiate between the person who needs help and the person who only needs reassurance. On a freak-out, the person may scream loud and long, become agitated, become unable to 'contact' another person, sob uncontrollably, or retreat to a corner and tremble. You can intervene in these crises in such a way as to relieve the tripper's anxiety and aid him in relocating himself within a more positive space.

Make contact with a calm question such as 'Are you in a place you don't want to be?' The person may respond, or continue to freak. Don't be hurt or frightened if she doesn't respond immediately. Unaggressively continue with surface questions or statements. 'When did you drop? Do you want the music on? Where are you at now? I'm here to help you. You are here at your place with friends.' Give the tripper a handle so that she can contact you. Try to let her know where she is, that it is a safe place, that she can trust those she is with, and that the bad experience will pass. Listen, and offer reassurance. It is often helpful to tell the tripper, 'Flow with it, let go. It will all be clear later. Relax, let go.' Avoid ridicule, censure, and playing guru – don't attempt to make sense out of the verbal content for the tripper. Encourage them to talk. Respond simply and honestly. The person will usually get comfortable within an hour. It is well to have a second person with you, or close by, if you are helping a person bring themselves down. If you get tired, the second person can take over. It is best for the three of you to spend time together before the first helper leaves. If the tripper becomes violent, be cautious. Restrain only when he actively strikes out. Frightened people are strong and aggressive when they imagine an attack on their person. Call more friends, or stronger and more experienced friends. In this situation, and other drug emergencies, don't get in over your head. Don't be afraid to request help, or back off from a potentially dangerous person. You may have to call an ambulance. If this is necessary, try to accompany the person to the hospital. Follow them so that they don't get fucked over. If a person becomes unconscious, or begins to convulse, get them to a hospital immediately.

You can use the same approaches with a person who has an acute panic reaction on grass (this does happen – usually with an inexperienced smoker or people who turn on when they are already in the midst of a stressful emotional state) or people on speed runs. A word on speed. There are reports of fatal overdoses on speed. People can also become violent and paranoid on speed, and extremely depressed after a run. People who use a lot of speed are in the midst of a chronic drug emergency. Urge them to seek structured help.

It is a poor idea to give downs or tranquillizers to a person who is freaking out. The drug you give may initiate a dangerous situation in the person's body. You never know what is in a tab that is said to be acid, mescaline, etc. Secondly, aborting a trip with the aid of drugs may prevent a person from working through the difficulty which brought on the bad trip. This may be the cause of flashbacks. It has been determined that depriving a person of dream time can cause flip outs. The situation where you abort a trip with another drug is quite similar.

Drug Overdoses

Most fatal overdoses result from an excess of opiates, barbiturates, or combinations of barbs and alcohol. When people inject drugs, they sometimes 'go under' right after they shoot up. They come around or someone slaps them awake for a brief period of time. Then they nod out again. Lots of times they never wake up. The drugs have depressed breathing beyond the capacity to support life. People take fatal ODs hours after they get off. It takes a while. You can play doctor and shoot them full of salt, coke, or speed, waste time, feel important, complicate an already dangerous bodily condition, or you can get them to an emergency ward as fast as you can. The tools and skills to save an OD victim are to be found only in a hospital. Being in the middle of an od situation is frightening in that someone may be dying, and to save them you may have to face the possibility of doctor and cop hassles. But then it is equally confusing when someone dies in your presence. There is always realistic guilt. Disposal of a dead person's body is heavier than a run to the emergency ward. How do you respond? Stash any drugs you have on you. Try to slap the person around and get them walking. Head for the nearest hospital, or call an ambulance. Meet the ambulance outside – say you found the person there. If you can get them to the hospital, do so fast. Once again, say you found him outside your house. The police or hospital officials have no right to detain you. You are simply a good citizen helping a fellow, though unknown, citizen. If the person stops breathing, start mouth to mouth. Tilt the head back, remove foreign objects from the mouth. Pinch the nose closed and breathe a lung full of air into the victim's mouth. The chest should raise and then deflate again. Repeat until the person can breathe on his own. Don't wait for the person to stop breathing before you respond. If you can't slap a person awake, head for the hospital. If the person comes around, don't let them go under again, and don't leave them alone. If a person has ODed on methadone, he can be fine for two hours and suddenly die. Methadone is very long acting. The same is true of barbiturate overdose. A person often cops barbs at intervals. The ones he took an hour ago may knock him out, but the pills he dropped twenty minutes ago will kill. Never try to induce vomiting unless the person is quite alert. Usually, inducing vomiting is effective only in the first fifteen minutes after a person drops pills. Any later the person will strangle on their vomit because their gag reflex is knocked out. In the hospital the stomach can be successfully pumped.

The OD victim has put you in a funny place. It is she who has taken the overdose, but you must decide whether or not to attempt to save her life. You have to deal with those changes. He has to deal with the hospital changes. You don't have to take any 'Why the fuck did you take me to the hospital? I would have been OK,' bullshit from anyone who gives himself a drug overdose and starts to die in front of you. Their response is only one of guilt. It is not unhip to save someone's life.

The Most Common Drug Emergency

The most common drug emergency happens to millions of people every day. They are slowly killing themselves and destroying those around them with downers, speed, heroin, and alcohol. If this is you, or someone you care about, there is a drug emergency. These people don't do it alone. They have more than enough help from our society. America has the best of everything. If you want the best drugs there are for fucking up people, America has these drugs. A mime of our cultural madness is what people do to dance their death dance with America's drugs. With Thorazine hospital oranges, with Mexican reds the CIA-Federales ignore in their macho shoot-outs with peasant grass growers, with the princess amphetamine that wires a person into a 'groovy chick', with federal tax, state tax, sales tax, value-added tax, tax stamp inspector, assistant chief tax stamp inspector, chief tax stamp inspector, director of chief tax stamp inspectors, nicotine and alcohol, with killer street acid for children, with political mafia smack, scag, duja, junk, horse, dope, tagic majic, boy, heroin, shit, shit, shit. If you, or someone you relate to, punches a hole in their arm, there is a drug emergency. If you are on a speed run, ask the wall people if you have a drug emergency. If you can't sleep without barbs, or you wonder how many goofers are behind your bottle of wine, someone is telling you something. But maybe you can't hear anyone because you found out there isn't anyone there. Do you put so many drugs into the only body that you have, that you have lost your body and locked your mind into itself and you are all alone, all alone? If this is your reality, seek out a change with others who are changing. You cannot change yourself alone, or with others who are not changing, or without others who are changing. Those who will accept you are here, but you must find them in fucked-up America. Only you can find them. They are there.

If you really care about someone who is in a constant drug emergency, you know what to do. Try to discover a way of communicating this to them. If you always scream the message, whisper it. If you always whisper, scream.

32. People's Psychiatry Sheet 3: Suicide

Cynthia Ganung and Michael Glenn

One extreme way our society destroys us is to make us destroy ourselves. Anger and hopelessness about our situation is turned inward: rather than group together to change the oppressive conditions affecting our lives, many of us withdraw, become lost in our depression and try to kill ourselves.

Suicide is serious. Eighty per cent of people in this country admit to having had ideas of suicide. About two million people alive right now have a history of at least one attempt on their lives. Once a minute someone tries to kill themselves in this country. About twelve per cent of people who have failed will kill themselves on another try within two years. This sheet is aimed at trying to prevent needless suicide. We're not arguing whether people have a right to kill themselves or not. About eighty per cent of people who kill themselves seem to have asked for help in some way. This sheet hopes to help each of us be more responsive.

Suicides which are unsuccessful are called 'attempted' suicides. About eighty-five per cent of attempts fit this pattern. Some people think that because a suicide fails, it means the person wasn't serious about it, or was only 'looking for attention'. They call such attempts 'gestures'. We should avoid the American success/failure trap. A failed suicide is still a signal that things are seriously wrong. People who make an attempt will try again unless their situation changes. It's a mistake to think that, once someone has recovered, everything's OK.

The politics of suicide are clear once you understand who's trying to kill themselves. Alienated people, people who feel half-dead, grieving and lonely people, people who feel worthless, oppressed people – urban black people, American Indians –

these are the ones who try to end it all. Often the people with the sharpest sensitivity to the hopelessness of their lives make attempts: they refuse to play the hypocritical games our society demands. Heroin users court suicide daily.

Women make three times as many attempts as men (although men 'succeed' more). Women typically choose pills or poison, while men attempt to shoot or hang or cut themselves. The sexist power patterns of our society are echoed in this fact.

Anger in oppressed people is righteous rage: it should be focused on the people and institutions which oppress us, at the ruling class: not on our own minds and bodies.

Here are a few facts which can help you deal with someone who might be suicidal:

– Most of us have had thoughts of killing ourselves. Usually we do not act on these thoughts because we have other alternatives open to us, or because we feel too helpless and passive. Once suicide becomes a real alternative, though, it can be pursued repeatedly. Most people who reach this point *want* someone to talk to them and help; part of them does *not* want to die. Many who complete suicides were desperately seeking help and did not actually intend to kill themselves.

– Certain facts are known about people who might seriously consider suicide. People are statistically more likely to try to kill themselves if the following are true: (a) they've made a prior attempt, (b) they've actually threatened to kill themselves, (c) they have a chronic physical illness, (d) they've recently lost someone close to them, (e) they have severe money problems, (f) they have relied heavily on drugs or alcohol, (g) they have a relative who killed himself. In addition the more concrete plans people have made, the more serious it is: making a will, talking about death, writing suicide notes, setting a date for suicide and figuring out the way they will kill themselves, making no plans past a certain future date, giving away special possessions, etc. People more likely to go ahead with suicide plans are those who are feeling acutely upset or sad all the time, who feel totally disorganized or exhausted, or who have lost all interest in the world. People who have alienated themselves from body feelings – they can cut themselves and feel no pain – are also likely to hurt themselves. The most important indicator of suicide thoughts is the feeling that there is no hope for things to change, that suicide is the only answer.

– When people who have been very depressed for a while suddenly become cheerier without any apparent cause, it may signal that they've resolved to kill themselves. This may be especially true of people who tend to keep their feelings to themselves. It is important to maintain contact with a person after a suicide attempt as nearly half of all suicides occur within three months after a person has come out of an emotional crisis.

– About two-thirds of male suicides and over half of female suicides are over forty-five. This is part of the oppression of the elderly in our society; leaving people feeling useless, isolated and suffering with no available solution. We should be alert to older people's situations and try to understand and respond to their oppression.

– Very often the suicidal person has either withdrawn from other people or feels totally cut off and rejected. Often, this may be an *accurate perception*. It is important to reach the close persons towards whom the suicidal act (anger, guilt, blame) may be directed. When possible the person's friends and relatives should be mobilized to provide support and bring about changes. At times suicidal people are cut off from everyone and the person who helps may be the only one who really does care for them at that time. This is a heavy burden to take on, a serious responsibility. These people may need close and continued personal contact through a period of time. If you can do this, do it. If you cannot, don't promise what you will have to fall down on. Your relationship with the person can make a critical difference and rejection would just make suicide more likely. It is ideal for a group to help so that more emotional support is available and people can work together to help the person bring about changes in their life situation.

Suicide Emergency

If you find someone who has just tried to kill themselves, act quickly. If they are cut and bleeding, apply first aid (check Red Cross manuals, etc. on this) and get them to a hospital or clinic. If they are unconscious, make sure they are breathing and their heart is beating – otherwise give first aid – and get them to a hospital. If they are drowsy keep them awake and – if they are getting drowsier – get them to a medical facility. If you take a person to a hospital, try to stay with them and make sure they get prompt and helpful treatment. If you can find out what the person took and they look in no serious danger, try to keep them awake, talk to them and see what has gone on.

If they have taken some drug or chemical, try to find out what it is. If you don't know what the drug does, call the nearest poison control centre or drug hot-line.

Don't hesitate to ask others to assist you in helping. If a person is violent, trying to hurt themselves and others, try to get help to hold them in a reassuring manner. Try to maintain both emotional and physical contact with the person and be straight with them as to how you are feeling and what you are willing to do to help them.

After the emergency or if the person isn't seriously ill, try to use the moment to deal with the life crisis. First try to understand what the problem is, share your feelings, and then engage in active approaches to solve the problem. The person may be angry with you and initially reject your help but later on they might understand your willingness to be involved as a sign of caring for a sister or brother. People who are really alone and very despondent might need to find a different place to stay, a different job, etc. Try to find out the resources available.*

* A good emergency reference is: *Emergency Medical Guide*, by John Henderson, McGraw-Hill (paper).

A Final Word

Ultimately the responsibility for our lives rests with us. No one should feel they can totally protect a person from suicide if that is what they really want to do. Some suicides – people with terminal illness, people who have much physical or emotional pain – may be unavoidable. But *most* suicides are preventable. 'Do your own thing' is not a correct philosophy to follow when it's a matter of a sister or brother's life, and they are essentially uncertain and conflicted about what to do. We have all been messed over. By reaching out to someone, you may be able to help save their life and bring them back into the struggle.

33. Number Nine:
Creating a Counter-Institution

Dennis Jaffe

Number Nine was created in October 1969 as a service for young people in crisis. It was founded by a group of young people who found the frustrations and internal contradictions of working within the existing mental health system too great. It represents an attempt to create an alternative model of a service institution which helps people change, and which also is politically relevant in that it hastens the adoption of its humanistic values by a wider segment of society. I want to discuss several themes in Number Nine's development, not because we have solved any basic dilemmas, but because our struggles highlight some of the concrete issues that come up when one seeks to apply radical approaches to personal growth as a service to a specific community.

Getting Started

Before we could open a crisis clinic for young people we had to make sure we were on their side. The young people we knew (mainly white and middle-class like ourselves) had a basic and massive distrust of their parents, their teachers, their government and much of what they saw around them. They had developed a counter-culture of institutions, media, and ways of relating which had the trust, if not the outright allegiance, of a majority of their peers. As a result of the development of this culture they were sensitive and resistant to efforts to depersonalize them, adjust them, change them against their will, or blackmail them by withholding achievement. The young people we knew were introspective, self-critical, idealistic, and demanded moral honesty from adults who wished to work with them.

When given the chance they could define concretely what they wanted. If we were to build up enough trust to make our venture successful, we had to learn to embody the values of the counter-culture. It would be presumptuous, for example, to try to 'treat' their problems, because the nature of their dilemma, as they defined it, was to develop new and more meaningful ways to relate. Our services could not be those who had answers helping those who didn't, because we ourselves were searching for answers to the same questions, and trying to actualize the same values. From the first, we had to develop a style of collaboration.

The founders, a small but fairly representative group of young people, most of whom had lived through several stages of the radical movement, had a two-fold task. First we had to break free personally from the traditional assumptions about service that would crop up in their behaviour if the planning process was not highly self-critical and open to new information at every step of the way. We also had to constantly see feedback from the community and evaluate our efforts in terms of whether we responded to real needs, and whether our clients felt helped. We very quickly found that it would be a long time before we could settle on any one type of service as being right. We expected to constantly try new projects and never develop a stable set of procedures and programmes, which meant that any static concepts of organization would be useless to us.

In order to develop a flexible and responsive service, we decided to concentrate on our own personal growth as a staff, and this has turned out to be one of our chief attractions to volunteers. Our feeling was that if we worked among ourselves to actualize our values in our own relationships, we would be likely to embody these values in our service to others. Concentrating on our own growth and openness as a community also allowed us to become comfortable in criticizing each other, which is crucial to any community which does not want to institutionalize and structure in its own blind spots.

With a vague and ambiguous collaborative structure we set out to offer service to young people in a radically new way. We chose a name, Number Nine, from a Beatles song, which would be easy to remember and identify us in a way that mental health clinic would not. We knew of centres in other cities which operated switchboards, referral and counselling services twenty-four hours a day, offered emergency housing for runaways, dealt with bad drug trips, and helped in family crises. All of these seemed valid needs, and no other services in New Haven seemed to accept responsibilities in these areas. We decided that our services should be offered free, and that we could build greater trust and respect confidences by not asking names. We felt also that this would be the best defence against police interference with our drug or runaway counselling.

Number Nine opened two weeks after the planning process began, with $100, a free storefront from the Redevelopment Agency, an apartment/crash pad borrowed from the Free School, and telephones on credit. After a tremendous initial influx of volunteers to form the staff, and young people with various problems phoning and coming in, we were able to attract donations and $13,000 in foundation funds to buy a condemned house to fix up, hire seven staff to work full-time, and meet expenses. We now have about fifteen full-time staff who make from five to twenty dollars a week, plus room and board at our house. We have ten spaces in our house for people who are going through personal or family crises and need a place to stay for a short time, and we have a psychedelic bus and rock band which travel around and give shows and help out at rock festivals, which sometimes also bring in money. We just moved into a four-storey building which we can use for such new programmes as an alternate high school, personal growth centre, and creative art centre.

This illustrates both the opportunity and the need for creative expansion of current views of social services. All of our activities grew out of our interaction with young people, and dialogue about what they needed for growth in a world which they saw as largely hostile. While psychotherapy, encounter groups, family counselling, and other social services form a large part of our work, they seem to take on meaning and relevance by their connection to our other activities. Our activities are unified through our growing, and still largely fuzzy, conception of ourselves as a community within a larger alternative culture which is working for broad changes in the fabric of our society.

Making Contact with Our Community

Traditional institutions have a passive idea of offering service – you open up, perhaps announce it to other professionals, and wait for people to come. If they don't like what they get, they can leave. Many such services, like court, welfare, or school counselling and mental hospitals, utilize compulsion to get their clients. We believe that a service has to justify itself to its clients, and constantly ask the community it serves whether it is seen as useful. This cannot be done by bureaucratic means, as for example a committee, because these means are unlikely to attract those who might be critical or have fresh ideas to offer.

The best way to do this, we found, is to be in the community in as many and as active ways as we can. Our concepts come from the more active forms of community organization, where the first step is to fight the inertia and apathy of people who are accustomed to passive acceptance of a *status quo* they disagree with. In mental health the analogous problem is that people who seem to be in the greatest distress usually have defence mechanisms that keep them from actively seeking help even if it happens to be available. Ironically many mental health institutions take the attitude that people whose problem is an inability to accept their help should be punished. We sought to make our image as broad as possible, so that people, whatever their problem, would feel comfortable in at least trying us out. We also wanted to move out in the community, and offer many ways to get involved in our programme, so that we could reach those very people who are not usually helped because they deny their difficulties, get service agencies angry at them, or just put other people off.

We did this by being visible. We (1) sent staff to places in the community where we expected to find clients, (2) participated in other activities of the counter-culture, (3) advertised in media that young people responded to, (4) made our staff and our own community open to the point where people could drift into our meetings or office without having the burden of having to relate as a client, (5) created the bus and band, which was not only fun for us but demonstrated that we were involved in ways that young people respected.

As a by-product of our openness, one of the greatest problems we have is not being sure who is on our staff. We have a weekly community meeting to which anyone can come, and people are free to sit in on any staff meetings. Anyone can help out on such things as building our house, fixing up the storefront, or going out with the bus. We found that while diffuse boundaries cause a lot of confusion, it helped young people get to us who really wanted help but had difficulty admitting it. Often our community or staff meetings became therapy sessions or feedback, where people got the kind of information they would get from therapy, without ever having to put themselves down by asking for it directly. They accepted it in that context, where they might not otherwise, because that was the way we operated and they respected that. So far this procedure has sufficed to deal with difficult problems of social control, where someone creates a lot of tension in others or is disruptive. We try to get at the meaning of a conflict rather than resolve it restrictively by creating rules or boundaries.

The greatest problem we had in starting was to create trust in the entire youth community. We found that suspicion of any agency, even a new radical one like ours, ran almost to paranoia. Several times we found ourselves the victim of rumours that we were informers, which were not generated out of malice, but were due to genuine misunderstandings or foul-ups by our staff. We always dealt with such situations by going to the people we knew were critical and trying to work things out. We found that young people demanded an almost complete moral purity from an institution, and were put off by any dealing that showed we were less than they wanted us to be.

We tried to maintain informal networks at each local high school and stay in touch with the 'freak' community by sending our staff to hangouts and talking to people. They are aware of our shortcomings and our failures, but as time goes on they begin to see our honesty and our pluck in remaining open despite them, so we are beginning to outlive our criticism. Bringing our bus to festivals, even if at first we were astonishingly inept showmen, has brought us a visibility and energy in meeting people and learning about their problems that we could not have gotten any other way.

How we are helpful

The ways that we help clients have travelled far beyond the traditional limits of counselling, due to the incredible range of possibilities offered to us through the new media and forms of growth/self-expression developing with the counter-culture. Other than a few basic ground rules, our basic principle has been experimentation. Some of the organizers had experience with psychotherapy, as well as community organizing and political confrontation, and our style is a blend of these two influences. We have tried to look critically at each of our preconceptions about helping others, in order to get back in touch with the whole person and his dilemmas. Our method at first was to be available as listeners from the moment a person came in or phoned up. We would try to look as openly as possible at all aspects of the situation that was presented. Through questions we tried to get our client to look at other aspects of his situation. We responded naturally out of our own understanding and experience with other situations, often going into some of the seeming contradictions in what the client was saying, or helping him to explore other outcomes than hopelessness.

Some general characteristics of the youth counter-culture are an emphasis on immediate experience, dealing directly with people, knowing one's feelings, and a willingness to look directly into areas of anxiety. We tried to incorporate these into our counselling style. In addition, we learned from our clients that one of the primary characteristics of a personal crisis is the storage and inability to discharge strong feelings. A goal for counselling then is to help people recognize and deal with feelings around their situation, for example, towards family or boyfriend. We also began to include all the revelant people in the session, because we began to see that resolving a situation required work by all the main characters. This led us into family counselling and groups of friends or couples. Now more than one-third of our clients (about ten new contacts a day) eventually have one to four lengthy family sessions. We were surprised at our clients' willingness to call in their families, even when in the past they had dealt with parents by rebellion or flight. Parents also had little trouble cooperating, which is leading us to feel that people do not really wish to maintain a generation barrier, but are forced into it by feelings they do not know how to understand. We have found that our involvement and immediate service has impressed parents as much as it did our clients.

Another aspect of our method is our involvement in all aspects of the situation; not merely counselling but also obtaining other services, jobs, or housing. We originally had planned to make many referrals to outside agencies. As we began to get feedback about the outcome of our initial referrals, we found that most of them (if they ever got there) were rarely dealt with in a way that they felt was helpful. We began to sense that our difference in values and commitment to building an alternative culture made us acutely sensitive to the irrelevance and lack of responsibility of other agencies to our people. When we did make referrals, as for abortions or legal aid, we found that we had to take initiative to ensure that our client got service, and offer counselling around the legal or medical services that was needed. We began to view referrals as an adjunct to what we did, so that we felt responsible to go with our clients, and maintain contact until they obtained relief from the problem they brought in. We tried not to narrow or evade responsibility to help with any problem, to act as a parent or friend would. In contrast, agencies define responsibility only for providing a specific kind of service, so that for example a psychiatrist would feel that he only had to do therapy.

We began to deal with many people having difficulty breaking free of their parents, getting close to other people, or dealing with an educational system that seemed irrelevant and unconcerned about their welfare. We developed a variety of groups around common themes and issues, both scheduled and spontaneous. Our association with the Free School led us to work with high-school students in initiating educational reforms in schools and outside. We took the initiative when, for example, large numbers of young people came in about difficulties from a single source, to act as ombudsman or mediator on behalf of our clients. This year we will have a lawyer working with us in the very important and usually ignored area of civil and constitutional rights for young people.

Another service that developed is the residential crisis centre. We found that there was no place where a young person could go when his parents were having difficulties or were for some reason unable to take care of him, where a person could work out the transition of leaving home to work, for runaways to deal with their problem and reconcile themselves with their parents, and for a score of other difficulties. Usually, a youngster in such a situation ended up in jail or a mental hospital, starting a cycle which very soon made him feel either bad or crazy. The house environment is flexible and still in the process of defining itself. Most of our full-time staff live in the large house as a commune, and residents hopefully become part of the ongoing community for their stay of up to a month. We try to offer a free and open place for young people to look into themselves and receive shelter and support for that process.

The staff

Our staff represents another radical departure from established institutional policy. Basically, we did not find that education or credentials had any relationship to intelligence, sensitivity, or ability to help others, and so we have never looked to professionals for our staff. (We do, however, utilize some professionals as consultants, and in many cases their experience and involvement has enabled us to understand better what we are doing.) We felt that young people who had learned by experience, who had gone through personal crises themselves, were the most suitable to help others, provided that they had worked out their difficulties sufficiently to enable them to focus energy on another person. Many of our full-time staff originally came as clients. The staff consists mainly of high-school students and dropouts or vacationers from college, with a median age of twenty. Most of our staff have used drugs, many have been addicts or in mental hospitals, and all of us are in the process of searching for an identity and meaningful work as part of a movement to change society.

We see working at Number Nine for a year or so not as a career, but as a stage of our own growth, which combines community service with a meaningful learning and growth experience. This short-term and educational aspect leads to the tremendous energy and dedication in the work the staff does. Since we constantly incorporate new faces, we hope to withstand rigidifying or loss of commitment as an organization. We hope we are a school for community leaders in social change. Each of our staff, as he graduates (without certificate), should be prepared to work in and form a growth-oriented institution.

The training process is the work itself. A new staff member initially watches others working and counselling, and then takes initiative to get involved in one of the projects or develops a new one. Our whole culture is training, because outside norms are overturned as much as possible, and our staff must develop a way of dealing with each other that is different from the way they have before. Alternative cultures were first artificially created in T groups or encounter groups for training or growth, and our educational nature stems from the extent to which we can actualize these new values in our culture and help people overcome personal difficulties that inhibit them from operating on this level. Our meetings are analogous to counselling sessions in that we discuss all aspects of a situation, including our feelings, and then collaboratively reach a decision. Leadership comes from being involved to the point of having the relevant information to make a decision, or having the energy to carry it out and take responsibility for it. Thus, learning, growth, and leadership are all defined in terms of effective action, which is in sharp contrast to educational institutions whose criteria are largely irrelevant to action.

Our history over the first year can be looked at as an experiment with various styles of leadership. After the first three months it became apparent that the concept of pure participatory democracy was not working, in that three of the founders were doing the greatest share of the work and decision-making. This was due to their greater experience in radical service organizations and to the fact that they had arranged for funds which paid them to work full-time for Number Nine. Other staff felt guilty about not working as much, found it harder to initiate action, tended to defer in making decisions, and had personal difficulties and outside pressures on them. The three who were assuming more and more leadership found themselves in the position of therapists to other staff members. They became the directors, which concretized the differential in leadership, and made the directors more comfortable in exercising authority.

As Number Nine grew and found funds to hire others to work full-time this structure became inadequate. The new staff began to develop the skills that the directors had, and the structure developed some of the drawbacks of the hierarchical organization structure. The directors felt that nobody was taking responsibility, while the staff felt the directors held them back. During the summer the entire structure was called into question, and the three directors stated that they wished to be relieved of their responsibilities by the staff, although they would remain in the organization for a further year. They wished to devote more time to looking critically at Number Nine, and helping other organizations get started. The staff elected six of the ten full-time staff members to be directors, which corresponded to the staff members who felt comfortable exercising initiative and making decisions in ambiguous situations.

Number Nine as a community

Although we are an institution and an organization, Number Nine tends to think of itself as a community. This is in line with the counter-culture assumption that working and living should not be separated, and that people should be open and intimate in work relationships. In addition, the staff mostly lives together, so that social and housekeeping activities are integrated with our service work.

The reason for the emphasis on community, and the attempt to include its volunteers and clients in its activities, stems from our concept of what 'cure' we offer people in difficulty. Traditionally, improvement in therapy is based on adjustment to the usual situation, or gaining enough independence from the therapist to leave him. Since we are orientated towards rejection of the *status quo*, we must do more than help the person to some degree of comfort with himself. We try to offer him an alternative society if his growth through counselling leads him to want to commit himself to personal or social change. Our community tries to do this, so we would not necessarily see 'cure' as getting to the point where a person leaves us, or loses his dependence on us. Instead, we would define his dependence based on the quality of his participation, and invite clients to join us. Many clients join the staff, or hang around while they continue to absorb what we have to teach or offer. We encourage this, to the point where we have a fairly firm policy of not asking anyone to leave. We can tolerate having disturbed people around because we have a wide range of acceptable behaviour, and because we are persuasive in asking people to look into the effects of their behaviour. We enlist support by creating the feeling that we are moving as a community towards goals a young person might share, and are asking him to participate. We have less difficulty with discipline than a school or hospital, which takes few pains that its goals are shared with its inmates.

We have been praised and criticized because at times we seem like a religious community (or a fantasy system). We have 'rites' at rock festivals and inspire a religious devotion to our values, and use openness and group pressure to communicate and enforce our norms. Many of our people also use drugs and seek a communal consciousness, and we have frequent intense encounter groups. This is a valid way to look at what we do, to say that we are just changing values rather than improving them. Our 'religion' seems to be fairly effective in building a shared and worthwhile set of values, while most other institutions currently are failing in that area. We have found that it is this sense of a religious community, where people are close and dedicated, that most often accounts for young people coming to us in the numbers that they have. The meaning that we represent to them, while partly based on a fantasy, is the reality on which we build their own sense of themselves, and faith in their ability to do what they want, and find out what they want, despite depressing world or home situations. This community feeling is a form of creative energy that seems more powerful than psychotherapy alone for producing personality change.

The fears, avoidances, and depressions caused by trying to live at this level produce crises in our community and in its members, so that we have a constant source of powerful learning situations to face. A primary function of the directors is to utilize personal and group crises, such as shared frustration stemming from a fear of getting close, or goofing off based on unresolved anger, as learning opportunities. This increases each staff member's comfort with his own strong feelings, and willingness to look at them. There seems to be no better training for counsellors. The constant ability for Number Nine to disarm serious crises by resolving them not in the restrictive sense of making rules to prevent them in the future, or making informal social norms to avoid such threatening issues, but through actively dealing with what is happening in a way which leads to greater understanding by each person, is probably the source of its great strength and great attractiveness as a working and growing community.

Number Nine as social change

In a political sense, we feel that a community like Number Nine, if it can survive and grow, will pose a constructive threat to education and social service institutions. First, we will prove to bored and tired bureaucrats that their jobs do not need to be dull or frustrating. We can show that satisfaction will lead to better service. We can demonstrate to community mental health clinics why they lose so many customers, and frustrate so many others.

We can develop and practise with new modes of counselling from a wide variety of sources, such as Eastern religions and growth centres. We can challenge schools to look into their concepts of the maturity and responsibility of young people by having their students working effectively helping others. We can also educate students to pose challenging questions and alternatives to their educational system. And we can educate parents who come to us to the social changes that are happening, and perhaps make them fear them less. We are trying to be a model for the type of treatment, the kind of education, and the style of life that we want.

We do this in a way different from the confrontation policies we are more familiar with. Although we respect and many of us feel the need for serious political confrontation, we have decided that for our own survival and for our own values we will deal with the world differently. Since we see ourselves as a model of the kind of community we would like to live in, we have chosen to relate on this model to institutions outside us. In our current political situation violent confrontation seems in many cases to be the only way to obtain redress for the violence perpetrated on us. However our clients are primarily middle class and white, and for the large majority of them violence is not and never will be their style. We do not feel a need to reach those who have already been politicized, but rather seek young people who are not yet ready to recognize and deal with violence for what it is, and what it is doing to people around us. We see ourselves as recruiting new people to a movement towards massive cultural changes, rather than working with old faces.

Our contacts with adults have a similar aim. We try to make ourselves visible, and engage many people in dialogue. We do this by modelling our community as much as we can outside. For example, in our frequent talks to PTAs, community groups, or mental health workers we do not give lectures. We rather try to conduct exchanges, which, similar to our meetings and counselling sessions, deal as much as we can with the feelings and reactions of those whom we are addressing. Instead of providing a lot of information which can be misunderstood, we work to lessen the fear and hostility that keep adults from getting into meaningful encounters with young people. We practise subtle confrontation. For example, we would send a former patient to address a hospital staff, or a high-school student to a PTA, or ask parents who ask us questions about drugs why they can't ask their child or read a book about it. We do not blunt or soften our message for our audience, but we try to offer it in a context of friendliness and basic respect for what our audience has to say. We try to plant a seed of doubt in their prejudices, that will lead them to look further into the counter-culture. We are armed with the knowledge that we have more fun, and that we are nice people, even if they don't think so at first. Adults who hear us usually come out feeling better about us and themselves.

We try to create a change in each interaction we have with the community, in such a way that those we contact come back for more. We encourage people to visit us when they are suspicious, and include them if they come to our meetings. Gently but firmly we hope that people will begin to respond to what we have to say. We offer workshops and seminars for parents and families. When they say they want to get involved in our work, we do not discourage them or put them off. We of course mention our financial needs, which are considerable, but we also tell them that we would like them to gather their friends for an evening discussion with some members of our staff, at their home. In this way we can not only solicit funds, but communicate to a small group the meaning of what we are doing. This is community organization at its core. We ask our adult friends to help us by talking to other groups. This is the crux of our method of working for radical social change, and it presupposes that other groups, especially in the political sphere, are working and recruiting actively from people who have worked with us. This may be a naïve conception, but at an individual level it has been responsible for some powerful personal learnings by adults, has informed them about the nature of our critique of society and enlisted their aid in carrying the message further.

This paper has looked, in a somewhat oversimplified and naïve way, at some of the issues that have been worked on by a community that is trying to develop a cultural alternative that goes with its critique of the current cultural norms. The hard issues of how to stay alive, how to deal with our own upbringing in a culture that we now resist, and how to get things done with a new set of values have had as much to do with how we developed as our ideals and values. We feel that experimental organizations like ours form a sort of transition stage where values such as human potential can be actualized, as a concrete message that such things may indeed happen. We feel that such organizations cannot exist only in the laboratory, but must be visible and operate within the political reality of a community.

R. D. Laing in Pelicans

The Divided Self

'Dr Laing is saying something very important indeed ...
This is a truly humanist approach' – Philip Toynbee
in the *Observer*

'It is a study that makes all other works I have read on
schizophrenia seem fragmentary ... The author brings,
through his vision and perception, that particular touch of
genius which causes one to say "Yes, I have always known
that, why have I never thought of it before?" ' – *Journal of
Analytical Psychology*

Self and Others

As in his other works, Dr Laing here attempts to focus on
specific facets of the problems of human relationships in
the light of a theory that comprehends these facets within
a non-fragmented vision. He draws on diverse sources;
psychoanalysis, phenomenology, American studies of
families and on the insights of drama and the novel.

Sanity, Madness and the Family

with Aaron Esterson

And in Penguins:

Knots *

*The Politics of Experience and
The Bird of Paradise* *

* *Not for sale in the U.S.A.*